Stanley Abbey and its Estates 1151-c1640

A Cistercian monastery and its impact on the landscape

Graham Brown

BAR British Series 566

2012

Published by

Archaeopress
Publishers of British Archaeological Reports
Gordon House
276 Banbury Road
Oxford OX2 7ED
England
bar@archaeopress.com
www.archaeopress.com

BAR 566

Stanley Abbey and its Estates 1151-c1640: A Cistercian monastery and its impact on the landscape

ISBN 978 1 4073 1040 4

Printed in England by 4edge, Hockley

All BAR titles are available from:

Hadrian Books Ltd
122 Banbury Road
Oxford
OX2 7BP
England
www.hadrianbooks.co.uk

The current BAR catalogue with details of all titles in print, prices and means of payment is available free
from Hadrian Books or may be downloaded from www.archaeopress.com

Frontispiece. Extract of John Speed's early seventeenth century map of Wiltshire showing the area centred on Pewsham (Chippenham) Forest. Stanley lies on the northern edge of the Forest.

PREFACE

This volume largely comprises a PhD thesis that was undertaken at the Centre for English Local History at the University of Leicester, and was awarded in 2012. It assesses the impact of a Cistercian monastery on the landscape and how, in its turn, the landscape influenced the monastery. It also tests some of the traditional views on the early ideals of the Cistercians such as their attitude to colonisation, land clearance, administration of their territory and dealings with secular society. This study also goes beyond the monastic period and examines what effect the suppression of the monastery had on the landscape and community.

The research of monasteries has tended to be rather insular and concentrate on the recording of their standing fabric or the excavation of the church and conventual buildings; however, this volume approaches the subject from a different perspective and examines not only the abbey but its territory using archaeology, architecture, documents and map evidence in a holistic, 'landscape' manner.

In order to understand why the monks chose Chippenham Forest for their monastery the geomorphology of the region and the pre-monastic landscape is first assessed since it probably affected later colonisation.

Using the earthwork survey plan of the abbey, features within the precinct are identified. It is clear that, following its Suppression, the west range of the abbey was converted into a mansion house with gardens and parkland beyond, which are revealed on the plan. Similarly, archaeological evidence would suggest that similar conversions were undertaken at some granges.

The abbey's granges were located in diverse locations; some were in isolated positions while others were on the edge of existing settlements. It is also clear that the monks held manors at an early date, but within some of these manors there were also granges, thus the monks held a compact blocks of land in severalty, but also owned the demesne with tenants owing dues to the abbot.

Graham Brown
Amesbury
Nativity of the Blessed Virgin Mary. 2012

CONTENTS

FIGURES

TABLES

ABBREVIATIONS

AP	Aerial photograph
Ag Hist Rev	Agricultural History Review
Archaeol Cambrensis	Archaeologia Cambrensis
Archaeol J	Archaeological Journal
Architect Hist	Architectural History
BL	British Library
British Archaeol Rep	British Archaeological Report
Bodl	Bodleian Library
BRO	Bristol Record Office
Cal Anc Deeds	Calendar of Ancient Deeds
CBA Res Rep	Council for British Archaeology Report
Cal F of F	Calendar of Feet of Fines
Cal Lib R	Calendar of Liberate Rolls
Cal Pat R	Calendar of Patent Rolls
Cal Close R	Calendar of Close Rolls
DM	Devizes Museum
EH	English Heritage
IPM	Inquisitions Post Mortem
JBAA	Journal of the British Archaeological Association
L & P Hen VIII	Letters and Papers Henry VIII
Med Arch	Medieval Archaeology
NMRC	National Monuments Record Centre
NMP	National Mapping Programme
ODNB	Oxford Dictionary of National Biography
Proc. Hants. Field Club	Proceedings of the Hampshire Field Club
Proc Prehist Soc	Proceedings of the Prehistoric Society
RCHME	Royal Commission on the Historical Monuments of England
RCHMS	Royal Commission on the Historical Monuments of Scotland
RCHM(Wales)	Royal Commission on the Historical Monuments of Wales
SHC	Surrey Heritage Centre
SMR	Sites and Monuments Record
Somerset Archaeol Nat Hist Soc	Somerset Archaeological and Natural History Society
Surrey Archaeol Collect	Surrey Archaeological Collections
Trans Bristol and Gloucestershire Archaeol Soc	Transactions of the Bristol and Gloucestershire Archaeological Society
Wiltshire Archaeol Nat Hist Mag	Wiltshire Archaeological and Natural History Magazine
WSA	Wiltshire and Swindon Archives
Yorks Archaeol Soc	Yorkshire Archaeological Society

ACKNOWLEDGEMENTS

The genesis of this volume was an earthwork survey I undertook of Stanley Abbey while employed with RCHME. During my research it soon became apparent that, apart from an early twentieth-century excavation, little was known of the abbey and even less of its territory, and it was this paucity of research, not only at Stanley but other monastic landscapes I have worked on that convinced me of the validity for such a study.

I would first like to acknowledge the advice from Professor Chris Dyer whose patient and perceptive comments helped enormously in my research. I would also like to acknowledge my former colleagues at RCHME and English Heritage (EH). Deborah Cunliffe drew the earthwork plan of Stanley for the initial report, and my plan of Bowden Park. Elaine Jamieson kindly provided her plan of the Mendip Hills and her map symbols, and discussed with me at length aspects of my research. Helen Winton and Fiona Small of the Aerial Survey and Investigation Team at EH kindly provided the aerial photographic transcription extract of the Thames valley and Lambourn Downs and advised on my interpretation of my own transcription of the Stanley environs. The NMR library staff at EH took an active interest in my study and were, as always, helpful in securing books for me. Other colleagues at EH, Paul Everson, Mark Bowden and Dave Field, keenly engaged in discussion on occasions on aspects of landscape archaeology and provided useful insights. Beyond RCHME and EH I have been fortunate in the help I have received from the staff at the Wiltshire Heritage Centre, particularly Steven Hobbs, who was extremely helpful and was able to draw on his immense knowledge of the archive. Other libraries and record offices that have provided assistance include the Wiltshire Sites and Monuments Record (now part of the Wiltshire Heritage Centre); staff at Devizes Museum; the county record offices for Gloucestershire, Berkshire, Somerset, Oxfordshire, Surrey and Bristol; Wells Cathedral Library; the library at the Institute of Historical Research, and the college libraries and archives at Christ College and Oriel College, Oxford, and the Bodleian Library. I would also like to thank the staff at the British Library and National Archive for their efficient assistance. Finally, but by no means least, my wife Lilian who has lived with the Cistercians for several years, and has been supportive in my research throughout.

The Aurelius Charitable Fund generously provided a grant towards the publication of the colour illustrations.

INTRODUCTION

The monastic Orders were amongst the largest and wealthiest landowners in England during the medieval period and their impact on the landscape was profound. Monasteries were a statement of power and prestige; they were specialised settlements, places of exclusion, but at the same time places of inclusion where visitors were received and alms given. At its centre was the sacred space, the church. Beyond the church and conventual buildings were a range of buildings including a guesthouse, infirmary and ancillary buildings such as mills, barns and other agricultural buildings. The monastery was also the hub of an outlying territory that provided the monks' needs. The monks may have drained, cleared and cultivated their land, but at the very least they 'formed' and 'managed' it for their specific requirements. This was particularly so for the Cistercians who sought isolated, desolate places for their monasteries where they could lead a more austere lifestyle. The Cistercians were also distinctive in the way they managed their territory from granges, another form of specialised settlement and traditionally seen as one of the hallmarks of their success.

Today, in an age and country where spiritual matters appear less relevant, it is perhaps hard to imagine how deeply medieval life was imbued with a sense of religion that permeated society. Central to this were the monasteries; their whole *raison d'être* was as places where monks could worship God and do His will with acts of charity through hospitality or giving alms to the needy, and labour around the monastery and in the fields. As far as the Cistercians were concerned this entailed a coenobitic lifestyle following the example of the likes of St. Antony of Egypt and the other 'desert fathers', and St. Pachomius (AD 292-346) the founder of the first monastic community, and later St. Benedict, who formulated a Rule which the Cistercians adhered to (Waddell 1998, xxviii; Thompson 2001, 19). Meditation and prayer were pre-eminent; prayer to God and prayer for the soul of their patron and for those in purgatory seeking redemption for their sins or, as the Book of Revelations puts it, for those 'come[ing] out of the great persecution' (Rev 7:14) on their journey towards heaven. Monastic life was dominated by the *Opus Dei*, the Work of God, which entailed the saying of the eight offices of the day that were signalled by the ringing of the church bells. These offices were interspersed with manual labour, reading, eating and sleeping. Manual labour was also seen as a basis for prayer and meditation rather than a distraction from it; idleness, after all, was the enemy of the soul. For the monk a monastery was the symbolic expression of the heavenly Jerusalem 'where, far from the world and from sin, one draws close to God, the angels, and the saints who surround Him' (Leclercq 1961, 55).

The presence of a monastery would have been a potent symbol to lay people in the surrounding area, those working in the fields and going about their daily lives, and the significance of the sound of the bells and the physical presence of such a powerful symbol of Christianity would have been understood by lord and peasant alike. Stanley Abbey, the subject of this research was such a Cistercian monastery; it was established in the mid twelfth century at a time of rebellion in the country and dominated the region and its inhabitants for over 350 years.

The Cistercians

The Cistercians have their roots in Burgundy, in 1098, when a group of monks led by their abbot, Robert, left their monastery at Molesme to found a new house. They wanted to follow more closely the Rule of St Benedict and lead a primitive lifestyle of poverty bereft of wealth and landed property. The site they chose was about twenty kilometres south of Dijon where they established a 'New Monastery', which later became known as Cîteaux. The abbey was located in heavily wooded country in an area portrayed as 'a place of horror and vast solitude' thus evoking images of the deserts of the East, but it was also an area that included 'a few peasant dwellings and most likely even an old chapel' (Lekai 1977, 14), which perhaps suggests that it was not so desolate. Robert returned to Molesme following representations from the abbey, and was replaced by Alberic who was the former prior of Molesme. Thus Alberic became the first abbot of Cîteaux. He was succeeded on his death ten years later in 1109 by the prior, an Englishman named Stephen Harding. Stephen was an influential abbot and a great scholar who oversaw the initial expansion of the Order; according to Lekai he was:

> 'the first person in the Order's history who can unmistakably be recognised as a creative genius. He inherited only one of countless reform-abbeys of some notoriety; he left behind the first 'order' in monastic history possessing a clearly formulated programme, held together by a firm legal framework and in the process of an unprecedented expansion' (*ibid.*, 17).

The success of Cîteaux was down to its ascetic ideals, which were what the new disciples were seeking, and its organisation, leadership and constitution ensured its success beyond the bounds of Burgundy. Much of this success can be attributed to the dynamism and personal appeal of one individual, St Bernard of Clairvaux (Clairvaux was a daughter house of Cîteaux) who was appointed the first abbot of the new monastery by Stephen Harding in 1115. For nearly forty years, until his death in 1153, St Bernard was a leading force in the politics of Europe and the monastic movement. This charismatic, contemplative monk was a prolific writer and 'the most widely read and influential ascetical theologian of the Middle Ages' who had the respect of popes and royalty alike (Lawrence 1984, 180). His fame as a preacher, his holiness and moral superiority, gave the Cistercian ideal the impetus to flourish. During his abbacy, sixty-five daughter houses were founded from Clairvaux, and throughout Europe the number of abbeys increased to 340 (Lekai 1977, 36; Robinson 2006, 21). The first half of the twelfth century was, therefore, a period of rapid expansion and evolution for the Cistercians as they defined themselves and formulated their legislative statutes and texts by which they were to live.

The Cistercian reform, which was part of a much wider monastic reform, was above all a movement of spiritual renewal and a much stricter observance to the Rule of St. Benedict. The Rule provided guidelines on all aspects of monastic life and the Cistercian ideals are encapsulated in their legislative statutes such as the *Capitula* and the *Carta Caritatis*. These regulations evolved over time into the Institutes of the General Chapter, which were subject to change and addition. They stipulated, for example, that new foundations were to be dedicated to the Blessed Virgin Mary, and comprise an abbot and twelve monks. Their lands were to be 'far removed from the dwellings of men', watercourses and meadows. Clothing was to be plain and inexpensive; their diet was to be simple and exclude meat. No monk was to stay outside the monastery, and lay brothers were to be admitted into the community to assist the monks in agricultural tasks. The monks' livelihood was to be derived exclusively from 'manual labour, from the cultivation of land and raising of animals', although the animals were for utilitarian purposes. Their land should not be too close to secular land, although they were permitted granges that were run by the lay-brothers; these granges were to be no more than a day's journey from the abbey. Sources of revenue from churches, burial dues, tithes, villages, serfs, taxes, or dues from mills, were also strictly prohibited (Lekai 1977, 26; Waddell 1994, 27-38).

Attitudes to property and land that was acceptable, and the methods of running their territory from granges are seen as the a hallmark of the Cistercian Order that was emulated by some others. The Cistercians, however, were not without their critics, particularly over the privileges and exemptions they obtained. Stanley Abbey, for example, obtained a papal inhibition in 1241 on 'any rectors of parishes in which the monks' sheep are pastured, to exact tithes of wool, milk, and lambs' (*Cal. Papal Registers Vol. 1*, 194). One individual who was particularly critical was Walter Map, although he was somewhat biased, he commented that 'they proceed to raze villages, they overthrow churches, and turn out parishioners, not scrupling to cast down the altars [...] every other invader has some pity, and spares something [...] These take every precaution that there should be no return' (James 1983, 93-5).

As far as their churches are concerned, although nothing

was prescribed in the regulations, their design was nevertheless influenced by the Rule and Cistercian ideals. The earliest churches were deliberately small and austere, but by the 1130s they were built on a much larger scale and developed a 'distinct architectural aesthetic' (Robinson 2006, 23). This style reflects the Cistercian life, a life of poverty and simplicity, and their churches therefore lacked ornamentation and coloured windows so prevalent in some monastic churches elsewhere. In other words churches were a suitable backdrop for prayer and devoid of distractions and a life that was essentially one of silence (Kinder 2001, 38).

In time, the rapid expansion had important consequences for the Order and their ideals were eroded. The annual meeting of abbots at the General Chapter at Cîteaux became increasingly difficult, particularly for those who had considerable distances to travel, which led to a dilution of their influence. In addition, although the General Chapter sought to maintain uniform standards of life and discipline, individual abbots had to deal with the practicalities of their environment. In well-populated and 'anciently settled' regions, such as England, the flood of benefactions of varying kinds and land availability meant that compromises had to be made to their early ideals. The most conspicuous deviation from the ideals was when the Savignacs joined the Order and were able to retain sources of income that were otherwise prohibited to the Cistercians. It was in this climate of change and compromise that Stanley Abbey was founded, and how the monks adapted to these circumstances is a principle theme of this study.

The Cistercians in Britain

The origins of the Cistercians in Britain can be dated to 1128 when the Bishop of Winchester, William Giffard, founded the first monastery at Waverley in Surrey with monks from the abbey at L'Aumône (Loir-et-Cher). Waverley was quickly followed by others at Rievaulx (1131) and Tintern (1131) and within the next quarter of a century, during the reign of King Stephen and the period of the Anarchy, a further forty-three houses, including Stanley, were established until 1152, when the General Chapter forbade any further colonisation. This, however, had little impact since monasteries continued to be established, albeit at a slower rate, until the final foundation in England at St Mary Graces, London, in 1350 (Burton 1998b, 7-33; Donkin 1978, 29; Knowles 1950, 208-66). There were also thirteen Savignac abbeys in England and Wales, including Stanley's motherhouse, Quarr (Isle of Wight), and in 1147 these communities were absorbed into the Cistercian Order (Knowles and Hadcock 1971, 110).

The distribution of Cistercian monasteries in England is particularly striking (Fig 1:1). It shows a cluster of abbeys in Yorkshire, but the majority lie in a swathe of land down the centre of the country and paradoxically some are within, or close to, the area referred to as 'champion' England or, as Roberts and Wrathmell prefer to call it, 'the Central Prov-

Figure 1:1. Cistercian houses, excluding temporary sites, in Great Britain and Ireland. The shaded area represents the 'Central Province' (adapted from Knowles and Hadcock 1971; Coppack 1998; Roberts and Wrathmell 2000)

ince' (Roberts and Wrathmell 2000). This was essentially an area of nucleated settlements and large open fields with the more dispersed settlements and smaller closes lying elsewhere. These monasteries, however, despite being in the Central Province, were on the fringes of settlement or in pockets of woodland; examples include Biddleston, which was in Whittlewood, Bruern in Wychwood, and Combe and Merevale in Arden. They were, therefore, not necessarily in truly desolate places; on the other hand they were not in the heart of what is regarded as Champion country.

3

In contrast the Savignac houses were widely distributed throughout England and Wales and mainly occur near the coast and only two, Byland and Jervaulx, lay on the fringes of the 'Central Province'.

The majority of monasteries were in existence for little more than 400 years when they were acquired in the mid-sixteenth century by a new 'social elite' who adapted their newly acquired assets to their own needs. The fate of the monastic territories varied and while some continued to be farmed in much the same way as they had in the past, others became the seats of the upper echelons of local society, the 'newly rich'. The mid-sixteenth century was also a time of great social upheaval that not only saw the largest transfer of land-ownership since the Norman Conquest, but also a time when there was continuing agricultural change as new crops and methods were introduced; land was also enclosed and some settlements abandoned. It was also a time of rebellion, religious suppression and persecution of the 'old faith'.

Archaeology and monastic sites

Archaeology has made a profound impact on our understanding of monastic sites although most research has been confined to the excavation of the abbey churches and conventual buildings or the study of the 'standing' fabric from an architectural perspective. In contrast relatively little research has been carried out of the precinct and, apart from their history, even less into the territories that supported these monasteries.

Archaeological research has a long pedigree. Following on from the nineteenth-century antiquarians, early researchers tended to concentrate on the excavation of the physical remains of an abbey resulting in the exposed foundations of the church and conventual buildings and where the documentary evidence was used to put the site in its historical context. At much the same time historical research resulted in the publication of several monastic cartularies, not simply because they were monastic, but for the wealth of material they contained on economic and social history. It was only in the past few decades that a more research-led agenda was put in place, but many of these studies were still purely archaeological, dealing only with the site and not understanding the community who lived there and managed the land, or how they related to the wider community.

THE STUDY

It is against this backdrop of monastic research that this book is set. It is a study of a single monastery - Stanley Abbey - and its environs and estates in the south of England; of how its plantation affected the landscape and how, in turn, the landscape affected the monastery. The abbey was of modest size and not particularly wealthy, nor did it have vast estates, and when compared to some of the better-known houses in the north of England and Wales, in many ways it is rather ordinary and nondescript. However,

rather perversely, its main attraction is that it represents many of the other Cistercian monasteries scattered across the country in that the nature of the evidence is fragmentary and rather diverse, but it is appropriate and rewarding to use a 'landscape' approach to such a study.

This research is distinctive since it goes beyond the church and claustral buildings and uses all forms of evidence to understand the monastic landscape. This landscape includes the precinct and wider environs, as well as the abbey's territory. Analysis of earthwork surveys is used to 'tease out' features within the precinct and on some granges, not only for the medieval period, but also the post-monastic landscape. In addition the mapping from aerial photographs helps us understand, for example, the extent of medieval cultivation and the areas of assarting. It also recognises that the pre-monastic land-use must first be understood since it may have influenced later, medieval colonisation. It seeks to identify how the monks perceived their landscape from a spiritual as well as utilitarian perspective, what influenced them in their siting of monasteries and granges, and their relationship to local communities. The study goes beyond the monastic period and questions to what extent the suppression of the monastery had on the region.

Aims of Study

This book, therefore, aims to assess the impact of the monastic settlement at Stanley on its landscape during the medieval and immediate post-Suppression periods and how the landscape in turn influenced the monastery. It tests many of the perceived traditionalist models of Cistercian settlement, of land-clearance, innovation, and the administration of their estates and questions some of the Cistercians' perceived attitudes to land ownership and dealings with secular society. Further, the study analyses the impact of the transfer of ownership following the Suppression and questions whether the monastery's demise had any significant affect on an already changing landscape.

In Chapter Two the pre-monastic landscape is assessed and questions why the Cistercians chose Chippenham Forest for their monastery.

Chapter Three examines the two monastic sites at Loxwell and Stanley. The chapter questions why these specific sites were chosen and whether they conformed to the Cistercian ideals. Using the earthwork survey the abbey's precinct is examined and an assessment made as to whether Stanley followed other Cistercian monasteries in its layout and features within the precinct. It also questions to what extent the Cistercians were different to secular lords, which may be apparent in the landscape setting.

Chapter Four examines Stanley's environs, the area beyond the abbey gate. It questions whether the Cistercians conformed to the ideals of the Order as far as their attitude to land acquisition in the environs of an abbey and assesses to what extent they cleared and colonised the region. It also questions the impact on the settlement and agrarian landscape in the Forest region and the monks' relationship with secular society. Finally, it questions to what extent Stanley differed from other Cistercian monasteries in their choice of site for their home grange and methods of colonisation.

Chapter Five examines Stanley Abbey's territory. It questions the Cistercian attitudes to land clearance and settlement depopulation to form their granges. Also, in a landscape that was already exploited, to what extent the monks at Stanley cleared and colonised the land. The early Cistercian statutes prohibited the ownership of manors, but did Stanley conform to this ideal? The ownership of churches and mills were also prohibited but did the monks at Stanley adhere to this or did they come to own them along with the benefits they generated?

The main theme of Chapter Six is the 'secularisation of the landscape'. In a period of dramatic change in the countryside, it questions to what extent the Suppression had on the region.

THE LANDSCAPE APPROACH

A landscape approach to the study of a region or settlement was first promulgated in the 1950s and 1960s by individuals such as Hoskins, Beresford, Finberg and Everitt. Crawford also made a valuable contribution in identifying the archaeological palimpsest in the landscape (Bowden 2001, 42). The strength of this approach is that it is multi-disciplinary and therefore likely to produce the most satisfying results; it uses sources such as the documentary (including place-names and field names), archaeological, architectural, and cartographic evidence, to understand the history of a place or region and to set it in its wider social and geographic context. It seeks to identify, analyse and interpret features such as the standing buildings, the field pattern, communication pattern, and settlement earthworks to 'reconstruct' the landscape. It also recognises that the inhabitants of an area or settlement depended on a particular territory and its resources for their living. In addition it attempts to understand how people perceived and interacted with their landscape. A landscape approach should not be confined to a particular period since the occupation of an area may be influenced by earlier settlement and land-use. There is also an awareness of the subsequent development in the post-medieval and modern periods.

Features in the landscape, be they natural or man-made, are invariably given a functional interpretation; they may, for instance, be evidence of settlement (the tofts and crofts, abbeys and castles), or agriculture (enclosure and assarting) but, in some cases, there may be a deeper, social or symbolic meaning. Archaeologists studying the prehistoric period have for some time recognised this symbolism in the landscape; Bradley, for example, has emphasised how 'natural places' such as caves, mountains, springs and rivers were perceived and given special status (Bradley 2000). However, symbolism can also be recognised in

later periods. The siting and dedication of churches, like those beside pagan sites or springs, probably had meanings beyond the 'convenience of place'. Religious or ritual symbolism is also evident in the way people thought and acted in their everyday lives; a good example, if rather subtle, is the sounding of the *Angelus* bell from monasteries and churches summoning people to pause in prayer during their daily toils, a practice dating to the eighth century in monasteries, and still observed in some countries today (Baulch 2005, 80; Fig 1:2).

Figure 1:2. The Angelus - a prayer to the Blessed Virgin Mary, a reflection and a time set aside from the toils of the day. In the background is the church. This scene would have been repeated throughout the Christian world and a potent symbol of the Church (painting by the French artist Jean Francis Millet dated to 1857-59 at the Musee d'Orsay, Paris).

A landscape approach could perhaps best be summed up by one of the letters of Bernard of Clairvaux when he wrote to Henry Murdoc, the third abbot of Fountains Abbey about Murdoc's study of the Prophets: 'Believe me who have experience, you will find much more labouring amongst the woods than you ever will amongst books. Woods and stones will teach you what you can never hear from any masters' (James 1953, 156). These words are equally apt for the detailed analysis of a landscape; books and documents go so far, but it also requires the field evidence and as Hoskins said 'the English landscape itself, to those who can read it aright, is the richest historical record we possess' (Hoskins 1955).

Recent projects that have used a landscape approach to good effect include regional studies of, for example, the upland regions of the south-west of England on Exmoor, the Quantock Hills, and Dartmoor, while in Scotland a large area of upland and lowland on either side of the River Don was investigated (Riley and Wilson-North 2001; Riley 2006; RCAHMS 2008). In a lowland region of England the Whittlewood Project examined a wide tract of countryside bordering Northamptonshire and Buckinghamshire and studied the settlement pattern together with the evolving land-use (Jones and Page 2006). There have also been several landscape studies of specific rural settlements and their territory such as Wharram Percy, Raunds and Shapwick. The Shapwick project, for example, examined the evolution of the early and late-medieval rural settlement patterns in the area. The varied strands of evidence, archaeological, architectural and documentary evidence, combined to show that the modern village was established by the tenth century (Gerrard and Aston 2007).

A landscape approach has also been used in the study of some abbeys and their territory. Examples include Evesham Abbey and Abingdon Abbey, although these studies avoided the actual abbeys and concentrated on their landholdings (Bond 1973, 1-63; 1979, 59-75). There are only three examples where the archaeology of an abbey as well as a study of its territory has been undertaken; these are the on-going research projects at Bordesley and Strata Florida, and the ground-breaking study of the Premonstratension abbey at Barlings in Lincolnshire (Astill *et. al.* 2004; Austin 2004, 192-201; Everson and Stocker 2011). The Barlings project studied the abbey and its 'home' estate through time; it included detailed analysis of the surviving earthworks and buildings, and an examination of the landscape that the abbey exploited. It also examined the probable ritual significance of the region as well as the pre-monastic and post-monastic landscape when the site of the abbey was transformed into a grand house with attendant gardens.

There has also been a landscape approach to the study of one of Garendon Abbey's granges on the White Peak in Derbyshire, that of Roystone Grange (Hodges 1991). The study involved fieldwork on dating the dry-stone walls, test-pitting, and the excavation of the foundation remains of three buildings that were interpreted as being part of the grange complex. The grange estate was also analysed, and showed evidence of cultivation and sheep farming. The study, although concentrating on the medieval landscape, also covered the prehistoric and post-medieval periods and put the grange in its wider landscape context.

REVIEW AND EVALUATION OF SOURCES

A landscape approach to the study of Stanley Abbey entails the use of a wide range of sources, which conveniently fall into four broad categories: the archaeological evidence, the documentary evidence, antiquarian research, and the map evidence.

Archaeological evidence

An excavation was undertaken during 1905 by the architect and archaeologist Harold Brakspear (Brakspear 1908, 541-81). The excavation was typical for the day in that it was primarily a case of following wall lines with no stratigraphic interpretation. Apart from the west range, the walls had largely been grubbed-out, presumably to be recycled as building material elsewhere. Within the precinct, Brakspear identified the likely position of the infirmary and chapel as well as several other features such as the inner gate and millpond. Finds from the site included a large

quantity of pottery from the area of the kitchen, floor tiles, fragments of lead, a stone coffin, an Elizabethan coin, and clay pipes.

It was some sixty-three years later, in 1968, before any further archaeological fieldwork was undertaken when the Ordnance Survey surveyed the site and produced an earthwork plan. In 1996 the RCHME carried out a more detailed analytical earthwork survey (Brown 1996; Chapter Three). As far as Stanley's estates are concerned, the Ordnance Survey has surveyed the earthworks at Richardson (Chapter Five). Further surveys were carried out at Langdon Wick, Codrington and Bowden Park during the course of this study.

Earthwork survey contributes to a landscape study in a way that is not possible from any other source. The survey plan, for example, reveals the form and condition of extant features at the point of their abandonment. The identification of features overlying others, or cutting them, gives us phasing, or a chronology to our plan, but in the absence of other evidence it will be a relative chronology rather than absolute. An earthwork survey is also useful in identifying 'episodes' that are not evident from other sources. For example, at Richardson the earthworks include a settlement, which is known from documents, but there are also extensive garden earthworks that are unrecorded elsewhere. However, a possible shortcoming of earthwork survey is that, although the demesne site, the moat, was identified, without the documentary evidence it would not have been possible to ascribe it as the probable site of the grange.

Aerial photographic transcriptions have also formed an important line of enquiry, and use has been made of English Heritage's National Mapping Programme (NMP) plans that include Stanley's estates. These are: the Avebury region, with the granges at Langdon Wick and Richardson; Mendip Hills and their land at Easton and Mercumbe; the Lambourn Downs and Thames valley with their lands at Lambourn and Wadley respectively.

The NMP transcription is at a scale of 1:10,000 and is therefore useful in giving large area coverage, but not the detail. The APs show the crop mark or soil marks of archaeological features; however, it may require several photographs taken at different times of the year to reveal features sufficiently.

Documentary evidence

Although no runs of accounts for the abbey survive there is a reasonable amount of documentation relating to grants of land and property during the twelfth and thirteenth centuries. A monk from the abbey produced a chronicle of England until 1270; in the same document there is also some evidence of the abbey (Bodl: ms. Digby 11). A calendar of the muniments of the abbey at the British Library has been published and includes some charters, papal bulls, and references to Stanley's estates. (BL: Harl. Ms. 6716; Birch 1875, 239-307).

Only two of the abbey's manorial court rolls survive, which date from the fourteenth century, as well as a ministers' account of 1292 for Langdon Wick grange, and an account for the Home Grange dating to 1415.

Figure 1:3. A seal from a deed of 1300 of Stanley Abbey relating to their mill at Ugford near Wilton (WSA: G25/1/207)

An indication of the growth and extent of the abbey's estates can be supplemented from State papers such as the *Calendars of Patent Rolls, Calendars of Liberate Rolls, Calendars of Close Rolls, Calendars of Ancient Deeds*, Pope Nicholas' taxation of 1291 (the *Taxatio*), the *Valor Ecclesiasticus*, and mid-sixteenth century Suppression documents.

The earliest published account of the history of Stanley Abbey was written by a local antiquarian, William Lisle Bowles, who was the vicar of the nearby church at Bremhill (Bowles 1828; Matthew and Harrison 2004b, 969). In writing the history, Bowles had access to charters and grants that were formerly in the possession of the Bayntun family, who had acquired the monastery and the majority of its estates following its suppression (Bayntun is also spelt Baynton, but for conformity Bayntun is used throughout). According to Bowles, these documents had not been seen by Dugdale when he compiled his *Monasticon*, or by any other historian. These documents are probably those that are now in the Wiltshire and Swindon History Centre, where others relating to the abbey's estates are also held (WSA 473; Fig 1:3).

Despite the scarcity of charters, what does survive gives an overall illustration of Stanley's estates and when they were acquired. However, it should be recognised that they have shortcomings since they were principally written to catalogue a transfer of land, but do not necessarily give details of the land in economic terms; this has to be supplemented where possible from other sources. For example, the only indication of Stanley holding land at Langley Burrell is in the schedule of the Tithe Award in the nineteenth century.

The scarcity of accounts and court rolls is also a drawback since they give an insight into land-use, land-holdings and population of an estate. Unsurprisingly the single account roll for Langdon Wick is sketchy, giving only values of work done and details of crops and produce. However, there is no indication of numbers of sheep or cattle, despite the mention of milk from ewes.

Antiquarian evidence

The antiquarian reports form an invaluable record of our abbeys and priories since they date from the sixteenth century and as such are the earliest accounts of the post-Suppression landscape. Travellers and diarists such as John Aubrey, John Leland and Celia Fiennes have all given invaluable accounts of various monasteries. For example, Celia Fiennes visited Hayles House, the successor of Hailes Abbey (Glos), in the mid eighteenth century and described the mansion house and chapel, which was the former abbot's lodging, prior to its destruction in the later eighteenth century (Morris 1947, 30).

Equally important were the early engravers and artists who portrayed monasteries in a 'romantic' setting. These illustrations constitute the earliest pictorial evidence of a site and as such are an invaluable resource; however, a degree of caution should be exercised with some since they were not always accurate depictions.

Unfortunately, while the interpretation of some monasteries have benefited from these early commentaries and illustrations, Stanley Abbey has been less well served, although the landscape and the fate of the buildings is evident from some rather sketchy observations. John Leland visited Chippenham in 1542 but the abbey, which by this time had been converted into a mansion house, was clearly not important enough to warrant a visit since he confined himself in describing the landscape between Malmesbury and Chippenham as being 'open [...] with fertile arable fields and grassland, but few trees' (Chandler 1993, 489). John Aubrey, a Wiltshire antiquary, visited the area in the mid seventeenth century and described Stanley as 'very rich land, but in a place in the winter time altogether unpleasant. Here is now scarce left any vestigium of Church or house' (Jackson 1862, 112). The state of the house is again confirmed by John Britton who, in 1814, described the buildings as 'entirely destroyed, having been taken down many years ago for the sake of the stone and other material [...]'. Some foundations extending over a large area and glazed tiles were still visible, as well as some stonework (Britton 1814, 532). The final antiquarian comment was fifteen years later when the Revd. Bowles described the site of the abbey as:

> 'now marked by the extent of broken ground, the remains of fishponds, a few pieces of columns and Norman tiles found on digging, and part of a stone coffin, once the last depository of the proud abbot, and which now serves the inglorious office of a pig's trough' (Bowles 1829, 81).

Map evidence

Maps are a crucial part of any landscape project since they show the changing patterns in settlement and land-use over time, as well as giving topographical relationships. The earliest map of the area is Saxton and Speed's county maps dating to 1579 and 1611 respectively (frontispiece). They mainly depict the river network, woodland, and settlements, including Stanley, as well as the parkland.

The earliest accurate map of Wiltshire is Andrews and Dury's map of 1773, which was surveyed at approximately 2 inches to the mile. It shows topographical detail such as relief, rivers, and the principal communication and settlement pattern. The map is significant since it was produced before the coming of the railways, the establishment of some turnpike roads, and parliamentary enclosure.

There are also several estate maps, although none date before the third quarter of the eighteenth century. In addition, enclosure and tithe maps are invaluable since, in some cases, they show the extent of some of the grange estates as tithe-free land and contain field names.

Finally, Ordnance Survey maps, particularly the First Edition maps and geological maps, have been extensively used. The earliest depiction of Stanley Abbey is in fact on the 1st edition 6-inch Ordnance Survey map that dates to 1889.

LITERATURE REVIEW

Arguably the most influential historical study of monasticism in England and Wales is the work undertaken by the former Benedictine monk, Dom David Knowles. His books give an overview of monasticism in the country from the tenth to the sixteenth century (Knowles 1950; 1959). As far as the Cistercians are concerned he emphasises the whole ethos behind the Order. He sees their way of life made their monasteries different from the Benedictines; whereas the Benedictine abbeys were invariably near a centre of population, the Cistercians sought remote places. The precincts were also different; the Benedictines appear to mirror in many respects a lay or ecclesiastical lord's residence, whereas the Cistercians' precincts consisted of only the necessary monastic buildings, with simpler, if extensive, ranges of offices within the precinct. Knowles believes that the Cistercian ideal was to settle

on undeveloped land and to farm their land directly from granges. This traditionalist view has its supporters but has also been challenged by others (*below*).

In recent decades there have been further monastic studies, many either document-based or written from a historical geographers' perspective. They deal with a particular house, Order or region. Notable amongst the historical studies are those on the Cistercian houses of Rievaulx and Fountains, and Bolton Priory, a house of Augustinian canons (Burton 1998a; Wardrop 1987; Kershaw 1973). Historical geographers have also made a major contribution in studying, and in one case mapping, the colonisation of England and Wales by Orders such as the Cistercians and Augustinians (Donkin 1978; Robinson 1980, 2006; Williams 1998).

Turning to the Cistercian economy, several historians and historical geographers have carried out valuable research. One of the earliest was undertaken by Bishop in the 1930s where he defined a grange as being a predominantly arable farm, which was initially held in demesne. In his view, Cistercian granges were generally larger than those of the other 'new' Orders and were mainly created following the acquisition of wasteland, which they then set about clearing. What set them apart from the other Orders was that they sought to concentrate their land in consolidated blocks that was held in severalty. Their estates were not necessarily confined to a single township but may have included part of neighbouring townships. Bishop also emphasised the unpopularity of the Cistercians when they de-populated a settlement in order to create a grange, although he balances this by suggesting that they should be given credit for reclaiming and cultivating the land (1936, 193-214).

In contrast, Waites (2007) argues that Bishop's description of granges was rather unsatisfactory since, although there was an arable element on all granges, some had other functions depending on the resources in the area. Additionally, he questions Bishop's assertion that 'granges were created very rapidly' (Bishop 1936, 200) and instead sees the process as being more gradual and spread, perhaps, over one or two generations. He also maintains that the part the Cistercians played in the development of granges, although substantial, has been over-emphasised at the expense of the other Orders. The differences between Cistercian and Benedictine granges, Waites contends, were mainly due to the way the two Orders were organised. The Benedictines, for example, were part of the feudal system and held manors with tenants and as a consequence there granges were more akin to a manor house and cell. They also did not have a strong system of centralised governance, unlike the Cistercians, and their granges were thus more autonomous (*ibid.*, 59).

Further research was undertaken by Donkin who published several papers during the 1950s and 1960s, which were drawn together in a book entitled 'The Cistercians: Studies in the Geography of Medieval England and Wales' (Donkin 1978). In his opinion the formation of granges was the single most important contribution of the new Orders, particularly the Cistercians, to the landscape of the twelfth and thirteenth centuries, and the activities for which they are perhaps best known, land reclamation and sheep farming, were inextricably linked to the grange system. He suggests that a fully developed Cistercian grange was usually arranged around one or two courts; buildings within these courts varied depending on the function of the grange, with many having a simple oratory or chapel. Although the Cistercians were renowned for their sheep farming, he also emphasises the importance of their cattle farms, horse studs and industrial exploitation.

Using examples mainly from Meaux Abbey (Yorks), Platt goes beyond the historical geographers' notion of Cistercian estates and uses archaeological and architectural evidence to plot the form and extent of granges and their territory (Platt 1969). He makes a clear distinction between the grange, which he sees as being the farmstead, and the grange estate, the land exploited from the grange. Arguably, Platt's most significant contribution to the Cistercian debate was his recognition that many of their estates could be mapped using the evidence from Tithe Award maps since their land was largely tithe-free. Platt's method of mapping estates has been used to great effect by Hockey for Quarr Abbey (Isle of Wight), and on a much larger scale by Williams in Wales (Hockey 1970; Williams 1990).

Platt also emphasises that the more remote Cistercian monasteries were responsible for extensive programmes of land clearance and enclosure, and where there were existing peasant communities they could be transplanted and resettled elsewhere. This view, and many of the assumptions of their distinctiveness, has been analysed by Burton (1998b; 1999). In a detailed study of Rievaulx Abbey charters she found that there was, for example, no evidence that the occupation of the abbey site involved the dislocation of any previous settlers, although at one of the home granges a settlement was probably displaced or absorbed into the community. Elsewhere, there are instances where the coming of the monks may have deprived or removed the settlers but at others, their settlements invariably became granges, implying that they were either reduced in size or depopulated (Burton 1998b). In her view, the novelty of the grange system lay in the consolidation of estates for the greater efficiency of management, and in the reliance on *conversi* (lay-brothers) and hired labour rather than manorial services. This, by implication, ruled out the possession of manors and manorial rights. As Burton points out 'manorial exploitation was the antithesis of what came to be seen as the classic Cistercian practice' (Burton 1999, 244).

This is at variance to Alphonso's research where she questions the notion of the Cistercian 'ideal'. This traditionalist view, which was expounded by the likes of Bishop, Platt and Knowles, sees the White Monks colonising unpopulated areas and resorting to large-scale land clearance, and where the direct exploitation of their land from consolidated blocks was farmed directly by *conversi* and hired labour from a network of granges. In Alfonso's opinion, the most contentious part of this model is that the Cistercians were reclaimers of waste and creators of new arable land out of a wilderness and cites many recent studies to show the contrary; she also questioned the belief that the Cistercians lived outside the manorial system in their early years (Alphonso 1991, 3-30).

Berman undertook a major research project of the forty-three Cistercian monasteries in southern France that were created in the mid-twelfth century where their controlling, centralised nature show parallels in their settlement in England. The research was document-based, nevertheless it has been the most in-depth study so far undertaken into the economy of the Cistercians on the Continent. One of her findings was that they were not the 'pioneers' or 'frontiersmen' that they were once portrayed, but rather that they should be seen as entrepreneurs and managers who introduced a new type of monastic agriculture. In addition, many of their abbeys in the region were established on former hermitages or monasteries founded by earlier reformers, and it was these earlier settlers who 'reclaimed' the land, not the Cistercians; their granges were mainly created in previously settled land since there was little 'new' land at this time (Berman 1986, 1-179).

Research into the Cistercian settlement and economy in Wales has been undertaken by Williams (Williams 1984; 2001). In common with Berman he found that several Welsh granges were sited on former Celtic hermitages; however, apart from this they do not appear to differ much from their English counterparts although the incidence of chapels at the grange appears to be greater. The larger granges were in the upland, pastoral regions where estates of up to 5,000 acres were known. Williams has also identified a number of Cistercian manors, which he sees as being a transition from a grange economy to a manorial structure following leasing and considers the two terms, 'grange' and 'manor', as being interchangeable.

Robinson has undertaken an in-depth study of the architecture of Welsh Cistercian monasteries (Robinson 2006). This seminal work is a particularly useful book since it covers the history of the Cistercians in Wales before turning to subjects such as temporary sites and an overview of church building in Wales. He goes on to analyse the development of the monastic churches from their earliest forms to the 'Bernardine' plan and Gothic, before detailing the development of the claustral buildings. Finally, there is a catalogue of all the Cistercian sites in Wales and the Borders, with architectural detail and history of each site.

Also in Wales, the RCHM(Wales) undertook the survey and analysis of the Cistercian granges in Glamorgan, which formed part of their overall analysis of the archaeology in the county. The granges belonged, in the main, to the abbeys at Neath and Margam and the fieldwork resulted in the most detailed plans of granges for any region in Britain. The study included an inventory of the sites with their history and the principal components (RCHM(Wales) 1982).

The Cistercians, in common with other monastic Orders and secular landlords, did not retain direct control of their estates for long. Joyce Youings, in a study of monastic estates in England and Wales, found that during the period 1350-1450 there was large-scale leasing of demesne, either as compact blocks or piecemeal. This policy was not necessarily universal, with some estates not being leased until the early sixteenth century (Youings 1971a, 312). However, elsewhere, where leasing was more prolific, Donnelly suggests that by the sixteenth century little survived of the 'old grange economy of the Cistercians' (Donnelly 1954, 450).

Woodward sees practically no difference between the monastic and secular landlords as far as the management of their estates is concerned. The economic pressures that obliged the secular landlords in the sixteenth century to overhaul the management of their estates, to raise rents and renew leases operated equally upon the monks, particularly in the last two decades before the Suppression. Rising costs compelled them to find additional sources of income; the days when they could rely on pious patrons to increase their endowments were over, and the founding of chantries and schools was seen as a more fashionable outlet for patrons (Woodward 1966).

The Cistercians were heavily involved in sheep farming and the manufacture of cloth was particularly important in north-west Wiltshire (Carus-Wilson 1959; Mann 1959; Ramsay 1965) although there is no evidence that the monks at Stanley were directly involved in cloth manufacture. Another significant development occurred in the thirteenth century with the introduction of the fulling mill. Fulling was an essential process in the production of cloth, especially the long, heavy broadcloths that characterised the region. The mills were regarded as a manorial monopoly, in a similar way to the corn mills, and tenants were required to take their cloth to be fulled at the lord's fulling mill.

In contrast to the seeming plethora of monastic studies, apart from the notable exception of Barlings, relatively little has been undertaken into the 'afterlife' of the abbeys following their dissolution (Everson and Stocker 2011). Some were dismantled or destroyed and the material re-used elsewhere, while others were converted into secular residences, or the churches converted into parish churches (Gaimster and Gilchrist 2003; Tonkin 1997; Woodward 1966). In Hampshire, as well as some conversions, others were used as quarries for the new Henrican coastal defences along the coast (Hockey 1970, 237; Hare 1993, 207-227; Hare 1999, 17).

CHAPTER 2

SETTING THE SCENE

THE PRE-MONASTIC LANDSCAPE

INTRODUCTION

In Chapter Two the settlement and land-use patterns in the Stanley region to the end of the twelfth century are examined.

For any settlement to be successful there are several basic requirements including access to a source of water, fuel, building materials, as well as sufficient land on which to subsist. These factors apply to all settlements; however, monasteries are a particularly distinctive form of settlement and for the Cistercians, as with many other monastic Orders, the location of their monasteries was ideally to be in a place of real separation, not only geographically, but also from secular society. This tradition of separation goes back to the desert fathers of Egypt in the third century and in Europe these remote desert places are epitomised by areas of woodland, upland waste and marshland; Orderic Vitalis writing in about 1135 and at a time of rapid expansion of the Order, described how the Cistercians 'have built monasteries with their own hands in lonely, wooded places' (Chibnall 1973, 327). The Cistercians achieved this isolation at some monasteries, particularly those in the sparsely settled areas of northern England, at places such as Fountains, Furness, and Rievaulx, or the Welsh examples at Cwmhir, which was described as lying in a 'mountainous district remote from parish churches', or Strata Florida, was set in 'desolate mountains' (*Cal. Papal Registers* Vol. 1, 131; *Cal Pat R Hen VI, 1441-46*, 95); but for many, particularly for those in the more exploited and populated regions in the south of England, this remoteness was not always possible.

How, then, does Stanley Abbey compare; what first attracted the monks to Chippenham Forest? Were they able to find their wilderness or did they have to compromise by seeking as secluded a site as possible within what was an old-settled countryside? Early settlers would have been drawn to the region because of its resources: the river and its terraces would have provided ideal 'hunting grounds' for animals and fish; the extensive woodland where game was hunted and timber felled for building and fuel; and the fertile claylands which were suitable for settlement and cultivation, but was it also an environment for the Cistercians? In seeking answers to these questions it is first necessary to examine the area's landform, its geology, relief and soils, since these are factors that have an influence on whether it was suitable for monastic settlement. It is also necessary to understand how the region was settled and exploited in earlier periods, particularly the Romano-British and Anglo-Saxon periods, since the earlier patterns and land-use invariably have an effect on later, medieval settlement.

Aim of Chapter

This chapter analyses the environs of Chippenham Forest in order to establish its suitability for a Cistercian settlement. It is a macro analysis of the region and is followed in Chapter Three by a more detailed, micro analysis of the actual abbey sites.

The first part of this chapter is a brief description of the landscape that we see today, which sets the scene for the second part where three main themes are addressed: the geomorphology of the region and the wider environs; the evidence for pre-monastic settlement; and the Domesday landscape. Would a monk visiting a potential site have seen traces of earlier activity, and was the area the wilderness the monks desired?

LANDSCAPE SETTING

Stanley Abbey lies in north Wiltshire mid-way between the market towns of Chippenham and Calne. It is set within the 'Central Province' of England that extends across the eastern counties from Northumberland and north Yorkshire to Dorset and Somerset (Roberts and Wrathmell 2000; Fig 1:1, Fig 2:1). It is also an area that has been referred to as the wood pasture, or 'pasture lowlands' region of England and is exemplified by pasture fields, woodland, arable fields as well as heathland (Dyer 2000, 97-121).

Today, the area to the south of Stanley, within the former Chippenham Forest, there are extensive stands of woodland with arable fields on the higher plateaux on former heathland. Within this area there are also three parks that were carved out of the royal forest in the sixteenth and seventeenth centuries. The largest is Bowood Park, which was imparked in 1618 (Crowley and Freeman 2002b, 118). To the south-west of Bowood is Bowden Park, which was once part of Lacock Abbey's lands. Finally, Spye Park, which lies to the south of Bowden Park, and was formerly a medieval deer park before becoming the principal residence of the Bayntun family in the mid seventeenth century. Further south, beyond the parks, the land is more fertile and used primarily for market gardening; however, the area to the south of Chippenham generally has long been regarded as 'the garden of Wiltshire' (Daniell 1894, 43). North of Stanley the landscape can be characterised as one of small hamlets and farmsteads practising a mixed farming regime. The low-lying ground is particularly susceptible to flooding, which accounts for the small ditched and enclosed fields.

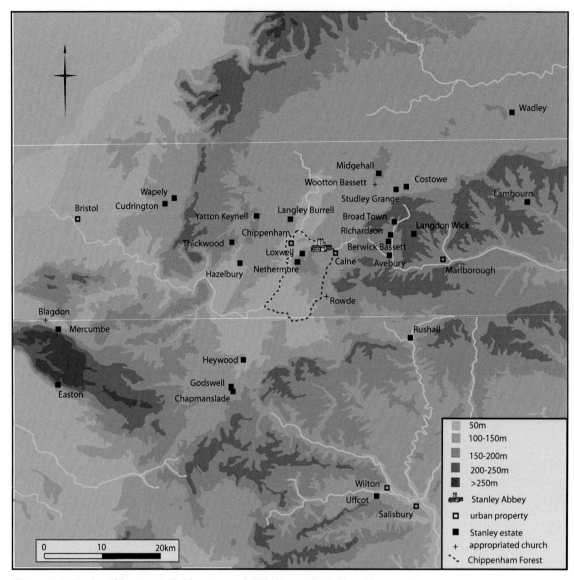

Figure 2:1. Stanley Abbey's main holdings in north Wiltshire and neighbouring counties

The main communication pattern is the east/west routes. The principal one is the M4 motorway to the north of the region. In addition, the older London road divides at Chippenham, one branch leading to Bath while the other leads to Bristol. There are two north/south routes. The first was the one linking Malmesbury and Chippenham, and south to Lacock. Another was the road between Devizes and Chippenham (Devizes was the administrative centre for Chippenham and Melksham Forests during the medieval period). Radiating from these roads and linking the settlements is a web of local roads and tracks. Only one road, the Chippenham to Calne road, was turnpiked during the eighteenth century, thus partly masking the earlier medieval route through the Forest.

GEOMORPHOLOGY

This part of the chapter questions whether the Stanley region was the 'desert' the Cistercians sought by examining the area's landform. This is followed by an examination of the wider region where Stanley had its territories.

Stanley Region

The soils and underlying geology, together with the drainage pattern, are all factors in determining the suitability for monastic settlement and land-use pattern. To the west of the River Avon lies an area referred to by Barron as the 'Stone Belt' of the Wiltshire Cotswolds, which extends west as far as the county boundary (Barron 1977, 35; Fig 2:2). On either side of the river are the gravels on the first river terrace bounding a narrow band of alluvium. Overall, the gravels are particularly narrow but broaden out to about 1.5km on the west bank near Lacock, and further north near the small hamlet of Avon. Beyond, the gravels are overlain by a discontinuous band of Kellaways Clay and further west on the Cotswold dipslope, by rubbly limestone mixed with sand known as Cornbrash and Forest Marble limestone of the Great Oolite Series. To the north of Chippenham, in the area of Langley Burrell, the Kellaways Clays give way to Kellaways Sands in the area of Bird Marsh and Langley Burrell (British Geological Survey (BGS) – Bath, sheet 265).

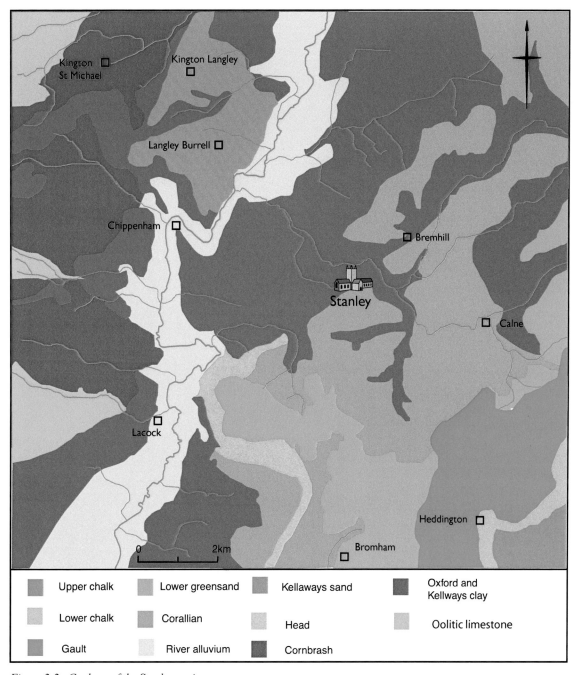

Figure 2:2. Geology of the Stanley region

On the eastern side of the Avon, beyond the alluvium and first river terrace, is the Clay Vale that separates the Stone Belt from the Chalklands (Barron 1977, 53). This broad band includes a further expanse of Kellaways Clay overlain by Oxford Clay that covers much of the low, wide plain to the east of Chippenham and Stanley, and the Corallian limestone ridge on the higher plateaux further east. This Corallian outcrop rises steeply above the Clay Vale and presents a striking prospect when viewed from the west, but in the east it dips gradually towards the chalk downlands. The outcrop extends in a north-east/south-west direction through the area and is composed mainly of Coral Rag with Bremhill on an 'island' of Lower Calcareous Grit. Opposite Lacock, and following the contours of the steep slope, is a broad band of landslip, or head, measuring up to 800m in width, which gives way to an outcrop of

Lower Greensand on the plateau. This Greensand is economically significant since it contains a layer of ironstone that has been exploited since at least the Romano-British period (*p. 17*). Compared to the limestones of the Stone Belt, the Clays are impermeable and unless drained, they are frequently covered by flood water; this is particularly so in the area to the east and north-east of Chippenham, near Stanley and Tytherton Lucas, where the land rarely rises above 60m OD.

Two rivers, together with a number of minor tributaries, drain the region. The most prominent is the Avon, which rises to the north of Malmesbury and flows south and ultimately emptying into the Bristol Channel (Fig 2:3). To the north of Chippenham is the confluence of the Avon and Marden; the latter river rises on the Marlborough

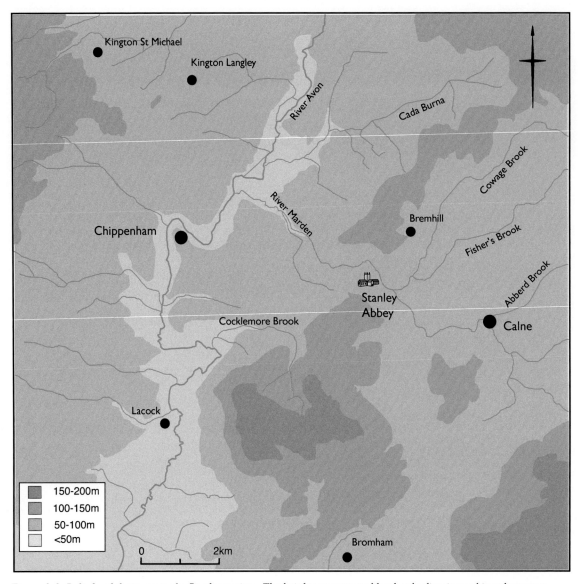

Figure 2:3. Relief and drainage in the Stanley region. The heights represented by the shading is used in subsequent distribution maps.

Downs near Calstone Wellington and flows west, through Calne and Stanley, before joining the Avon. Several minor streams meander from the higher ground to join these two rivers. The principal ones to the east of the Avon are the Cade Burna and Cockelmore Brook. Cada Burna is an unusual name and is probably a personal name meaning 'Cada's stream'. It was first mentioned in 937 and may be associated with Cadenham, which lies near its headwaters (Gover *et. al.* 1939, 5, 87). Cockelmore Brook rises at Nethermore within Chippenham Forest and was also referred to as 'the stream of the Pewe' in 1304 (Gover *et.al.* 1939, 5). As far as the Marden is concerned, there are three main tributaries: Cowage Brook, Fisher's Brook, and most importantly as far as Stanley is concerned, the Abberd Brook, where the abbey had meadowland. On the west side several streams rise on the Cotswolds dipslope and flow east to join the Avon.

The soils vary, but in the main accord with the underlying geology. Extending east from the River Avon the soil is predominantly of the Denchworth Association, which is slowly permeable and waterlogged in winter. Artificial drainage is essential if cultivation is to be successful. On the rising ground beyond the first river terrace there is a change to a more loamy soil and where the underlying geology is landslip the soils are more suitable for grass. Further east on the higher ground at Bremhill the soils are deep and well drained, and are better suited for cultivation. Further south, on the Lower Greensand, the soil is again well drained and easily cultivated (Findlay *et. al.* 1984). These light, warm and easily worked soils are well suited to cultivation of market garden crops (Fry 1940, 214-5).

On the west side of the River Avon, and as far as the Cotswolds, the soils are principally of the Sherbourne and Evesham 1 Associations. In the north, they are naturally well drained and therefore suitable for cultivation and grass. Elsewhere, on the higher ground and in areas of woodland, the Evesham 1 Association soils tend to be waterlogged if no drainage exists. However, where there is drainage, the land is good for agriculture (Findlay *et. al.* 1984).

14

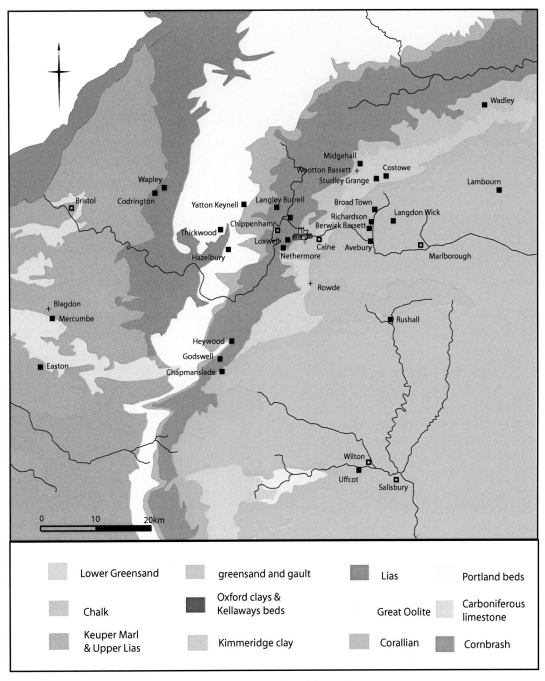

Figure 2:4. Simplified geology of the area of Stanley Abbey and its estates

In summary, the low-lying region in the environs of Stanley was an area of extensive clayland rising in the south to the Corallian limestone ridge, which is dominated by heath and woodland. The land near Stanley is slightly undulating and the clay soils are prone to waterlogging and it is here that there are several marsh and moor field names, which would have been perceived as a suitable 'desert' by the Cistercians.

The Wider Region

Beyond the Stanley region the abbey's other territories were widely distributed in north Wiltshire and neighbouring counties. These were on a variety of rock formations and soils, which emphasises how the abbey exploited different landforms to produce a varied economic base.

The most dominant formation in Wiltshire is the chalk downlands of Salisbury Plain and the Marlborough Downs, accounting for 52 per cent of the county (Fry 1940, 162; Fig 2:4), but it was the Marlborough Downs and the Lambourn Downs in Berkshire where some of Stanley's principal estates lay. This area is ideal for sheep and corn husbandry. The distinctive grasses and herbs provided the ideal habitat for the close-cropping of the turf, which also accounts for the scarcity of tree cover (*ibid.*, 184).

The chalk downland is composed of three zones: Lower Chalk, Middle Chalk, and Upper Chalk, the latter is capped in places by clay-with-flints. The chalk is an extremely thick rock, up to 400m in places, and is very permeable. It also weathers well resulting in the undulating nature of the landscape with deeply incised coombes and subtly round-

15

ed hills. The Lower Chalk on the Marlborough Downs forms a level terrace, or bench, measuring up to 6km wide and rising about 75m above the Clay Vale (BGS - Marlborough, sheet 266). In contrast to the other two zones, the soil here contain few flints and is well drained and as a consequence it is more suitable for cultivation. Above the Lower Chalk is the Middle Chalk that contains flint where the upper beds outcrop at the surface. The division between the two is striking, with the Middle Chalk escarpment rising some 70m in less than 500m. Drainage here is more rapid than the Lower Chalk soils and it is used for pasture and cultivation. The Upper Chalk is less suitable for cultivation because of the high levels of flint, but was more suited to sheep walks and grazing for cattle.

Slicing through the chalk downlands are several rivers and streams. The most prominent on the Marlborough Downs being the headwaters of the River Kennet (Fig 2:1). These streams and rivers, as well as the winterbournes on the higher ground, are underlain by alluvium with river gravels extending on either side. Settlements developed here, and they were also well suited as meadowland.

Stanley also had several estates on the Clay Vale to the north of the Marlborough Downs, as well as on the Cotswolds and Mendip Hills. Those lying on the Clay Vale and Cotswolds are similar geological formations to those in the Stanley region apart from Codrington and Wadley (Glos), which lies mainly on clay of Lower Lias formation, extending into limestones of white and blue lias (BGS - Bath, sheet 265). At Wadley, some land was on Corallean limestone while to the north it was clay.

The geology of the Mendip Hills comprises layers of carboniferous limestone beds that extend along the upper reaches and onto the plateau (BGS - Wells, sheet 280). These limestones, like the Chalk and Cotswold regions, are generally well drained and were used extensively during the Middle Ages for pasture. There were also large tracts of woodland and minerals such as lead and silver, which were exploited since at least the Romano-British period (Atthill 1971, 40).

PRE-MONASTIC SETTLEMENT AND LAND-USE

The second theme analyses the evidence for pre-monastic settlement in the Chippenham Forest region. The study of a single monastic landscape, such as that at Stanley, allows research to achieve a greater depth of understanding of a particular Order's impact in a regional and national context; however, the study should not simply be confined to the medieval period since its settlement, the siting of its granges and how its lands were used, as well as the importance of their Rule, were all factors that were influenced by earlier settlers, as well as the landform. The prehistoric, the Romano-British, and particularly the Anglo-Saxon patterns of landholding and exploitation may have influenced later colonisation and should be considered at the outset. Equally, we should be aware of the effects of the

transition following the Suppression, such as the change in land-ownership, the cultural differences between regions, the agrarian changes brought about by disafforestation and enclosure, which are all important factors of how the land was later perceived and exploited (*Chapter Six*).

Little systematic archaeological fieldwork has been undertaken in the region and many of the finds have been the result of stray finds by individuals or as a result of 'developer led' investigations, particularly in the area to the south of Chippenham. The area is also largely pasture and therefore the potential for systematic field-walking is reduced. Much of the evidence for Romano-British activity is the result of antiquarian interest and early twentieth century fieldwork; individuals such as Stukeley, Skinner, the Cunnington's, and Hoare, were all involved at one time or another here.

The Prehistoric Landscape

There is ample evidence for prehistoric activity in the Stanley region and although it had no impact on later medieval settlement it nevertheless points to the extent to which the resources were used, which areas were settled and which were avoided. Much of the evidence comes from finds along the Avon valley emphasising the exploitation of this riverine and marshland landscape by hunter-gatherers, while on the higher ground on the east bank of the Avon, in the area of woodland and wood pasture, there are several Iron Age sites and stray finds. Fieldwork and excavation in Chippenham, particularly in advance of building development, has produced a wealth of evidence of occupation from the Mesolithic to the medieval period, indicating that the town was always a favoured place of settlement and exploitation. Further east, on the Chalk, Neolithic and Bronze Age material and barrows are more prolific.

The earliest evidence of man's presence in the region dates to the Palaeolithic period and comes in the form of a flint flake from Langley Burrell (NMR: ST 97 NW 33). Mesolithic material is more prolific and is generally found near the streams and rivers although there are isolated finds on the eastern escarpment above the river valley. The largest concentration, however, was along a small stream in Langley Burrell and included about sixty flints. This site was probably a 'working area' and, because of the evidence of burning, was possibly a temporary settlement (DM Acc Register 1982, 95, 150; NMR: ST 97 NW 26). Elsewhere there were other smaller working areas along the stream.

In the Neolithic period more settled communities cleared and cultivated the land. In the Stanley region their presence is mainly apparent at Chippenham where potsherds and flint tools have been found as well as a pit containing worked flint and bone, and on the Chalk there is a long barrow close to several Bronze Age round barrows. Isolated finds such as flint axes have also been found along the Avon valley attesting to its continued exploitation. Similarly during the Bronze Age there have been finds of flint at Chippenham, and a stone mace-head was recovered from near the site of the abbey, although its precise provenance is unknown (SMR: ST 97 SE U05). Also, the geology of Stanley, and the place-name, would suggest that there was exposed stone. Perhaps this was a natural outcropping, but the name may derive from a single stone or perhaps even ritual stone settings (*Chapter Three*).

Iron-Age occupation appears to be mainly at Chippenham and on the higher ground away from the rivers and streams where there are several finds as well as a small promontory enclosure overlooking the Avon valley. The enclosure, which is roughly rectangular, has a single bank and ditch and is about eighty metres wide. Samian and Romano-British coarseware potsherds are thought to be associated with a later phase of occupation (NMR: ST 96 NW 5). Finds mainly occur in the area that was later to become Chippenham Forest, partly on Lower Greensand, which suggests that iron was being exploited here.

The Romano-British Landscape

Evidence for the Romano-British period is more conspicuous than for the prehistoric period simply because of the durability and proliferation of artefacts such as pottery, which is less friable, ceramic building material and metalwork; however, prehistoric activity was also probably greater than the archaeological evidence would suggest, but remains largely hidden from us.

The Romano-British settlement pattern in north-west Wiltshire appears to have been one of predominantly villa estates with smaller dispersed farmsteads in the valleys (Fig 2:5). Within the Stanley region, on the high ground on the east side of the Avon, several villa sites have been identified, most lie within what later became Chippenham Forest. There is also an embanked enclosure and a small, nucleated settlement at Sandy Lane, which has been identified as *Verlucio* in the Antonine Itinerary. It lies almost at the mid-point on the Roman road that traverses the area between *Cunetio* (Mildenhall, near Marlborough) and *Aquae Sulis* (Bath) (Corney 2001, 29; Rivet and Smith 1979, 493-5). This enigmatic site is situated on a band of Lower Greensand and survives partly as an earthwork in woodland with the remainder defined as a faint earthwork feature in fields on the opposite side of the Roman road; it forms a rectangular enclosure covering about three hectares (Corney 2001, 29-30). The occurrence of coins, pottery and building material in the vicinity would suggest that the settlement was once much larger and probably spread beyond the confines of the enclosure.

The nature of this site can only be alluded to since there has been little modern archaeological work, but based on evidence elsewhere, Corney (2001) has suggested that there would have been a *mansio* here and was presumably used as a staging post; however, iron slag and kilns in the area also points to substantial industrial activity and it may be that it was a regional administrative and distribution centre for this industry. There is also limited evidence of a mili-

tary presence with finds such as an ornate bronze buckle dating to the second or third century as well as a fourth century buckle (Griffiths 2001, 62, 68). A comparable site to *Verlucio* is the settlement at Charterhouse on the Mendip Hills where lead and silver were being mined from at least the second century. Within the settlement orbit there was an enclosure of similar size to *Verlucio*, a detached settlement, and an amphitheatre (Fradley 2009, 99-122).

Several villas occupy the high plateau. Within Bowood Park, for example, there are two probable villas. One of these, Nuthills, was partially excavated and interpreted as a winged-corridor villa. Finds in one room included the remains of painted wall plaster as well as rough sandstone flooring and the base of a fountain. The finds appear to span much of the Romano-British period and included pottery, coal, animal bones, and a brooch dating to AD150-200. Thirty-six Roman coins were also recovered from the vicinity (NMR: ST 96 NE 11; Lansdowne 1927, 49-58). The second villa was found in 1779 by labourers landscaping the park close to Bowood House. Although no dating was proposed, a tessellated floor, ashes, charcoal, pottery and six skeletons were found (NMR: ST 96 NE 9; Lansdowne 1927, 58-59).

Another villa lies much closer to *Verlucio* and, although no wall footings have been found, the incidence of surface finds such as pottery and flu-tiles, points to a large building (NMR: ST 96 NE 2; Hoare 1812, 124).

Perhaps the most substantial villa, however, was the one discovered near Bromham in 1765 and excavated by the local landlord, Sir Andrew Bayntun. He uncovered baths, tiles, and a tessellated floor. It was excavated again in 1840 and 1880 when further foundations were uncovered suggesting that it was a corridor villa with at least seven rooms (Hoare 1812, 123; Oliver 1881, 299-302).

Closer to Stanley, on Red Hill, finds included a bronze figure of the goddess Minerva with traces of a Romano-British building nearby. This site has been interpreted as a possible temple (Bowles 1828, 77; NMR: ST 97 SE 1).

Iron slag, sometimes in association with charcoal, has been found at several places on the Lower Greensand plateau. The working of this material would imply a managed woodland landscape and a source of water. Some of this iron slag has been dated to the Romano-British period because of the association with Roman pottery and coins with the slag, while in two cases they date to the medieval period; there are also several other sites that were undated. However, much of the evidence is from nineteenth-century antiquarians' fieldwork and some of the industry may be post-Roman. Iron working was undertaken in northern Wiltshire in the Middle Anglo-Saxon period, at Ramsbury, where an iron smelting site and smithy dating to the late eighth to early ninth century was excavated (Haslam. *et.al.* 1980; Hinton 1990, 44). The Stanley region could also have produced iron during the Anglo-Saxon. On the Low-

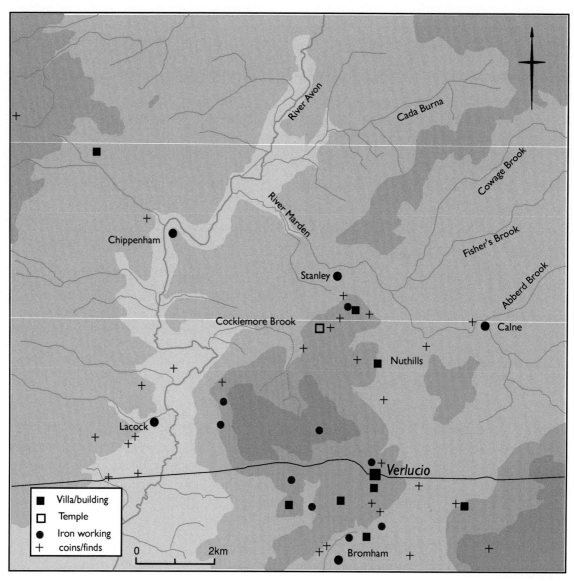

Figure 2:5. The Romano-British evidence

er Greensand plateau above Lacock a recent excavation revealed evidence for ironstone quarrying and smelting continuing into the medieval period at places such as Nash Hill and Bowden Park (Wilts SMR: ST NW 461, 480), while documentary sources mention several iron smelting sites elsewhere within the royal Forest. This 'industrial zone' on the high plateau, deep within what later became Chippenham Forest, appears to be the main focus of villa settlement during the Romano-British period and some of the villas, rather than being purely agricultural, may have been industrial centres. The major Roman road that traversed the area and iron ore deposits probably influenced the development of this settlement, although the fertile soils in the Bromham area are well suited to agriculture and would have been a contributing factor.

To the west of the Avon finds of Romano-British pottery and other artefacts are more sporadic but nevertheless points to a dispersed settlement pattern of small farmsteads. These deposits are concentrated above the flood plain, either beside the streams that feed into the Avon, or on the higher ground of the Cotswold dip-slope. Aerial

photographs have also revealed a possible Romano-British settlement dating to the first and second centuries near Lacock (Anon 1993, 159-60). A bronze weight in the form of the head of a goddess (DMDB 1991.6) and other finds, suggests a high status complex here. Further north, at Allington, crop-marks enclosing a possible small farmstead have been confirmed by excavation to be robbed-out walls (Canham 1982, 9; Wilcox 1987, 7).

The area to the east of Chippenham, as far as Stanley, lacks evidence of Romano-British settlement or land-use; however, in view of settlement and field boundaries found during excavation in the Chippenham region, a similar number of farmsteads could have existed, but cannot be discovered in the modern pasture fields.

As far as communications are concerned, the *Cunetio* to *Aquae Sulis* road is the only major Romano-British road in the region. Its route across the Avon lay to the south of Lacock and although there is no evidence of its precise route across this wide flood plain, it would probably have been negotiated via a causeway. On the west bank coins have been recovered from several places close to the road, suggesting, perhaps, small 'ribbon' settlement. This major road probably formed part of a more extensive network of local roads and tracks that linked settlements to their market centres and access to fields and woods.

The economy of the area was probably based on a mixed agricultural regime with industrial activity on the higher ground in the woodland on the east side of the Avon. Branigan (1977, 71) suggests that the Cotswolds, for example, was an area suitable for growing wheat and barley; however, unlike the chalk downlands, the earthworks of 'Celtic' fields are absent in the Stanley area. However, to the southwest of Chippenham, field boundary ditches dating to the Romano-British period and oriented north/south, reflect a similar pattern to others to the north of Chippenham (Bateman 2000) suggesting a partially enclosed landscape.

In summary, the evidence shows that the region was a long settled and exploited landscape throughout the prehistoric and Romano-British periods. In the area of Stanley, although the earliest evidence is from the Bronze Age, for the twelfth-century monk visiting the area for the first time there may also have been other visible features such as ancient field boundaries, or perhaps standing stones if this is the origin of the place-name (*Chapter Three*). Iron-Age and Romano-British activity predominates in the wood pasture across the higher plateau, while on the lower ground, the river terraces and wide alluvial plain, there were probably dispersed farmsteads.

The Anglo-Saxon Legacy

Branigan (1977, 93-108) suggests a hiatus in the mid to late fourth century when a number of villas in the region were damaged or destroyed although many were later re-occupied, some albeit at a much reduced scale. For example, the villa at Cherhill, which lies 6km to the east of *Verlucio*, there was a mosaic floor dating to the second half of the fourth century overlain by a hearth, which raises the possibility that it was re-occupied, or later used as an industrial site either in the sub-Roman or early Anglo-Saxon period (Pollard and Reynolds 2002, 158-160). The ending of Roman coinage in Britain indicates the ending of Roman influence; however, many of the late coins are particularly worn and some have been clipped suggesting that coinage may have continued to be the currency of exchange for some time after the Roman withdrawal (*ibid.*, 182).

The Environmental Evidence

The environmental evidence for the region is lacking but evidence from elsewhere provides potentially useful insights into what the Stanley landscape would probably have been like at this time. The end of the Romano-British period has, until recently, been seen as one of woodland regeneration following the abandonment of arable fields (Turner 1981). This is supported by fieldwork from a number of sites; on the Groveley ridge to the west of Salis-

bury, for example, 'Celtic' fields and a Roman road lie in woodland which was still substantial at the time of the Domesday Survey. Work by Dyer in Gloucestershire has shown that the abandonment of the Romano-British settlements was followed by woodland regeneration (Dyer 1994, 57). Similarly in the Whittlewood project area in Buckinghamshire and Northamptonshire pollen evidence revealed woodland regeneration over areas that had previously been cultivated (Jones and Page 2006, 60, 106). This regeneration was, however, by no means ubiquitous. In some parts of the country cultivation continued and in some cases there was intensification into at least the fifth century (Dark 1994, 144). The villa at Barton Court, Oxfordshire, for example, was soon re-occupied by Anglo-Saxon settlers following its abandonment at the end of the Romano-British period, and the environmental evidence indicates that arable farming continued (Tingle 1991, 70).

In the Stanley region there is little evidence of 'Celtic' or Romano-British fields apart from near Chippenham. However, the prevalence of 'moor' field names, coupled with the extensive areas of woodland recorded at the time of the Domesday Survey, would suggest that there was a less intensive level of cultivation and that the wood pasture landscape on the high plateau prevailed in the centuries following the Roman withdrawal (Fig 2:6).

The Archaeological, place-name and documentary evidence

The archaeological evidence, together with the presence of topographical names of Latin or British origin, points to a survival of a British population in the Stanley region. Eagles (1998, 40) has shown that the westerly extent of known early Anglo-Saxon sites in Wiltshire lies in an arc extending from Purton in the north to Market Lavington in the south, and bordering the Calne and Cherhill area where two probable British pennanular brooches were found. One of these brooches was found within Oldbury hillfort and dated to the sixth century, while the other was found 'near Calne' and dated to AD 450-550 (Youngs 1995, 130). This evidence, coupled with the apparent lack of early Anglo-Saxon sites in neighbouring south Gloucestershire, suggests an extensive British territory in north-west Wiltshire that continued until the seventh century (Eagles 1998, 40).

The place-name evidence supports the archaeological evidence. Perhaps the most noteworthy near Stanley is the Marden, a river name which, although not recorded until 937 when it was known as Merkeden, is an OE word meaning 'boundary mark' or 'boundary valley' (Ekwall 1968, 278; Gelling 1984, 99). This river borders the posited British territory with a cluster of Britonnic habitative names such as Calne, Chittoe, Cherhill, Quemerford and Calstone nearby. A further British name is the Avon that derives from Abon, meaning 'river', which was first recorded in AD688 (Ekwall 1968, 21).

Stanley also lay within *Sealwudu* (or *Selwudu*), a vast expanse of woodland that derives from the Britonnic *coed mawr*, or 'great wood' (Gover *et. al.* 1939, 15). It was

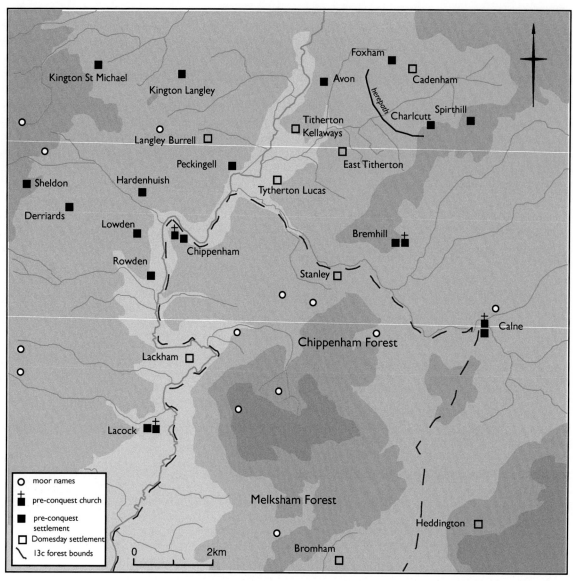

Figure 2:6. The post-Roman evidence in the Stanley region. The map also shows the thirteenth century northern bounds of Chippenham Forest, which probably reflects the area of woodland and wood pasture during the Anglo-Saxon period. Apart from 'Afletmore' which lies to the south-west of Stanley, the remaining 'moor' names derive from the OS 1st edition map.

recorded in AD705 when the bishopric of Sherborne was established 'to the west of Selwood' and remained an important natural boundary to Anglo-Saxon expansion until at least the ninth century (Stenton 1985, 65; Yorke 1995, 24). According to Grant the wood incorporated what later became the medieval royal Forests of Braydon, Chippenham, Melksham, and Selwood itself (Grant 1959, 391).

Settlement Evidence

The archaeological and place-name evidence, therefore, would suggest that the Stanley area should be regarded as a 'frontier' zone in the early Anglo-Saxon period with a British polity probably still pre-eminent. It is not until the ninth and tenth centuries that there is any firm evidence for an Anglo-Saxon presence in the region (Fig 2:6). Chippenham, or Cippenhamme, for example, was first recorded in AD853 in the Anglo-Saxon Chronicle when King Æthel-

wulf's daughter was married to Burgred, king of Mercia, 'in the royal residence which is called Chippenham' (Gover *et. al.* 1939, 89; Whitelock 1961, 43 note 10). The 'hamm' element in the toponym suggests that the main focus of settlement was in the bend in the river (Gelling 1984, 43) in much the same position as it is today. Despite its importance as a *villa regalis*, there is little archaeological evidence of Anglo-Saxon activity apart from the post-holes of a possible 'hut' and a ninth or tenth-century decorated iron spearhead and a Viking stirrup that were recovered from the Avon on the northern side of the town (SMR: ST 87 SE 400; Seaby *et. al.* 1980, 112; Anon 1990, 229). It is, however, tempting to see these latter two finds as dating to AD878 when Guthrum's army over-wintered here during his campaign against King Alfred.

Chippenham figured in the itineraries of the kings of Wessex during the ninth and tenth centuries, which suggests that it was a *villa regalis*, a 'central place', a meeting place where courts were held, disputes settled and trading undertaken. The marriage of King Alfred's sister here implies that the church was of superior status, probably a minster church. Perhaps a comparable place is Ramsbury, which was not a major settlement in the late Anglo-Saxon period, nevertheless it was a *villa regalis* and had a minster church (Haslam and Edwards 1976, 49).

In the late eleventh century Chippenham was one of only five royal estates in Wiltshire that was not assessed in hides or paid tax (Darlington 1955, 116) and therefore a place of some importance. In 1086 the population included forty-eight villagers, forty-five smallholders, twenty cottagers, and twenty-three pigmen, who between them had sixty-six ploughs. Although no burgesses are mentioned, its size and the large number of smallholders would suggest a change to incipient urbanism. Certainly by the mid-twelfth century it had been granted borough status and in 1205 there was a grant to hold a weekly market and annual fair (Beresford and Finberg 1973, 117; Kirby 1994, 72). Apart from the principal settlement others were in existence within the estate by at least the late eleventh century since Chippenham 'and its appendages' were to pay one night's revenue (Darlington 1955, 116). These dependencies may have included Sheldon, Lowden and Rowden (Brown 2001a). They form a cluster of 'dun' names that have been interpreted as meaning 'a hill, or very low ridge suitable for settlement' and according to Gelling it was a suffix that may not have been used much after AD800 (Gelling 1984, 141-2).

At Calne the medieval settlement lay on elevated land on either side of the River Marden and was, in common with Chippenham, the centre of a large royal estate and eponymous hundred. The north-west bank appears to have been the secular focus where the king had a residence; and it was presumably here that the witans of 978 and 997 were held. By 1086, Calne, with forty-five burgesses and seventy-eight smallholders, was a market town (Crowley and Freeman 2002a, 34-5; Darlington 1955, 115).

Elsewhere in the region, the only archaeological evidence of Anglo-Saxon settlement is a single sunken-featured building that was excavated at Derriards Farm, which lies on the river terrace to the south-west of Chippenham, while to the south of Sheldon three sherds of organic tempered ware pottery were recovered during field-walking (Anon 1991, 143; Chippenham College unpub notes).

Charters of the ninth and tenth centuries mention a number of settlements; in AD854 there was a grant of land at Hardenhuish (Sawyer 1968, S308), and Kington St Michael, including detached holding at Peckingell, were granted to Glastonbury Abbey in AD987 (Sawyer 1968, S866; Wilson and Tucker 1983). In 1065 Bremhill formed a thirty-seven-hide estate of Malmesbury Abbey with secondary settlements at Spirthill, Charlcut, Avon and Foxham (Akerman 1857). All these charters point to a process of fragmentation in the tenth and eleventh centuries, in these cases of royal estates to ecclesiastical institutions, which is witnessed elsewhere in Wessex (e.g. Hooke 1994, 83-95).

Early churches in the Stanley region

By the mid-eighth century, much of England had an established system of superior churches known as minster churches. Groups of itinerant monks operating from these churches were responsible for pastoral care for the laity within a *parochia*, which normally encompassed a number of what later became parishes. *Parochia* were based on secular *regiones* that perpetuated territorial units dating to the early Anglo-Saxon period (Blair and Sharpe 1992, 4). This minster system declined between the tenth and twelfth centuries as secular lords built manorial churches on their estates. Although some of the churches may have been manorial, minsters also established what Everitt refers to as 'secondary' minsters (Everitt 1986, 196). Over a period of time these churches acquired full or partial rights within their territory and became parish churches. Within certain parishes other churches or chapels were dependent on the parish church. By the thirteenth century, the proliferation of churches had ceased and the parish system had crystallised (Blair 1988, 14).

Three churches are listed in the Domesday Survey in the Stanley region, although they all may have had their origins in the ninth or tenth centuries. They were all of minster status or had many of the characteristics of a minster church. The first, and possibly the earliest is at Chippenham, and was assessed as having two hides and a value at 55s in 1086 (Darlington 1955, 116). The present church has twelfth and thirteenth century fabric, but has been mostly rebuilt in succeeding centuries (Pevesner 1963, 167); however, the fact that King Alfred's sister was married 'at the royal vill of Chippenham' in 875 (Whitelock 1961, 43 note 10), and that it was held by Bishop Osbern since before 1066 (Darlington 1955, 116), strongly hints that there was a church here in the later ninth century and that it was of minster status, probably the hundred minster. This is reinforced by its high value of £26 13s 4d in Pope Nicholas' *Taxatio* and the dependency of five chapels in the twelfth century (Astle *et.al.* 1802, 189; Kemp 1999, 88; Pitt 2003, 79).

The church at Calne had a higher value than Chippenham at the time of the Domesday Survey. It was assessed as having six hides and land for five ploughs, two of which were in demesne; in addition, prior to the Conquest, the church held a further five hides (Darlington 1955, 115). This evidence, coupled with the dependence in the twelfth and thirteenth century of the churches at Cherhill and Berwick Bassett, points to another minster (Crowley and Freeman 2002a, 34; Hase 1994, 53). The architectural evidence would suggest that the earliest part of the church was the narrow nave, which dates to 1160-70 (Pevsner 1963, 155). The third Domesday church is at Bremhill where the north-west angle of the nave has long-and-short quoins, which are characteristic of late Anglo-Saxon architecture. In addition, a short length of internal walling provides evidence of an earlier, aisle-less nave that had tall, thinner walls (Taylor and Taylor 1965, 6, 98; Pevsner 1963, 140). The church, dedicated to St Martin, who was a soldier turned monk, was part of Malmesbury's large estate and had at least two dependant chapels and was what Pitt termed an 'estate church' or 'estate minster' (Pitt 2003, 82-5).

There was also probably a church at Lacock in the late eleventh century, although it is not documented in the Domesday Survey. The evidence is tentative and relies on the church's dedication to St Cyriac, which is unique in Wiltshire. Elsewhere in England there are only ten other examples, most of which are found in the West Country (Arnold-Forster 1899, 171). The West Country distribution of this cult, in an area where a Britonic speech survived until at least AD750, and Lacock's position in an area of Wiltshire where the majority of the county's British place-names are found, would strongly suggest a pre-Conquest date for this church and dedication.

An old settled landscape

The environs of Stanley and Chippenham were, therefore, an old settled landscape. Following the Roman withdrawal, the evidence would suggest that fields were abandoned and the establishment of moorland with woodland on the higher ground such as the Lower Greensand belt, but by 900 the landscape was organised and settled. The moorland and wood pasture landscape above the Avon valley would seem the ideal environment for the Cistercian 'desert'.

THE DOMESDAY LANDSCAPE

The third section of this chapter examines the landscape evidence for the Chippenham Forest region in the late eleventh century, which is the landscape the monks would have witnessed and been familiar with. It questions whether the monks were truly settled in a desert, in a barren place that was separated from secular society.

Settlement

The Domesday Survey provides the earliest comprehensive picture of lordship, settlement and land-use, and shows that many of the larger estates in the Stanley region were either in royal or ecclesiastical hands (Table 2:1). Hooke points out that the settlements may not necessarily lie in the same location as the later eponymous medieval settlement and in any case the name applies to an area, not necessarily to a precise site (Hooke 1997, 28).

Land-use

The Domesday Survey shows that there were large tracts of woodland in the Stanley region and was an area that later became known as Chippenham Forest; however, the proximity of the woodland to royal centres would suggest that it was used for hunting during the Anglo-Saxon period and that the Normans were probably building on a pre-existing situation (Table 2:2).

It is noticeable that, apart from Stanley, there are no Domesday settlements in the northern part of Chippenham Forest suggesting that settlement was discouraged in the Royal Forest. The significance of this is unclear but given that it was one of sixteen settlements scattered throughout Wiltshire in 1086 held by Waleran, one of the king's huntsmen, it may be that Stanley was in some way connected with the hunting scene; perhaps there was a lodge here and used by the king when he was in Chippenham or Calne, or by officials who implemented forest law. Elsewhere in England, Hooke notes that 'certain manors were firmly associated with hunting, probably maintaining royal hunting

Manor	Domesday Name	Landholder
Chippenham	Chipeham	King
Stanley	Stanlege	Waleran Hunter
Cadenham	Cadeham	Earl Hugh
Tytherton Kellaways	Teritone	Osbern Giffford
Tytherton Lucas	Teritone	Edward of Salisbury
East Tytherton	Tedelingtone	Alfred of Marlborough
Hardenhuish	Hardenhus	Arnulf of Hesdin
Lackham	Lacham	William of Eu
Lacock	Lacoch	Edward of Salisbury
Langley Burrell	Langsfel	Edward of Salisbury
Bremhill	Breme	Malmsbury Abbey
Bromham	Bromham	King
Calne	Cayna	King
Heddington	Edingtone	Edward of Salisbury
Kington St Michael	Chintone	Ralf of Mortimer
Kington Langley	Langhelei	Glastonbury Abbey

Table 2:1. The Domesday manors in the Stanley region, some of which were in existence by at least the mid tenth century (after Hooper 1987)

Manor	Ploughs	Mills	Meadow	Pasture	Vineyard	Woodland
Chippenham (1)	100	12	100a	2x1 league		4x4 league
Chippenham (2)	2			4x1 furlong		
Stanley	1					
Bremhill	30	2	12a			2 league x 2 furlong; 4a
Lacock (1)	9	2	20a		0.5a	1x1 league
Lacock (2)	1		2a			
Kington St Michael	1	1	4a			6a
Kington Langley	16		15a	10a		1.5x0.5 league
Cadenham	2		5a			2x1 furlong
Langley Burrell	6		8a			6a
Tytherton Kellaways	6	10a				
Hardenhuish	4		12a			1x1 furlong
W. Tytherton (1)		0.25	6a			
W. Tytherton (2)	4	0.5	10a			
Lackham	10	2	15a			1x1 league
Calne	29	7	50a	2x1 league		
Calne (Church)	5	2		4x2 furlong		2x1 furlong
Heddington	6		10a	8a		8a
Bromham	10	2	40a	12a		5x3 furlong

Table 2:2. Land-use in the Stanley region at the time of the Domesday Survey. The manors that are in bold are those held by the King

lodges' (Hooke 1989, 122). An example is Whittlewood Forest, where the Domesday settlement at Wakefield appears to have been abandoned when it was taken over as a royal hunting lodge in the early twelfth century; and the subsequent development of Silverstone owes much to the establishment of another lodge, together with its chapel and fishponds, at this time (Jones and Page 2006, 172). A parallel in a monastic context is Faringdon, when it was found to be an unsuitable location the monks accepted King John's hunting lodge in the New Forest for the site of their new monastery, which became known as Beaulieu Abbey (Hockey 1974, xxxv).

By at least the tenth century extensive clearings had been created in Selwudu. Two of these lay to the north of Chippenham, at Kington Langley and Langley Burrell. Both incorporate the 'langley' element in their names, which means 'long clearing' (Gelling 1984, 205), and suggests an area that was probably one of wood pasture (Rackham 1986, 121). Place-name elements describe various aspects of woodland. *Lēah* is perhaps the most notable and is regarded as meaning 'forest, wood, glade, clearing and later became a pasture or meadow' (Gelling 1984, 198). Although most of these names date from the post-Conquest period, they may nevertheless describe a landscape that was already established by the late Anglo-Saxon period. Stanley is another *lēah* and despite no woodland being recorded here in the Domesday Survey, post-medieval field names with elements such as 'riding' and 'break', indicate the probable location of former woodland. Other 'lēah

place-names are first documented in the thirteenth or fourteenth centuries and may similarly represent assarting and settlement expansion; they include places such as Ashley, Henley, Bewley, Brocklees Farm and Thingley.

In the Domesday Survey, the size of the woods in the county are either expressed in terms of acres or by the length and breadth in furlongs or leagues, unlike Kent and Sussex, for example, which were assessed by the number of swine. Much of the woodland was described as *silva* (Darby and Welldon Finn 1967, 33). Although it is unclear to what type of woodland it refers it was probably mature trees or 'standards'. At Bremhill, apart from *silva*, there were also four acres (1.6ha) of *spinctum*, meaning a 'wood of thorns', implying mature trees and underwood (Rackham 1976, 108; Wager 1998, 3).

The Domesday Survey also shows that the area was a 'developed' landscape with large tracts of arable fields, meadow and pasture at Chippenham. Much of this cultivated land probably lay on the Oxford Clays to the south of the town on the wide fertile plain, while the meadow also lay to the south of the town on the river alluvium, in the area known during the medieval period as Eastmede. The number of mills also highlights how economically developed the region was; Chippenham alone had twelve mills, but elsewhere in the region there were over thirty. To the east of Chippenham, in the Stanley area the land was probably moorland, while on the plateau it was dominated by large tracts of woodland and wood pasture.

CONCLUSION

For the Cistercians, the desire for desolate, isolated locations for their monasteries meant that they sought 'desert' regions that were typified in north-west Europe by areas of woodland, upland waste and moorland. The Chippenham Forest region was well suited since it contained these basic ingredients. However, the Forest was also a 'non-desert' environment in settlement and land-use terms. Although the archaeological evidence points to periods of continual change as different resources were exploited, by the mid-eleventh century the settlement pattern was well established with the large royal estates and eponymous hundred centres at Chippenham and Calne, and Bromham another royal estate, with their hinterlands of dispersed farmsteads and small hamlets all bordering the forest. Land was cultivated; there were also extensive pastures and meadows as well as managed woodland. The ecclesiastical framework of minster churches and their dependencies was also in place, as well as the territory of the late Anglo-Saxon monastery at Malmesbury.

Therefore, the choice of a site for a monastery would have been a complicated agenda of what was desirable and what was achievable, and although the monks wanted to be separated from society, this was an 'anciently settled' landscape and therefore they had to compromise their ideals since they were invariably not far from the trappings of civilisation: the towns, hamlets, and road network. They also needed suitable land to cultivate. Their dilemma is exemplified by the remarks of a contemporary commentator, Walter Map, who described ironically how the Cistercians sought ' a place not uninhabitable but inhabited, clean, fertile, responsive to tillage, receptive of crops, embowered in woods, bubbling with springs, a very horn of plenty, a place outside the world in the heart of the world, remote from men in the midst of men, as wishing not to know the world yet to be known of it, as she who 'flies to the willows, to be seen as she flies' (James 1983, 75). Elsewhere in Britain, the Cistercians were prepared to negotiate for a site and not accept whatever they were granted. For example, when they took over a former Benedictine monastery at Old Melrose, they soon rejected it because it did not have sufficient arable land, and instead moved a little distance to Melrose (Fawcett and Oram 2004, 19).

CHAPTER 3

STANLEY ABBEY

INTRODUCTION

To many people, the ruins of a monastery are epitomised by places such as Fountains, Rievaulx, Byland and Tintern, where the building remains can be seen and appreciated in all their grandeur; however, this is not the norm and in common with many other monastic sites throughout Britain nothing survives of the church and claustral buildings 'above ground' at Stanley and all we have to rely on for evidence of its existence is the archaeological, architectural and landscape evidence. Analysis of these three strands in a holistic manner enables us to 'reconstruct' the siting and architecture of the abbey, its precinct and features within the precinct, and the whole complex can be understood as a building, a settlement of the Cistercian Order. In addition, the inevitable changes and development of the abbey, and its wider environment, which were caused by its fluctuating fortunes including the post-monastic phase, will be apparent in the archaeology.

The value of such an approach has been demonstrated at several Cistercian monasteries in recent years, most notably at Bordesley and Strata Florida. At Bordesley, excavation has revealed not only the form of the church but also aspects of the patronage and industry within the precinct. An analytical survey of the earthworks has identified the location of the church and cloister, and associated buildings, as well a change in the course of the river, the fishponds and at least two mills. Also, a study of the abbey's territory has led to an understanding of the wider monastic economy (Aston 1972, 133-6; Astill *et. al.*, 2004). This interconnected holistic approach places the abbey within a wider context and emphasises that it was a specialised settlement where the sacred and secular elements co-existed.

This approach is not confined to Cistercian houses. The excavations at the Augustinian monastery of Norton Priory (Cheshire) became one of the largest open-area excavations of a monastic site in Europe. As well as identifying the extent of the church and conventual buildings, there was an investigation of the precinct and the water management to the monastery, as well as the area beyond the precinct, which included analysing soil samples and field names to determine the pre-monastic landscape (Greene 1989; Brown and Howard-Davis, 2008).

Prior to establishing their monastery at Stanley, the Cistercians occupied another site, Loxwell, for three years. However, apart from aerial photography and limited field investigation, both of which were inconclusive, there has been no further archaeological work and we have to rely on the landscape evidence to understand its significance.

As far as the site of Stanley Abbey itself is concerned, archaeological fieldwork is confined to an excavation under-taken by Harold Brakspear in the first decade of the twentieth century and two more recent earthwork surveys, as well as aerial photographic transcription of the abbey environs. Brakspear's excavation, despite its shortcomings, is the only account we have for the layout of the monastery but, as more recent excavations on monastic sites have emphasised, there is potential for a re-appraisal of this earlier work. In addition, until recently precincts were poorly recorded and understood, the earthwork surveys therefore add an extra dimension to the excavated evidence and enable us to determine the precinct morphology and features within it. Analysis of the earthworks also enables us to appreciate how the Cistercians exploited this space and to compare and contrast it with other monasteries.

From the architectural perspective there is only one late-medieval building within the precinct. This structure was analysed by RCHME, but apart from a brief description and probable date there was no suggestion of its possible use (NMR: LB UID 316191). Elsewhere within the precinct there are fragments of medieval stonework re-used in some of the farm outbuildings, as well as a small footbridge over a former mill's tailrace, and revetting along part of the millrace.

Aim of Chapter

This chapter analyses the archaeological, architectural and documentary evidence for the abbey during the medieval period. It is divided into six sections. The first outlines the historical background of the abbey in order to put the book in context. The second section questions the suitability of Loxwell as a monastic site and also whether it conformed to the Cistercian ethos. It also seeks to identify what influenced the monks to occupy this particular site as opposed to any other. The actual location of the monastery has never been archaeologically verified, but the probable site is discussed, as well as what form the buildings may have taken.

The third section examines the evidence for the permanent site at Stanley. It begins by identifying the shortcomings of Loxwell and suggesting reasons why it was occupied for such a short time. An analysis is then made of the pre-monastic landscape at Stanley and questions whether the place was a 'desert', or did the monks have to compromise their ideals. Contemporary landscape literature from three Benedictine monasteries in England would suggest differing interpretations and that far from being desolate, inhospitable places they were in fact imbued with a special symbolism. Can we see this symbolism at Stanley?

The fourth line of enquiry examines the existing archaeological evidence by examining Brakspear's excavation in order to ascertain the morphology of the church and conventual buildings. This is followed by an analysis of the RCHME earthwork survey plan by spatially 'placing' the excavated evidence in the precinct and interpreting the earthworks within the precinct.

The fifth section, the discussion, is an examination of the archaeological and architectural evidence. The shortcomings of the early nineteenth century excavation are put in context with more recent excavations elsewhere. It also uses the earthwork evidence to determine the abbey layout, features within the precinct and compare it with other Cistercian precincts.

Finally, the sixth section questions to what extent Stanley can be seen as a 'landscape of lordship and seclusion'.

HISTORICAL EVIDENCE

Stanley Abbey was a daughter house of the former Savignac abbey of Quarr on the Isle of Wight (Knowles and Hadcock 1950; 1971, 125). In 1149 Quarr was granted land at Loxwell by the Empress Maud and her chamberlain, Drogo but it was not until 1151 that the abbey was founded (Dugdale 1825, 563; Cronne and Davis 1968, 666). Early grants to the new community included land in Chippenham Forest and a stretch of meadow beside the River Avon near Lacock (WSA: 473/4). Further afield they were granted a hide of land at Lambourn (Berks) and an important estate at Wadley, which lay along the Thames valley (Birch 1875, 280; WSA: 473/5).

Three years after the initial foundation, in 1154, the community moved to Stanley in the King's manor of Chippenham. The site chosen was a low-lying area on the banks of the River Marden some 2km upstream from its confluence with the River Avon.

The abbey grew in wealth and status. Although no comprehensive foundation charter survives, Richard I's confirmation charter of 1189 lists the abbey's holdings just thirty-five years after the community's move to Stanley. Their land was concentrated in Wiltshire in the region of Chippenham Forest and to the south at Chapmanslade and Godswell, but also included land on the Mendip Hills, the Isle of Wight, and Berkshire. The monks held urban property in Calne. They also held the moity of a fulling mill at Peckingell and the church at Blagdon on the Mendip Hills (Dugdale 1825, 565; Birch 1875, 281-3). In 1227, Henry III confirmed Richard's charter as well as other gifts to the monastery (Birch 1875, 294; WSA: 473/40).

In 1204 the community had grown sufficiently to enable them to send a colony to found a daughter house at Graiguenamanagh in Ireland under the auspices of its patron, William Marshall, earl of Leinster (Stalley 1987, 245). The General Chapter had not sanctioned this colonisation and as a result the abbot of Stanley, Nicholas, was deposed. The following year, however, he became abbot of Buckfast in Devon (Chettle and Kirby 1956, 273).

Although Stanley Abbey had no single patron, benefactions were made by several individuals until about 1292 when the acquisition of land seems to have all but ceased (Chettle and Kirby 1956, 271), around the time of the Statute of Mortmain in 1279, which was specifically designed to control and licence the growth of ecclesiastical landownership (Raban 1982, 1). However, the abbey continued to acquire property and rents into the fourteenth century, albeit more sporadically. For example, in 1310 the abbey was fined for having contravened the Statute of Mortmain (WSA: 473/31), and again in 1324 rent in Staverton was confirmed to the abbey 'notwithstanding the Statute of Mortmain' (*Cal Pat R Ed II, 1321-1324*, 359).

The thirteenth century appears to have been a period of consolidating estates and relative prosperity for the abbey. An indication of its wealth when compared to the other forty-eight Cistercian houses in the province of Canterbury can be gleaned from its contribution towards the £1,000 gratuity to King Edward I in 1276. It shows that Stanley Abbey, with a payment of £21 6s 8d, was the third highest after Beaulieu which paid £23 6s 8d and Warden's payment of £22 13s 4d (Hockey 1974, 254).

During the following century Stanley's granges and estates began to be leased, a trend that was replicated throughout the country on both ecclesiastical and secular estates. The earliest surviving lease dates to 1317 and relates to the manor of Wadley (*Cal Pat R Ed II 1313-1317*, 658); this was followed twelve years later by Codrington, and in 1330 by Heywood grange and the advowson of the church at Yatton Keynell (*Cal Pat R Ed III 1327-1330*, 419, 484). Further leases are documented in the mid-fifteenth century; in 1448, for example, Wadley was again leased, but this time to Oriel College, and twelve years later several estates, including those on the Clay Vale and Cotswolds were leased (*Cal Pat R Hen VI 1446-1452*, 180; *ibid. 1452-61*, 640).

The abbey's financial woes are highlighted in 1323 when Robert de Hungerford was appointed to assist the abbot in the management of the abbey's estates, and the following year several were leased specifically because of their debts (*Cal Pat R Ed II, 1321-1324*, 350; *ibid. 1324-1327*, 11). Hungerford's ties with the abbey were further enhanced when he later alienated a messuage in Salisbury for a chantry to be celebrated yearly in the abbey on the anniversary of his death (*Cal Pat R Ed III 1327-1330*, 335). Hungerford was succeeded in 1341 by John de la Roche, and seven years later by Gilbert of Berwick (*Cal Pat R Ed III 1340-1343*, 351; *1348-1350*, 199). The financial difficulties were partly alleviated when the king granted the advowsons of the churches of Rye (Suss), Rowde and Wootton Bassett (Wilts) with leave to appropriate them. He also granted them his profits of the fishing fleet at Rye (Chettle and Kirby 1956, 271).

Building work on the abbey started following the move from Loxwell in 1154, but within fifty years these buildings were being rebuilt (Brakspear 1908, 544). This new work was aided by indulgences from the Bishop of Salisbury, Roger Poore, and Fulk Basset, Bishop of London, to those who helped with its rebuilding (Birch 1875, 270). In 1222, Henry III granted wood and stone to the monks for their church and in 1246 he gave oaks from which the choir stalls were made. The following year the monks entered their new house, which implies that the east half of the church at least had been completed (Brakspear 1908, 545). Two decades later, in 1266, the church was completed and dedicated, like all Cistercian houses, to the Blessed Virgin Mary, by Walter Wylye, Bishop of Salisbury (Chettle and Kirby 1956, 274). Elsewhere within the precinct building work continued and in 1270 a new refectory had been finished (*ibid.*). In 1292, the monks were granted a licence to dig stone from the king's quarry in Pewsham (Chippenham) Forest for five years 'to build houses of their abbey and a wall around them' (*Cal Pat R Ed I 1281-1292*, 484). The abbey was probably constantly being repaired and new buildings constructed; as late as 1535, some of the buildings were described as 'newe builded' (Gilchrist Clark 1894, 311).

Little is known of the achievements of the abbots of Stanley apart from one notable exception, Stephen of Lexington, who was abbot in 1223-1229. Stephen came from an influential Nottinghamshire family that included four brothers; one became a judge, another was a steward in Henry III's household, while a third became Bishop of Lincoln. Stephen entered the Cistercian order at Quarr Abbey in 1221 following theological training at Oxford and two years later he was elected Abbot of Stanley. His most notable achievement during his abbacy was in 1228 when the General Chapter asked him to visit the Irish houses and restore regular discipline that had broken down, and it was probably as a result of his success that he was elected Abbot of Savigny, the mother-house of the former Savignac community, in 1229 (Matthew and Harrison 2004c, 683). Later in the same year he, along with the bishops of Bath and Coventry, was responsible for the inquiry into the canonisation process of St. Osmund of Salisbury (Rich Jones 1883, 85, 87). He went on to become Abbot of Clairvaux in 1243, and it was here that he left his most lasting legacy when he set up academic training at a college in Paris, the Chardonnet, for Cistercian monks. This college was later replicated at Montpellier and Toulouse and most notably in an English context, at Rewley Abbey, Oxford (Matthew and Harrison 2004c, 683).

Hospitality was an important part of monastic life, be it giving alms at the abbey gate, being a place of pilgrimage, entertaining the upper echelons of society, or providing accommodation for guests and corrodians. As well as entertaining visiting abbots, there were several royal visitors to the abbey, which presumably entailed considerable preparation and display. In 1282, Edward I, who had specifically granted stone to the monks for the construction of a chamber for his use, made two visits both lasting two days. In 1308, Edward II also visited for two days (Birch 1875, 300). As part of the wider Cistercian community, the abbot of Quarr was obliged to visit the abbey to ensure that the monks were conforming to the requirements of the Order. Only two such visits are documented which, according to Hockey (1970, 25-7), would suggest that there was little of concern about Stanley, unlike Quarr's other daughter house at Buckland where there were more visits. These visits were clearly important events; in 1205, for example, the abbots of Savigny and Quarr were at Stanley for an election and it was here, in the chapter house, that Abbot William of Quarr resigned his office (Hockey 1970, 27; Bodl: mss Digby 11, f. 149, f. 175).

Following the Act of First Fruits and Tenths in 1535, which resulted in the compilation of the *Valor Ecclesiasticus*, Stanley Abbey's net income was assessed at a little over £177 and as a result it suffered the fate of the majority of the 'lesser monasteries' with an income of less than £200 and was dissolved in February 1536. At this time there were nine monks and one novice as well as forty-three servants and a schoolmaster (Gilchrist Clark 1896, 311). Thomas Calne (or Morley), the last abbot, received a pension of £24 and was appointed suffragan bishop at Marlborough in 1537 before moving on to become a priest at Bradford-on-Avon. What became of the monks following the suppression is unclear, but apparently they did not go to Beaulieu as has been stated (Chettle and Kirby 1956, 274; Hockey 1970, 231-3).

In June 1536, eight of Stanley's granges and estates were granted to Sir Edward Seymour, Viscount Beauchamp. However, the bulk of Stanley's estates were sold for the sum of £1,200 in 1537 to one of the local gentry, Sir Edward Bayntun, who was chamberlain to no less than three of Henry VIII's wives, and who lived at nearby Bromham (*L & P Hen VIII* vol. 10, 143, 526; WSA: 473/227).

MONASTIC SETTLEMENT AT LOXWELL

The second section explores why Loxwell was chosen as the monastic settlement. The first indication we have of a monastic involvement at Loxwell is a charter, which is dated at Devizes on 13th April 1149 and reads:

> ... be it known that I give and concede to God and St Mary of Quarr in the Isle of Wight in perpetual alms, Loxwell, to make at that same a capital abbey, for the welfare and well-being of lord Geoffrey, duke of Normandy and count of Anjoir [...] and that the abbey of monks in the aforesaid place shall hold in liberty and quietness all the liberties and customs that the lady Empress, my mother, and I gave and conceded to lord Drogo last of my mother's conceded just as we gave them to the same Drogo our Chamberlain which the aforesaid words [works] have given and confirmed ...' (Cronne and Davis 1968, 666).

Loxwell is situated deep within Chippenham Forest and later place-names would suggest that it was in a landscape of woodland and heath, and therefore appears to have been well suited to the Cistercian ideals since it was in a metaphorical 'wilderness', a 'desert', which in biblical terms was a terrible place of solitude 'full of fiery serpents and scorpions, an arid land where there is no water' (*Deuteronomy* 8: 15). But why was Loxwell chosen and not somewhere else? Was there something special about this particular place? Did the monks comply with the Statutes of the Order as far as the process of founding an abbey? Finally, what sort of buildings would we expect to see?

Founding the abbey

The process of establishing a monastery could be quite a protracted affair. At Grace Dieu (Monmouthshire), for example, it took nine years, while the Savignac community that set off from Furness Abbey in 1134 eventually settled at Byland thirteen years later having moved location five times (Williams 2001, 12; Burton 2006). These, however, may have been rather extreme examples. The process would be initiated by an invitation from a benefactor to settle in a particular area. Approval from the local diocesan bishop, in Loxwell's case Salisbury, and the agreement of the General Chapter would then be sought, and finally the area would then be inspected to ensure its suitability (Robinson 2006, 49-50). In order for the monastery to be viable, sufficient benefactions would also be required. The initial charter to Quarr Abbey is not particularly illuminating, but presumably they went through the process since one of the witnesses of the confirmation charter was Robert, Dean of Salisbury Cathedral (Cronne and Davis 1968, 666).

Abbey	Foundation date	Distance from Loxwell (Km)
Loxwell	1151	
Kingswood	1139	39
Tintern	1131	69
Hailes	1246	123
Flaxley	1151	91
Cleeve	1198	141
Bruern	1147	73
Faringdon	1203	52
Thame	1137,1140	106
Netley	1239	114

Table 3:1. Distance of Cistercian abbeys in the south of England from Loxwell

Cistercian statutes also laid down the minimum distance between their monasteries and granges: monasteries were to be no less than ten burgundian leagues apart (about forty kilometres) while granges of different monasteries were to be at least two leagues apart (about eight kilometres) (Waddell 2002, 56, 200). Analysis of the Cistercian monasteries in the south of England shows that these minimum distances were largely adhered to. The only exception is a borderline case, that of Kingswood Abbey, which lay thirty-nine kilometres away (Table 3:1). However, as Waddell points out, a degree of flexibility to this rule is implied

since, in 1158, when there was a dispute over distances, it was settled by 'eye survey of the judges' and not done by 'measuring lines' (Waddell 1994, 29).

The Site

Location and Suitability

Bowles (1828, 90) has identified the nineteenth-century farm, Loxwell Farm, as the location of the monastic site. His assertion is based solely on the place-name and the occurrence of springs here; however, while he may well be right, there is no evidence to substantiate his claim. None of the present farm buildings, for example, are earlier than the mid-nineteenth century, nor are there any settlement earthworks or cropmarks in the vicinity. The farm is situated in an elevated position on the edge of dense woodland overlooking the Avon valley, which would seem ideal for the Cistercians (Fig 3:1). However, it is also in a constricted position since the ground soon falls steeply to the west towards a north/south re-entrant along which the Cocklemore Brook flows. This brook rises about 1.5km to the south and flows north and then west to the confluence with the River Avon. A minor tributary rises at Loxwell and joins the brook about 400m to the north-west of the farm.

Loxwell is also only 400m from the Chippenham to Devizes road, which was a major thoroughfare throughout the medieval period. Equally important was another route that lay two kilometres to the south of Loxwell, the London to Bath road, which was a major route since the Romano-British period (*Chapter Two*). Loxwell therefore had all the basic requirements for a successful settlement: a source of water, building materials, fuel and land, and access to good communications, and for a monastic settlement it was also set within a 'desert' since the region was sparsely settled and relatively undeveloped; however, the proximity of the roads and settlement on the lower ground meant that the monks had to compromise to a degree their ideals.

Following the community's move to Stanley, Loxwell became a grange and it is probable that the monastic buildings were adapted as farm buildings. But whether the nineteenth century farmstead overlies any medieval buildings is unknown. Indeed, evidence from several granges supports a dislocation in the post-medieval period: at Langdon Wick, for example, the grange complex was sited nearly 300m from the present farm although it was probably within the grange's outer court (Brown 2005b). Similarly the moated grange at Richardson was about 200m from the eighteenth-century farmstead. There are, however, cases where the later farmstead probably does overlie a grange, or includes medieval stonework in the building. The most conclusive example is at Codrington where part of the manor house dates to the fifteenth century, and includes a chapel. Other examples are Merecumbe and Midgehall. It seems likely, therefore, that the monastic buildings at Loxwell, (and later grange buildings), either underlie the present farm or are close-by (*Chapter Five*).

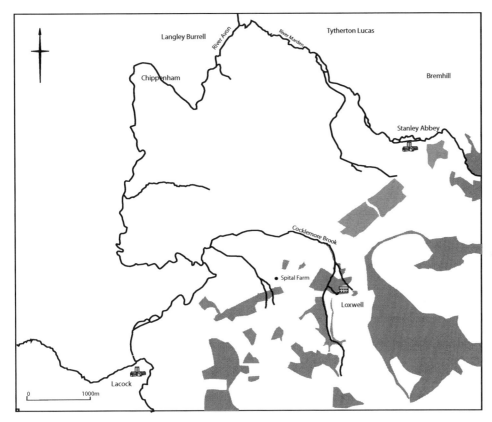

Figure 3:1. The probable site of the temporary site at Loxwell in relation to the permanent site at Stanley and the towns of Chippenham and Lacock. The extent of woodland in the nineteenth century is shown in grey (re-drawn from OS 1st editiion map).

Religious Symbolism

A possible reason why Loxwell was chosen for the monastery is its potential religious and political symbolism. The religious symbolism is alluded to in the place-name, Loxwell. It was clearly a significant, recognisable area in the mid-twelfth century since it was actually named and described as being 'a singular and romantic spring on the summit of a hill in Pewsham forest' (Chettle and Kirby 1956, 269). In the early documentation the site was variously described as being at *Lockheswellam*, *Drogonus funte* or Drownfont. From a charter dating to about 1151, for example, Matilda and her son, Henry Duke of Normandy, granted 'to God and St Mary of Drogo's spring [...]' (WSA: 1213/1). Another charter of about the same date confirmed a gift of a hide of land in Lambourn 'to the monks of Drownfont' (Dugdale 1825, 563). Also, when Jocelin de Bohun, Bishop of Salisbury, confirmed gifts at Loxwell and other places he used the name Drogonisfonte and Locheswellam (*Cal Anc Deeds* vol. 4, A8890; Kemp 1999, 142).

The significance of these names is that all the second elements are either 'spring' or 'fountain' names. The first element in *Locheswellam* may be a personal name, but the second element, 'wellam', is an Old English name for a spring or stream (Gelling 1984, 30); either would suit Loxwell since there are several springs and a stream in the vicinity, but there is no evidence of an earlier settlement. The more significant name, however, is *Drogonus funte*. Here the first element is again a personal name, presumably named after Drogo although this seems rather unusual, but the second element derives from a Latin loan word '*fons*'

or '*funta*'. Gelling suggests that this word is quite rare and was different from normal spring names and was used to describe a spring 'which was characterised by a Roman building work' (Gelling 1984, 22). She also suggests that it was unlikely that the Anglo-Saxons used a word of Latin origin for an ordinary spring (Gelling 1978, 86). It may also imply a survival of the Latin language in the area, which has already been alluded to (p.19). In Wiltshire there are only three other examples of funta place-names: Urchfont, Teffont and Fovant, all of which are in the south or centre of the county (*ibid.*, 83-6). Given the archaeological evidence of Romano-British activity in the region and that north-west Wiltshire, which included what later became known as Chippenham Forest, was possibly an extensive British territory until the seventh century (Eagles 2001, 199-233), it is conceivable that the spring at Loxwell was formerly a pagan or early Christian holy well, and is perhaps emphasised by its evocative description as being 'romantic' (Chettle and Kirby 1956, 269).

In 1214 an aqueduct, about 2.3km long, was completed along the contours from Loxwell to the new abbey site at Stanley (Bodl. mss Digby 11, f. 178). Despite there being other springs closer to the abbey, why was Loxwell specifically chosen? Could it be that it was seen as perpetuating the sacredness of the spring and therefore used in ceremonies in the conventual church as well as providing clean water. A possible parallel can be seen at Louth Park Abbey (Lincs) where the monks constructed a conduit, known as Monk's Dyke, from St. Helen's well to their precinct (Gurnham 2007, 25; White n.d., 143). Similarly at Strata Florida Abbey, one source of water to the precinct was from a holy well at Dyffryn Tawel ('Valley of Silence')

29

where there are also the remains of a large building which has been interpreted as a small retreat or hermitage for the monks (Austin 2004, 197). It is of course also conceivable that the 'holy' wells may well have been given that status because the monks found that the water flowed consistently and strongly, implying that there was both a practical and religious reason for using them as a water supply. The construction of the aqueduct from Loxwell was clearly a major undertaking and the description emphasises how everything the monks undertook was with God in mind:

> 'In this year [1214] was the aqueduct, from Loxwelle towards the Abbey of Stanley in Wilts, completed by the Master Thomas of Colestune, abbot of the same house. This work he had begun in fear and trembling, but God and our Lord Jesus Christ and good St. John the Evangelist helping him, he completed it well and excellently, of whom may it be an everlasting memorial of thanksgiving' (translation in Marsh 1903, 235 of Bodl. mss Digby 11, f. 178).

Holy wells, as well as holy trees and other 'natural' features, were important elements in pagan and medieval Christian religious practice throughout Europe and it has been suggested that such cult sites represent a kind of vernacular religion that existed alongside churches, which may in fact perpetuate minor pre-Christian cult foci within a wider Christian landscape (Blair 2005, 475-8; Turner 2006, 132-33; Walsham 2012, 18-79).

The siting of monasteries and churches on previously pagan or early Christian sites is not uncommon; however, the symbolism of such a plantation can only be surmised, but perhaps it can be seen in some cases as a conscious effort to transform or further Christianise the landscape; this perhaps follows Pope Gregory's (590-604) instructions to St Augustine before arriving in England to: 'purify the temples and then turn them into churches, to adapt pagan festivals as celebrations of Christian mysteries and Christian saints, to emphasise continuities rather than confrontation' (Duffy 2011, 57). At the very least these sites perpetuate the notion of sacredness and therefore a place of religious significance. An early example is the monk St Boniface (c.675-754), while on missionary work to Hesse, Germany, felled a sacred oak dedicated to Thor and built a chapel on the site out of the wood (Farmer 1978, 63). At Wells (Som.) a holy well formed the eastern end of the Anglo-Saxon minster (Rodwell 2001, 85). The large quantity of worked flint and pottery recovered from the area also attest to prehistoric activity here. In the words of Rodwell, 'it [the springs] was a place where the forces of the underworld were made manifest, and where a local religious focus could most naturally emerge' (ibid., 53).

The Cistercians were not averse to site their monasteries near or on previously sacred places. Examples include Roche Abbey, which was founded on an existing chapel, and a chapel and springs were in the area of Fountains Abbey. At Hailes the abbey was built beside the twelfth century church, while at Revesby Abbey, as well as depopulating the existing village when they arrived, the monks also used the church as their temporary church. Names of abbeys such as Kirkstead may also suggest either a place with a church or an ecclesiastical estate (Everson and Stocker 2008, 89; Robinson 1998, 159). In Wales the most compelling example of a monastery being sited at a pre-Conquest religious site is at Margam, where there are several stone crosses dating to the ninth and eleventh centuries from a probable Welsh church or monastery (Robinson 2006, 49). There is also evidence of early Christian memorial stones in the vicinity of the abbey sites at Neath and Strata Florida (ibid). Further afield, in Ireland, of the forty-three Cistercian monasteries that were established in the country, five were situated on Celtic sites some of which were at abandoned sites while others transferred their allegiance to the Cistercians (Aston 1993, 75; Carville 1982, 7, 118). In Italy one of the early Cistercian foundations along the Po valley was the abbey of San Bernardo di Fontevivo, which was established in 1142. The place-name is suggestive of the former landscape with the first element fonte, meaning spring, and the second, vivo, meaning living – a living spring.

Political Symbolism

As far as the political symbolism is concerned, the abbey at Loxwell was founded at a time when there was an upsurge in monastic settlement during the anarchy that ensued in the reign of King Stephen (1135-1154). It was during this period that the upper echelons of society, the barons, attempted to re-assert the power they had following the Conquest. They did this by siding with either Stephen or his rival Matilda and building a network of castles in order to consolidate their power (Hill 1968, 23). These same barons were also the greatest benefactors of the Cistercian Order in England (ibid., 27). As Hill states 'the same state of feudal disorder which prevailed on the continent for much of the twelfth century, where the private castle and the local feud were not forbidden, provided the political and psychological backdrop for the expansion of the most influential Order [the Cistercians] of the century' (ibid.).

Knowles sees the main reason for the development of the Cistercians as coming from the renaissance of spiritual life and centralisation of ecclesiastical discipline after the Gregorian reform movement while others have cited acts of piety (Knowles 1950, 191-227). While this may be partly true, there were other underlying reasons why the Cistercians were favoured. One was that they were far less expensive to establish than a Benedictine house. A Benedictine monastery required a large number of buildings as well as an extensive range of estates whereas the Cistercians, with their ethos of poverty and austerity and preference for underdeveloped land, required far less. The barons therefore made no great sacrifice in founding a Cistercian monastery, since the financial outlay was negligible (ibid., 246-47). These men built monasteries as a visible testament to their power and position; the monastery can therefore be seen in many ways as a status symbol of the patron.

Loxwell was founded by Matilda and her chamberlain, Drogo, but why was Quarr Abbey chosen to provide the monks to colonise it? It was by no means the closest, Kingswood, Tintern, and Thame, which were all founded in the 1130s at much the same time as Quarr, were all closer and presumably similarly well established by this time. Perhaps the main reason was that Quarr's patron was Baldwin de Redvers, a prominent adversary of Stephen, which would presumably have meant that the abbey was also sympathetic to Matilda's cause. In a similar way to the importance of castles in the landscape the founding of a monastery can be seen as another way of making a lordly statement of power and influence in a particular area. It can also be seen as being a stabilising or pacifying influence during a period of interminable struggle.

As well as royal patronage, there were several others who granted land during this initial phase of settlement at Loxwell and Stanley. The Basset family were one of these early benefactors. They held a small barony in the early thirteenth century and also held the manors of Wootton Bassett, Berwick Bassett, Winterbourne Bassett and land in Broad Town, where Stanley had land (Matthew and Harrison 2004a, 259). A further example of patronage, albeit somewhat later, is Fulk Basset who was Bishop of London in 1241, who gave indulgencies to those who helped with the construction of the second abbey church (Chettle and Kirby 1956, 274). The family also had close ties with William Marshall, Earl of Pembroke, and it was he who endowed land at Graiguenamanagh (Ireland) in 1204 to found Stanley's daughter house (Stalley 1987, 245).

The Early Buildings

What form the monastic buildings at Loxwell took is unknown, and since there was a change of use after only three years it is unlikely that they would have been particularly extensive or perhaps even completed, but evidence from elsewhere gives an indication of what form they may have taken.

According to the early Cistercian statutes there was a minimum acceptable level for any new monastery and no new abbot was to be sent to a new place unless certain requirements had been fulfilled. The buildings required included an oratory, refectory, dormitory, guest quarters and a gatehouse, all of which would probably have been constructed in timber which, by their very nature, would be quite ephemeral and consequently leave little archaeological evidence. The responsibility for the construction of these buildings would normally have been the patron and would have been done before the arrival of the new community although, as Ferguson has shown, there were instances when the founding abbey raised the first buildings and also where the monks did the work themselves (Robinson 2006, 50; Fergusson 1983, 74-86). At Hailes there is no mention in the abbey's chronicle of buildings being erected prior to the monks' arrival instead, when they arrived from their mother house at Beaulieu (Hants), they 'set up their tents at Hailes mill' and it was not un-

til five years later that 'a fine church, adequate dormitory, dignified frater and a large spacious cloister walk with adjoining buildings' were erected (Winkless 1990, 9). Similarly at Forde the monks occupied a house called Westford until their buildings were constructed, while at Pontigny (Yonne, France) the community established themselves in an existing chapel (Fergusson 1983, 75). Instances where a patron was responsible for the building work include Thame, Pipewell and Meaux (*ibid.*, 78).

The archaeological and architectural evidence for buildings at temporary sites in England is particularly elusive although there is a possible example at Brightley Abbey near Okehampton (Devon), which was founded in 1136 but abandoned by 1141 when the community moved to Forde. In his research of the buildings, Upham argues that the stonework in some of the farm's outbuildings may incorporate part of the original Cistercian monastery (Upham 2006, 151-64). Documentary sources also provide an indication, albeit scant, of buildings at some temporary sites. At Old Byland, which the Cistercians occupied for only five years before it was reduced to a grange, the buildings appear to have been quite rudimentary and not the expansive conventual layout of the later permanent site; it was here that 'they built for themselves a small cell [...]' (Burton 2006, 13).

In summary, Loxwell had the necessary resources for a successful settlement, but in addition it had the separation from society the monks sought. They were drawn to this place because of its isolation, its 'desert' qualities epitomised by the woodland. The springs may be seen as providing 'legitimacy' for the monastery, perhaps perpetuating an already religious site, but now a powerful Christian symbol. Although the monks were separated from society, their ideals were compromised since it was a relatively congested landscape where they were not too distant from the trappings of habitation with its markets, trade and road network. As for the buildings, we should not expect to find the more conventual range of church and the claustral buildings set around a cloister, but rather they were probably quite rudimentary and constructed of timber.

ESTABLISHMENT OF THE ABBEY AT STANLEY

In the third section an examination of the permanent site at Stanley is made and questions whether this site was a more suitable 'desert' for the monks. First, however, an analysis of the possible reasons for the move to Stanley is made and suggests what the landscape was like in the mid-twelfth century.

In 1154 the monks moved to Stanley, which was within the King's manor of Chippenham (Dugdale 1825, 563). The new site was on the south bank of the River Marden and 2½ miles from the market towns of Chippenham and Calne. Why the monks remained for such a short time at Loxwell is not entirely clear but they were by no means unique in occupying a place on a temporary basis. Elsewhere in England and Wales twenty-nine Cistercian abbeys, or thirty-three per cent of the total, moved location at least once before finally settling at their permanent locations (Knowles and Hadcock 1971, 110-28). This seems inordinately high, particularly when compared with the Augustinians where only 10.5 per cent changed site (Robinson 1980, 76). However, this lower figure may reflect the differences in colonisation whereby the Augustinians took over some churches and former Benedictine houses as their abbeys, which were clearly well established.

The reasons for these moves have been debated at length (e.g. Aston 1993, 78; Bond 2005; Donkin 1978, 31-6; Robinson 2006, 47; Williams 2001, 9). Aston cites the need for a better water supply as being the probable reason for the moves for four abbeys (Kingswood, Bindon, Beaulieu and Strata Florida), while climatic reasons and flooding are given for several others (Aston 1993, 78). In the border regions along the Marches and Scottish border, conflict and raids appears to have been the cause for the move of Grace Dieu and Diealacres (Donkin 1978, 35-6). One of Byland's temporary sites was at Hood where the monks spent four years, but the site was thought 'too restricted for the construction of an abbey' for the growing community (Burton 2006, 11).

As far as Loxwell is concerned, Donkin has suggested the lack of water as being a probable reason for the move but, as we have seen, there was abundant water (Donkin 1978, 34). Aston (1993, 78) suggests that the constricted nature of the site was probably the over-riding reason, and while there is merit in this, an equally plausible explanation is that it was never intended to be anything other than a temporary site while a more suitable one was found.

The pre-monastic landscape

At the time of the Domesday Survey, as we have seen, Stanley was a small territory amounting to one hide and three virgates of land with one plough and ten acres of meadow. It was one of Waleran the Hunter's sixteen estates in Wiltshire and, as well as a settlement, there may have been a hunting lodge here (*p. 22*). The population at Stanley was small, amounting to only three villagers and three smallholders (Darlington 1955, 151). What became of the inhabitants following the move from Loxwell is unknown; however, given the evidence from Cistercian houses elsewhere they may well have been moved from the site or recruited into the ranks of the hired labourers, or become tenants. In the case of Stanley it is likely that the settlement was a dispersed pattern, probably comprising farmsteads situated on the slightly higher ground to the north-west of the abbey in the same general area of later settlement, and therefore any physical disruption would have been minimal. They may also have become tenants of the monks, or perhaps a 'non-monastic presence' remained.

The evidence of land-use of this pre-monastic landscape is alluded to from three sources: the place-name, the topography, and the documentary evidence. As far as the place-name is concerned, the second element of Stanley is an Old English *lēah* name, meaning 'forest, wood,

glade, clearing' (Gelling 1984, 198). Coupled with the first element, 'Stan', it appears that it refers to a stone clearing (*ibid.*, 205) although there are few noticeable stony outcrops here. It may refer to the rising ground towards Studley, which lies to the east of the abbey, where the Ordnance Survey suggested that there was settlement evidence (NMR: ST 97 SE 14). However, more recent fieldwork suggests that the earthworks are more likely to be geological landslip, not settlement (Brown 1996). Another alternative, but equally plausible interpretation given the later ritual nature of the landscape, is that there was a prehistoric standing stone here.

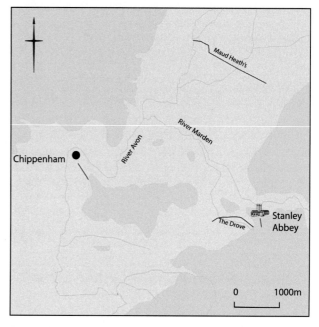

Figure 3:2. The causeways indicated by the red lines in the Stanley area. The lighter shade is land under 60m OD and therefore the possible extent of the marshland.

The archaeological and documentary evidence indicates that Stanley was a marshland landscape, and therefore well suited to the Cistercian ideals. The archaeological evidence hinges on the incidence of causeways and the ditched field boundaries. There are four causeways in the immediate vicinity of the abbey, and it is noteworthy that most lie on land lower than 60m OD apart from the causeway leading to the abbey, which is a little higher at 62m OD (Fig 3:2). This suggests that the 60m contour was possibly the maximum extent of the marshland and that settlement and cultivated land was on the slightly higher ground. The first causeway extends south from Chippenham and is named as such on the 1st edition OS map. Near the abbey there is a long curving causeway (known as the Drove in the nineteenth century) that ultimately linked Chippenham to Stanley. The third causeway leads from the precinct towards Close Wood and was probably constructed at the same time as the precinct boundary. Finally, to the north of Chippenham is Maud Heath's causeway, which was constructed in the fourteenth century (WSA: 473/51). While the latter two causeways are medieval, the dating of the first two is less clear. It is conceivable that the one at Chippenham fossilises the course of an earlier route across the

River Avon around which the town developed. The Drove may also be medieval; it had clearly gone out of use by 1773 (Andrews and Drury map) and probably much earlier, perhaps at the same time as the fields were enclosed in the sixteenth and seventeenth centuries.

The documentary evidence is explicit. In the early thirteenth century there were twenty-three grants to the abbey that specifically mention the marshland and woodland that lay on the south side of the abbey. To take just one example, a grant from Edmund, Lord Gacelin, who was lord of the manor of Chippenham, concerned '[...] his right of pasture in the wood called the More. Namely, from the entrance to the abbey to a close called *Affledmore* and from the marsh under the Moor to the top of the hill which divides the said wood and Moor' (WSA: 473/28.39; *Chapter Four*). The other grants use the same terms and it is clear, therefore, that the monks established themselves in a marshland region that was used as common pasture.

What was the relationship between the monks and their landscape; how did they perceive it? They may have regarded it as a former religious site given the possibility of a standing stone, but there was perhaps additional symbolism in how they perceived their environment. The notion that the landscape was a metaphorical '*locus horroris et vastae solitudinis*' may be true since it was in a relatively 'untamed' marshland, but they may also have regarded it in a similar way to the Benedictine monasteries at Glastonbury, Ely and Ramsay where twelfth and thirteenth century literary sources describe their topography as an island *loci amoeni*, a 'delightful place' set in a watery wilderness that asserted a regional and national identity and imagery (Clarke 2006, 67-89). The reclaiming and cultivation of the land was seen as spiritual work. These abbeys were situated in marshland and set apart in terms of status and prestige, but where they were also seen as 'endowed by God with beauty and sacred gifts' (*ibid.*, 69). In other words, although they were desolate places, there was also plenty of potential at each site. In biblical terms the wilderness was 'a waterless place [but where God] brought you water from the hardest rock, who in the wilderness fed you with manna that your fathers had not known' (*Deuteronomy* 8:16). Stanley was in a similar landscape to these abbeys in that it was on an 'island' between marshland and river, and yet it was an area where the monks could look inwardly within their cloister enclosure and devote their lives to God but at the same time, outwardly, where by their labours they could transform the land to their needs.

The Cistercians' literature also shows how they regarded their monasteries. St Bernard of Clairvaux defines a monk as a 'dweller of Jerusalem'. A powerful statement of the city where Jesus died; it is clearly not meant literally, but a place far from the world and from sin, where one draws close to God. St Bernard goes on to say: 'Jerusalem means those who, in this world, lead the religious life; they imitate, according to their powers, by a virtuous and orderly life, the way of the Jerusalem above' (Leclercq 1961, 55).

The Life of Jesus is therefore central to their whole being. This is reflected in the architecture of their churches, initially at least, which were characterised by the simplicity and lack of ornamentation (Kinder 2001, 38).

But how did secular society perceive the monasteries? Orderic Vitalis gives a tantalising hint when he says that having built their monasteries they 'thoughtfully provided them with holy names, such as Maison-Dieu, Clairvaux, Bonmont, and L'Aumône and others of the like kind, so that the sweet sound of the name alone invites all who hear to hasten and discover for themselves how great the blessedness must be which is described by so rare a name' (Chibnall 1973, 327). This suggests that they were highly regarded; they were set apart and seen as prominent, potent symbols of Christianity in the landscape.

Place-names also indicate how the monks perceived the land. Creighton notes, in the context of castles, how many have habitative names and are known by the eponymous settlement in which they stand. He also notes that several have Norman-French toponymns that appear to illustrate the new Norman lord's perception of the landscape. He cites examples containing elements such as 'bel' and 'beu', meaning 'fine' or 'beautiful', where the name refers not just to the castle but also it's setting (Creighton 2009, 41-2). The same holds for monasteries, although there are fewer examples. Of the Cistercian monasteries in England with Norman-French names, several have topographical names. Rievaulx and Jervaulx are 'valley' names from the Rye and Ure valley respectively, while Roche takes its name from its rocky environment. Meaux was formerly 'Melse' meaning 'lake or pool with sandy shores', but the name evolved following the Norman Conquest and the establishment of the monastery. It is thought to be associated with a French abbey at Meaux, which was originally named in Old French, 'Meldis' (Smith 1937, 44; Gelling 1984, 29). Another Norman-French example is Beaulieu. This name perhaps has added significance since the first element is 'beu', while the second element suggests a clearing, a beautiful clearing. An example from Wales is Grace Dieu, which has religious connotations since the name suggests thanks to God. Perhaps it was named for its eventual founding after several moves and troubled beginnings.

THE ARCHAEOLOGICAL EVIDENCE

The fourth section examines the archaeological and architectural evidence for the abbey and its precinct.

Brakspear's excavation

Harold Brakspear and a small team of four labourers excavated Stanley Abbey over a period of 'several months' at the end of 1905 (Brakspear 1907, 493-516; 1908, 541-81). The site had already been extensively quarried for stone before Brakspear's time and, apart from the west range, and the lines of some of the walls could only be traced by the robber trenches; nevertheless, he was able to uncover much of the layout of the monastery (Fig 3:3). In addition, he also planned and identified several features within the precinct (Fig 3:4).

Three main types of stone were used in the construction of the abbey. The first was rubble-stone, which probably came from the monks' quarry in Chippenham Forest. This was at Bycombe near Loxwell. Higher quality oolitic limestone was used as ashlar and came from their quarry at Hazelbury on the Wiltshire Cotswolds. Finally, the columns, capitals, and bases of the cloister and chapter house were made from a hard blue lias rock, probably from the Keynsham area.

The church lay on the south side of the cloister. This is unusual in Cistercian houses since most were sited along the northern side. Stanley was one of perhaps thirteen examples in England and Wales with this configuration (Robinson and Harrison 2006, 134). The reason for this difference is likely to have been topographical since a river or stream lay along the northern side of all these monasteries and in order for the water management to function most ef-

fectively, the church was ideally sited along the south side with the 'service' buildings close to the river. Also at Stanley the Cistercians did not own land on the northern side of the river, which would have enabled them to build their abbey in a more conventional manner. Elsewhere in England, Rievaulx Abbey, because of the topography, was another exception, but in this case the church had to be aligned almost north/south and positioned on the east side of the cloister with the conventual buildings also terraced into the hill-side. A lower position could have been chosen, but this would have been on the river alluvium; in addition, the position of the church on the escarpment meant that it had a longer period of daylight than would otherwise have been the case in this deep valley. An east/west orientation therefore, although desirable, was not essential.

Brakspear identified two phases of stone church, which presumably reflected the Cistercian style of austere architecture, although the excavated evidence is far from clear. The only surviving stonework from the first phase, which dates to the second half of the twelfth century, appears to

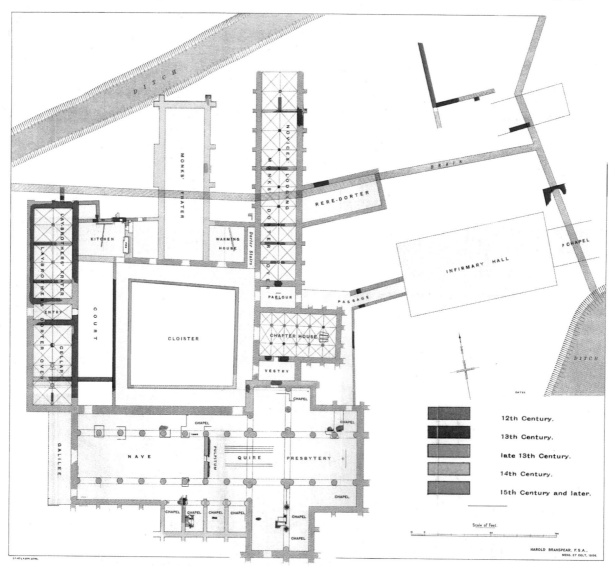

Figure 3:3. Brakspear's excavation plan (after Brakspear 1908, facing 541)

be a small fragment of the north and west walls of the north transept, parts of the walls to support the choir stalls, and perhaps the foundations of the nave arcade. The choir wall on the northern side survived to a greater length (6.5m) than the southern wall. The gap between the two sets of stalls was 2.9m wide (Brakspear 1908, 552-3).

The second phase occurred during the first half of the thirteenth century when the church was 'rebuilt or greatly enlarged' and consecrated in 1266 (*ibid.*, 552). The main changes appear to be in the presbytery, which was enlarged to three bays with aisles and two chapels at the east end. The foundations of the east wall were marked by a trench. However, the base of the first pier in the north was found, and a portion of a screen wall measuring 0.71m thick. Brakspear speculated that this wall continued under the other arches and separated the presbytery from the aisles in a similar fashion to Tintern and Fountains.

The south transept was of three bays and had two chapels against the east wall whereas the north transept, because of the claustral buildings, could not be similarly enlarged. The two columns of the east wall of the south transept appear to have been destroyed by mining or by the use of props. In plan, these columns comprised four half-circles surrounded by eight detached columns. The arches were of three mould-ed members and had hood moulds, but no vaulting ribs were found suggesting that the transept was not vaulted. The crossing was marked by the holes of the grubbed out piers.

Although there was no evidence of a tower over the cross-ing, Brakspear suggested that there would have been one and that it would have been a low construction and narrower from east to west than from north to south (*ibid.*, 552).

The nave had north and south aisles and measured 40m long by 10m wide; it comprised eight bays. There was evi-dence for six pillars, tiles, a burial, and possible chapel in the north aisle. In addition, a 'mass of foundation of its [south ailse] south and west walls remains in the south-west angles'. The architectural evidence for the walls of the nave is fragmentary, and Brakspear considered that they could be ascribed to either the twelfth or thirteenth century, i.e. first or second phase build. However, he thought that the original nave would be the same width as the transepts based on the spacing between the two choir stalls, which he thought was too narrow. At the west end there was a Galilee porch (*ibid.*, 558-9).

Later, in the first half of the fourteenth century, there were additions to the second stone church when four chapels, and possibly more, were constructed on the exterior face of the south wall of the nave. Fragmentary evidence of flooring was found in two of the chapels but was more extensive in a third. Here tiles were found bearing motifs of leopards of England, chevrons of Clare, and three lions rampant. The *pulpitum*, separating the choir from the nave, was built. The lower part of the west screen wall survives; it was 0.86m thick and had a doorway measuring 1.2m

wide in the centre (*ibid.*, 559).

The cloister lay to the north of the church and was marked by trapezoidal level area that measured 32m by 30.5m (*ibid.*, 561-2). Surrounding it were pentice-covered walks, which had been re-built in the fourteenth century, possibly at much the same time as the side chapels along the nave, with a series of arches resting on dwarf walls on the clois-ter side. On the west side a section of a well-preserved tiled floor marked a wide lane or court.

The east range comprised the vestry, chapter house, par-lour, and monks' dormitory at first-floor level. The ves-try was attached to the north transept of the church, and although it appears to date to the thirteenth century, an inserted doorway on the north wall was probably a post-dissolution feature indicating that this part of the abbey was in use in the later sixteenth century (*Chapter Six*). The most imposing chamber was the chapter house, which measured 18.5m by 9.25m and had six bays. Beyond the chapter house was a narrow parlour with a passage, which led to the presumed infirmary. North of the parlour was a twelve bay sub-vault, and apart from one small section the side walls, had been grubbed out. Attached to the east range were further robbed out trenches, which Brakspear interpreted as the monks' latrines (*ibid.*, 562-68).

Along the north side of the cloister was the warming room, refectory, and kitchen, but there was no evidence of a *lava-torium*. Apart from a fragmentary part of the north wall of the refectory, the remainder had been grubbed out. The refectory was orientated north/south and was 37m by 9.2m (*ibid.*, 569-71). No evidence for an earlier refectory, which would presumably have been orientated east/west like oth-er early refectories, was found.

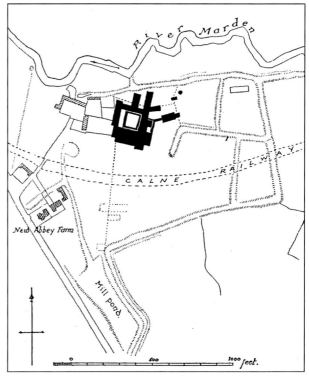

Figure 3:4. Brakspear's plan of the precinct (after Brakspear 1908, facing 548).

The west range was nine bays long and divided almost centrally by a small entrance. There were four bays to the south of the entrance and five to the north. Based on the evidence of the pilaster buttresses, this range possibly dates to the twelfth century; however, there were also fifteenth-century or later internal walls (*ibid.*, 571-74).

On the eastern side of the east range was a small section of walling dating to the twelfth and thirteenth century, as well as part of the drainage system. To the south of this walling, close to a prominent water channel, was a rectangular building whose lines only survived by the robber trenches, which was interpreted as the infirmary hall with a possible chapel on the eastern side. There was however a large amount of building material but this appears not to have been analysed. The outline of the infirmary hall measured up to 36m by 16.5m; the width indicating that it was probably ailsed. To the north of the chapel foundations were revealed spanning a drain which were interpreted as a possible latrine. Between the infirmary and millrace was a circular feature, which Brakspear interpreted as a dovecot (*ibid.*, 574-6). The infirmary hall probably dates from the thirteenth century, and may have replaced an earlier, possibly timber construction in a similar manner to Kirkstall and Waverley, which were built in the twelfth century.

Although Brakspear did not excavate much beyond the church and conventual buildings, he produced a plan of the precinct and identified several features within it such as the inner gatehouse, possible mill site and the water channels surrounding the abbey (Fig 3:4). Cutting through the site was an abandoned railway line. During the construction of the line, several coffins were uncovered as well as walling (DM: 16.79). These coffins, situated on the south-east of the church, were probably part of the monks' cemetery.

Earthwork surveys

The earthworks at Stanley are striking in their scale and prominent survival that reflect a diverse and long history of occupation and land-use from the monastic period, through to a post-suppression phase when the abbey was transformed into a secular residence with outbuildings, attendant gardens and parkland, leading finally to its eventual abandonment and conversion to a farmstead (Fig 3:5). The analysis of the earthworks, therefore, unlike the excavation, provides a more 'holistic' view of the monastic and later developments, and enables the history of the site to be unravelled and understood.

The Archaeological Division of the Ordnance Survey undertook an earthwork survey of the abbey site in 1968. The resulting plan (NMR: ST 97 SE 2) shows little change from the plan produced for the 1st edition Ordnance Survey map, which was probably the one used by Brakspear. Several post-monastic features are evident cutting through the site, which includes the remains of a canal embank-

Figure 3:5. The earthworks at Stanley Abbey The site of the church and conventual buildings are marked by the earthworks below Old Abbey Farm (upper right). Curving through the site is a former railway-line with Abbey Farm in the angle between the road and railway (NMR: 15208/17. ST 9672/26 ©English Heritage).

Figure 3:6. Earthwork survey of Stanley Abbey and its precinct surveyed at a scale of 1:1000 (NMR: ST NE 2; after Brown 1996; ©English Heritage)

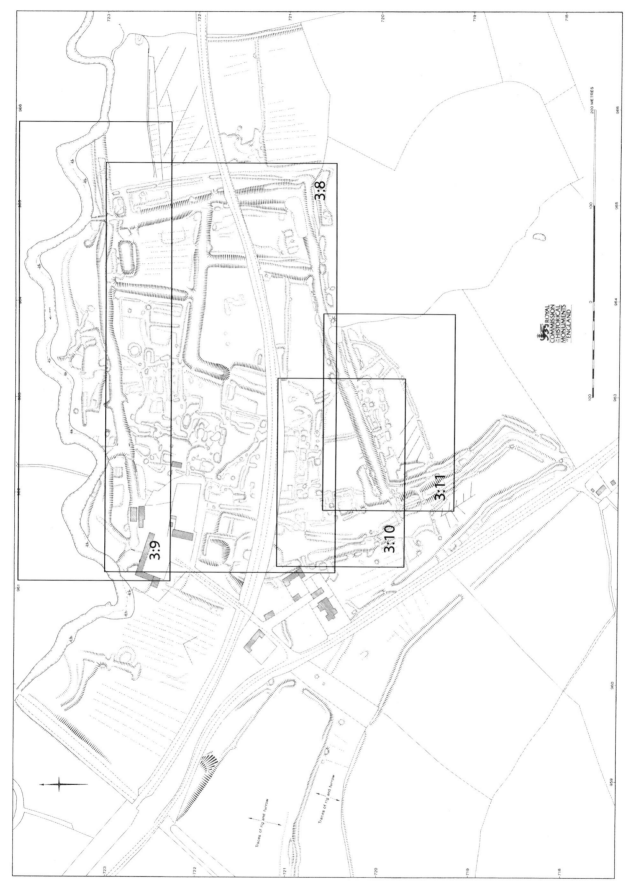

Figure 3:7. Earthwork survey showing insets

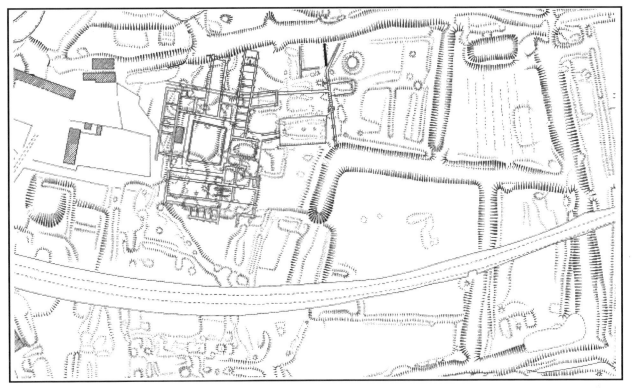

Figure 3:8. Earthwork survey overlain with Brakspear's excavation plan.

ment, a railway line, and a road that borders the southern side of the precinct. Within the precinct are two farm-steads, the northerly one, Old Abbey Farm, includes the only upstanding medieval building while the other, Abbey Farm, is situated on the southern side of the railway-line and dates to the nineteenth century. The site of the abbey was noted but not surveyed, and only a few earthworks within the precinct itself were plotted. In common with all their surveys there was little analysis of the site apart from the identification of probable fishponds and building stances on the southern side of the railway.

In 1996 the RCHME undertook a more detailed survey (Brown 1996; Fig 3:6). In order to simplify the analysis of the earthworks, the overall plan has been divided into several smaller, enlarged plans (Fig 3:7).

The precinct boundary is marked by a fragmentary bank and external ditch on three sides and the River Marden in the north thus enclosing an area of about 11.4 hectares (Fig 3:6). The boundary is most prominent along both the eastern and western sides where it stands to a maximum of 0.2m high. On the eastern side the bank (a) extends from a leat in the north to a point where it abuts a water channel in the south, suggesting that the channel is probably later than the bank, or that it has been re-dug at some stage. There are two entrances along the bank; the northerly one is slightly wider with a building platform on either side. A rectilinear enclosure to the south of the southern building platform may have been a yard or garden (b). Along the southern side the precinct boundary is more fragmentary. In the south-western corner a stone bridge (c) spans the channel linking the doglegged causeway to the precinct. Stone rubble in this area may be the remains of walling or

possibly the remains of an outer gate. On the western side the precinct boundary (d) extends from the modern farm buildings towards a railway-line beyond which its course is uncertain. It is marked by a bank and external ditch. To the west of the boundary there is evidence of ridge-and-furrow that extends west as far as the eighteenth-century canal embankment. A ditch and circular feature (e), the southern part of which has been back-filled, overlies the ridge-and-furrow. The purpose of this ditch is unclear, but there are three possible interpretations. First, it may be a later drainage ditch; second, it may be an extension to the precinct, in which case at its maximum the precinct was about fifteen hectares; third, since this area was part of the home grange (*Chapter Four*) it is more likely to be a ditched field boundary. Within the precinct there is a plethora of earthworks representing the church and con-ventual buildings, as well as other buildings and features associated with a monastic and post-medieval landscape.

The 'core' of the abbey

To the east of Old Abbey Farm are the amorphous earth-works of the church and conventual buildings. Without the aid of Brakspear's excavation plan, which is overlain on the earthwork survey, the earthworks would have been dif-ficult to interpret (Fig 3:8). The church is defined by scarps and banks that form a sub-rectangular feature along the southern side. The cloister occupies a level platform im-mediately to the north of the church. Fragmentary linear banks to the west mark the area of the west range with the remainder underlying building debris and a farm wall.

Along the east range is a circular depression (a) which marks the site of the chapter house. North of this are two

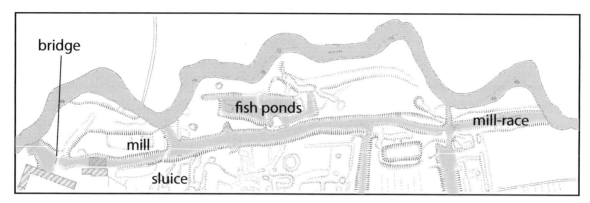

Figure 3:9. The mill and fishpond complex. Braided water channels are evident just to the south of the river. In the early seventeenth century the mill was a combined fulling and corn mill and it is likely that there were tenters nearby.

fragmentary parallel banks that define the side walls of the remainder of the range. To the east of the east range, and on a different alignment, is a rectangular earthwork, which is probably the site of the infirmary (b). To the north of the infirmary, and adjoining the east range, is a rectangular feature, which was probably the monks' latrine (c). The remainder of the conventual buildings' earthworks are quite fragmentary. To the east of the infirmary, and almost abutting it, is a slight ditch, which marks the course of a conduit identified by Brakspear. Further north, against the millrace, is a square enclosure, which is probably the site of a walled enclosure (e).

The area to the east of the abbey complex (d) is best interpreted as a garden and orchard, which is enclosed on the south, east, and north sides by a small bank. Sited on the 'quiet' side of the abbey near the infirmary, this complex of earthworks in their present form at least, as well as those in the two compartments to the south-east, probably date to the post-Suppression period, but probably overlie medieval gardens. Within this area are several slight scarps that sub-divide it into smaller garden compartments with a small circular mound mid-way along the eastern side. This feature may have been either a garden seat or small prospect. Another circular feature, interpreted by Brakspear as a dovecote, lies on the north-western side of the garden. The orchard (f) lies on a moated site to the east of the garden and is shown by the slight furrows that overlie a rectilinear building platform with a more recent pond on the northern side.

To the south of the garden and orchard are two rectilinear platforms or moat platforms surrounded, for the most part, by water channels. The eastern platform (g) has a spread bank, possibly walling, on the east and west sides with two building platforms in the southwest corner. The western platform (h) is largely devoid of earthworks apart from a fragmentary enclosure in the southwest corner.

To the south-west of the abbey is a large rectilinear depression, cut out of the natural scarp (j). It is bounded in the north by an 'L'-shaped bank with a further rectilinear enclosure to the east. This depression was probably a building stance with a garden or yard set within the enclosure.

Beyond the abbey complex and gardens there are several

earthworks reflecting a diverse land-use. The most distinctive and substantial are the ditches, or water channels. Their layout is unusual since, while some border the precinct, others extend at right-angles forming three moated sites. In addition, a slight ditch (k) on the southern side of the railway-line appears to turn towards a prominent channel in the north, suggesting the water management scheme is incomplete.

The mill and fishponds

Along the northern side of the precinct is a former millrace that flowed in a westerly direction from the river and provided water to a mill and fishponds (Fig 3:9). The millrace, now dry, is punctured in two places where the principal water channels empty into it, and by a small cutting on the north side that provided water to the fishponds. Towards the western end the millrace forks and a probable sluice, defined by a constriction and debris in the leat, would have controlled the water at this point; one branch leads back to the river while the other continues towards a pond. Stonework in the sides of the bank near the sluice indicates that they were revetted. The westerly channel narrows appreciably and, coupled with the increased depth, would suggest there was a mill here. This is probably the site of the combined fulling and corn mill mentioned in the early seventeenth century that lay within the precinct.

On the northern side of the millrace there are a series of depressions that mark the site of the fishponds, and several scarps and ditches, which may be earlier braided water channels. These channels, including the millrace before it was 'canalised', perhaps fossilise the pre-monastic landscape.

Gatehouse complex

On the southern side of the railway are several building platforms defined by rectilinear enclosures, some appear to have internal divisions while others are on two levels (Fig 3:10). On the southern edge of the precinct is a small bridge, which is the probable location of an outer gate. A partial lane, overlain by a deep rectangular depression, leads to a larger rectangular feature. The location of this feature, just inside the precinct boundary and close to the

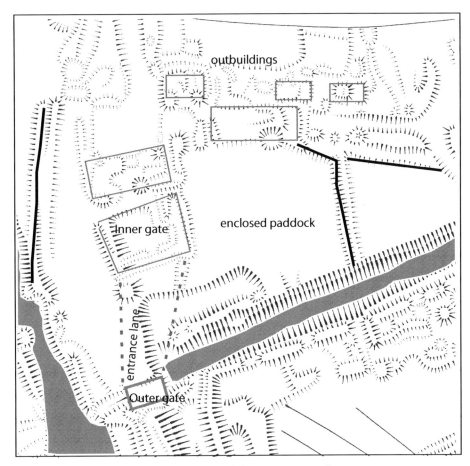

Figure 3:10. The gatehouse complex. The black lines represent walls.

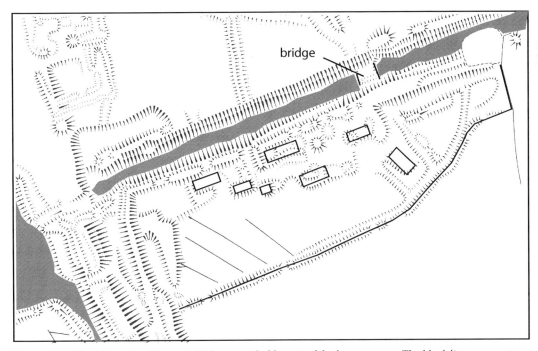

Figure 3:11. The 'extra-mural' zone, which was probably part of the home grange. The black line represents a wall or paling along the bank.

41

house. If this is the case, the outbuildings just beyond are probably associated with it and may include the guest accommodation, porter's lodge and stabling. In the angle between the inner gate and outbuildings is a small, enclosed paddock; while on the western side of the gate is a wide bank, which is probably the remains of a wall.

Extra-mural features

On the southern side of the precinct is a doglegged causeway that leads from the monastery towards Close Wood (Fig 3:6). On either side is a slight ditch that tapers on the western side but widens on the east. On the western side of the causeway, on lower ground, is a relatively flat area, which is bordered in the west by a bank. This area is another probable fishpond (Fig 3:6f). Within the pond are a series of herringbone drainage channels; these, and others within the area, reflect a post-suppression land-use when the area was being drained presumably to provide additional pasture. As we have seen, a contour leat was constructed in 1214 from Loxwell to Stanley; the course of this leat into the precinct would probably have been along this causeway.

On the southern side of the precinct, and abutting the causeway, is an enclosure defined by a curving bank with an internal ditch (Fig 3.11). On a ledge along the northern side are several building platforms. A slight hollow way can be seen leading from the gatehouse complex towards this point; there is also debris of a probable bridge in the channel. It is not entirely clear what this extra-mural area represents, but it is clearly later than the precinct and was possibly built during a period of economic growth in the thirteenth century and may be part of the home grange.

The Architectural Evidence

Old Abbey Farm, which lies close to the former west range, is the only surviving late medieval building within the precinct (Fig 3:12). The farmhouse dates to at least the late sixteenth or early seventeenth century but incorporates elements of an earlier, late medieval building. It is a two-storey building built principally of limestone rubble with brickwork and ashlar on the southern end. It is a six-bay structure, with the southern two bays having signs of smoke blackening to the roof indicating that it was once an open hall building. On the southern gable-end there are two blocked entries, which possibly led to former services. It is unclear how big the original building was, or its original function since it was re-built in the late sixteenth or early seventeenth century as a three-room lobby entrance plan building (NMR: ST 97 SE 8/67). It's position, however, on the west side of the abbey and close to the later Abbot's Lodging (which was in the west range), would suggest that it may have been a guest chamber, or an official's chamber. A similar example of guest chambers in this position can be seen at Tintern (Robinson 2006, 164).

On the southern side of the railway-line is another farmstead, Abbey Farm, which was built in 1862. Whether any

Figure 3:12. Old Stanley Abbey Farm, the only late medieval building within the precinct (south is to the right).

archaeological features were uncovered during the construction of the farm is unknown but given its position on the west side of the precinct, and the identification by Brakspear of a ditch along its northern side and building stances further east, it is probable that it has high archaeological potential.

DISCUSSION

In this section the excavation and earthwork survey evidence is analysed to determine the form and extent of the church and conventual buildings and features within the precinct, and is followed by a comparison with monastic sites elsewhere.

Brakspear's excavation methodology

In order to understand the excavated evidence it is first necessary to appreciate the methods employed by the early twentieth century excavators. Only with such an understanding can the strengths and weaknesses of their work be appreciated.

During the nineteenth century there was a change of emphasis in monastic studies and a more 'scholarly' approach was adopted that involved the study of the architecture of the ruins and the recovery of buried remains. Coppack sees this interest as being an attempt to re-establish medieval roots and a break from the eighteenth century classicism: a move which he asserts was led by both the Evangelical and the Anglo-Catholic wings of the established church. Abbeys were seen as a link to the medieval past which Victorian society could relate to with its notion of piety, patronage and Gothic architecture (Coppack 1990, 20). The archaeological excavation of places such as Fountains Abbey and Lewes Priory were in many respects important milestones in monastic studies since, for the first time, ground-plans were revealed and the recovered material was used to interpret the standing buildings. The recovery of pottery and architectural detailing at some sites, motivated by the arts and crafts movement as opposed to political ideals and ideas of religion, led to an appreciation of the craftsmanship and styles gion, led to an appreciation of the craftsmanship and styles of objects, but without an understanding of the archaeological context (Gerrard 2003, 59). These early excavations were, therefore, primarily concerned with the medieval fabric and gave scant regard to later, or indeed earlier periods. Some antiquarians, such as the clergymen W Bazeley and St Clair Baddeley who excavated Hailes Abbey, were more concerned with clearing the fallen masonry and rubble and revealing the monastic ground-plan for display to the public rather than recording the material properly (Bazeley 1899); however, there were others who adopted a more systematic and analytical approach to their excavations. One of these was Harold Brakspear, who is frequently associated with William St John Hope, and it was these two men who became the most prominent figures in monastic archaeology in the late nineteenth and early twentieth centuries. Their reports remain an invaluable source for our understanding of many monastic sites (Green 1992, 37). Brakspear was not a professional archaeologist, but an architect who was heavily involved in church 'restoration', but also undertook several excavations in his home county of Wiltshire and elsewhere in England and Wales such as the Cistercian houses at Waverley, Beaulieu, Rievaulx, Jervaulx and Tintern.

Brakspear's excavation technique, although for the time can be seen as revolutionary, would probably not stand up to much scrutiny today; it involved a combination of area excavation and trenching along the lines of walls in order to recover the layout of the abbey. The monastic plan was the ultimate aim, it shows the abbey layout in a variety of colour tints that were used to indicate the date-ranges of buildings and, importantly, his reports invariably included a plan of the precinct with suggested locations of some buildings. However, despite his undoubted conscientiousness, the rapidity and the use of labourers, throws into question some of his conclusions. For example, there are no section drawings, nor is there any concern for stratigraphy; parts of the plan appear to be conjecture, for example, the east wall of the presbytery (Brakspear 1919-20, 553); the recording of objects receives little attention; and the post-suppression phase is largely ignored. Looking at the photographs of Brakspear's fieldwork at Waverley it is clear that, in Green's words, the excavation 'seems to anticipate trench warfare; in other cases it looks like opencast mining' (Green 1992, 39). This comment, although seemingly harsh, does not necessarily apply to Stanley since Brakspear found that 'on the east side of the cloister were high mounds, on the south the frater was marked by a deep sinking' and 'further sinkings and mounds marking the position of the infirmary buildings' (Brakspear 1919-20, 547). He did not, however, 'reinstate' the site, but rather left it as a series of amorphous earthworks that we see today. Green also questions the reliability of some of the dates of the buildings at Waverley; he considers that those that had been dated using documentary sources were broadly correct, but elsewhere the architectural style is used, and where it is absent there appears to be a degree of guesswork (Green 1992, 39). Brakspear's interpretation of Cistercian monasteries was aided by the fact that their lay-

out followed a very similar pattern and he therefore knew what to expect; he would describe each range in some detail, but without providing much supporting evidence. As Kinder points out:

'So much has been written about the architecture, particularly the claustral buildings, that a popular belief has arisen that the plan of a Cistercian abbey is wholly predictable and can be reconstructed after finding a portion of one of the walls […]. In fact, no two identical abbeys have been found, although a general layout of the buildings around the cloister may be anticipated to some extent, at least in men's abbeys' (Kinder 2001, 37).

It is against this background that the excavation at Stanley should be seen. The evidence should not necessarily be taken at face value, but looked at critically with a view, perhaps, of shedding fresh interpretations. The example of Tintern emphasises the point where, following an excavation in 1919-20, the plan of the first phase church produced by Brakspear was considerably modified (Robinson 2006, 57).

The Church at Stanley

The excavated evidence would suggest that the church and conventual buildings underwent several changes, although there were essentially two phases of stone church building. Evidence from some Cistercian sites elsewhere however shows that the first buildings would probably have been a cluster of wooden structures, although there was no evidence for them at Stanley. At Meaux, for example, which was founded in 1151, the earliest buildings comprised a 'certain great house built with common mud and wattle [...]' and a chapel next to the house where the monks had, unusually, their dormitory on the ground floor with an oratory above (Fergusson 1983, 79-80; Coppack 1998, 27).

The possibility that there were earlier buildings at Stanley should be considered. For example, the cloister does not appear to have been excavated, nor the area to the south of the church. The potential for these areas is shown at Rievaulx and Cleeve. At Rievaulx a geophysical survey revealed evidence of a possible earlier aisle-less church within the cloister, while at Cleeve the foundations of part of a probable earlier church was found below the south transept (Fergusson and Harrison 1999, 46-48; Parker et. al. 2007, 80-81). Also, archaeological investigations at Fountains revealed the plan of a small rectangular structure beneath the crossing and south transept of the present church, as well as traces of a dormitory which, unlike Meaux, was separated from the church (Fergusson 1983, 81).

The excavation plan for Stanley shows little evidence for the first stone church, nevertheless Brakspear considered that it appeared to be similar to those at Bindon, Cleeve, Calder, Roche, and Buildwas; it would have had a short square-ended aisle-less presbytery, north and south transepts each with two chapels against the eastern side, a low tower over the crossing, and an aisled nave (Brakspear 1908, 552). However, this interpretation should be treated with caution since the evidence is so fragmentary. There is, for example, no evidence on the plan for two chapels in either of the transepts, or indeed evidence for the south transept. Brakspear was also unclear whether the nave arcade was of twelfth or thirteenth century date, but arguing for a twelfth. Tintern may be a useful comparison as far as the form of the first church is concerned despite it being founded twenty years before Stanley. At Tintern, where the church also lies to the south of the cloister, the first stone church underlies the north side of the nave of the Gothic church. However, it had an aisle-less nave, box presbytery, and transepts to the north and south, unlike Stanley whose nave may have been aisled.

There is more evidence for the second stone church when it was either 're-modelled or enlarged' and occupied by the monks in 1247, although it was not until 1266 that it was finally dedicated. This was followed in 1270 when the new refectory was completed (Bod: Digby 11, f. 184). The Gothic church measured 69m x 24m, a little smaller than the church at Tintern (74m x 25m) and, like Tintern, the *pulpitum* occupies the second bay in the nave. It had a larger presbytery than the first stone church with two chapels, and a nave of eight bays.

Further changes occurred at Stanley during the fourteenth century including the construction of several side chapels against the south side of the nave. Side chapels in the transepts and presbyteries of monastic churches were common; indeed there were at least four at Stanley and there was probably more, extending along the whole length of the nave. Their purpose was to provide additional space for the monks to celebrate Mass; however, the simple plan-form of many Cistercian churches meant that further space might have been required. One solution appears to have been to construct a row of chapels along the side of the nave, but significantly those at Stanley, whereas there was a side chapel on the north side of the nave, the other chapels were on the outside. This is extremely rare in Britain where only three other monastic examples, Buildwas, Melrose and Coggeshall, have been identified. It has been suggested that they may have been a continental influence where they are more common (Fawcett and Oram 2004, 137). At Melrose a row of eight external side chapels was built in the early fifteenth century - much later than those at Stanley; several appear to have been used as chantry chapels and the burial place for important families (*ibid.*). At Buildwas a single large chapel was built in the south side of the nave in the fourteenth century and is thought to have been a chantry (Robinson 1998, 80). At Stanley there is no evidence of their function but it is possible that they were used in a similar way to those at Melrose and Buildwas.

There is further evidence of this fundamental re-organisation of the liturgical space in the area of the nave when, in 1342, a 'separation' for the elderley and infirm monks be-

tween the monks' choir and the lay brother's choir and the mention of the Lady altar is documented (Chettle and Kirby 1956, 274). It is perhaps significant that these changes occurred at much the same time as changes in the management of Stanley's territory with granges being leased.

Figure 3:13. The twelfth-century lane at Byland viewed from the church. There are thirty-five niche seats along the east side of the lane.

The conventual buildings

On the north side of the cloister at Stanley stood the refectory. It was orientated north/south, which was the common orientation for Cistercian refectories from the later twelfth century (Harrison 2010, 122). Prior to this they were orientated east/west in a similar manner to Benedictine monasteries and presumably it was changed in order to accommodate the increasing numbers of monks. No evidence of this earlier phase refectory was found at Stanley; however, the almost total absence of building material makes a thirteenth-century single-phase interpretation questionable.

A rather unusual feature along the west side of the cloister, separating it from the west range, was a wide passage or lane. There are only a few such examples in English Cistercian monasteries and where they are found they have been interpreted as a way of further separating the lay brothers' accommodation from the cloister, and a similar interpretation can be proposed for the one at Stanley (Ludlow 2005, 71; Cassidy-Welch 2001, 52). They may also have been used as an assembly point for the lay brothers before they entered the church, which is perhaps highlighted at Byland by the seats (Harrison 1999, 20; Fig 3:13).

The fact that the cloister is not square is intriguing, particularly when the cloister at Pontigny is considered. Here the monastery lies on the south bank of the River Serein, with the church on the south side of the cloister as at Stanley. However, the cloister is trapezoidal, which suggests that the route of the water system existed before the construction of the abbey (Kinder 2001, 42). Although this explanation cannot necessarily be applied to Stanley, it nevertheless highlights the point that these buildings were not built in isolation.

Brakspear's excavation plan shows an L-shaped wall dating to the twelfth and thirteenth centuries with no buttresses on the north-eastern side of the conventual buildings, with a dovecot to the east, but he does not offer any interpretation. The walls appear to be the same thickness as the walls elsewhere in the conventual buildings. Comparing his plan with that of Tintern, which had a similar layout with the church on the south side of the conventual buildings, a rectangular building with no buttresses and a detached dovecot is evident in much the same place as that at Stanley; in this case it dates to the early thirteenth century. This has been interpreted as the Abbot's *Camera*, or hall (Robinson 2002). It is possible, therefore, to give a similar interpretation to the features at Stanley. This is perhaps supported by Ramy's research into abbot's lodgings where the most common location was in the area to the east or south-east of the east range (Ramy 1996, 27) – in much the same area as the feature at Stanley. Initially abbots lived communally with the monks in the dormitory; however, because of the need to entertain guests and carry out other duties without disturbing the community, separate accommodation with a kitchen, hall and possibly chapel became increasingly popular. The earliest evidence of this shift is at Rievaulx where the third abbot, Ailred, was given permission by the General Chapter to eat and live in the infirmary, probably because of ill health. In about 1157 he ordered a 'mausoleum' to be built for him near the infirmary. Later, with the demise of the lay brothers, the west range was also sometimes used as the Abbot's range.

The Precinct

A study of the excavated evidence of the abbey gives us a reasonably clear impression of the form and date of the church and conventual buildings, as well as its adaptation into a secular residence in the later sixteenth century; but in order to understand the precinct and its environs a more 'holistic' approach is needed. The earthwork evidence shows that the precinct contained a range of buildings, enclosures, water systems and route-ways, but what they are and their significance is largely a matter of conjecture at this stage; however, using a landscape approach a plausible layout can be proposed.

Precincts were the physical separation of the sacred space from the secular world offering tranquillity and seclusion to the religious community. It was also a potent symbol in the landscape, emphasising the area of exclusion as well as the status of an ecclesiastical elite in much the same way that castles were perceived. It was also the centre of a highly productive landscape where agriculture and industry co-existed with the spiritual life. Hospitality, be it for pilgrims, guests, or the giving of alms, were an important element of any monastic community, and it was from the gate that it was dispensed. The precinct could also be seen as defensive, particularly in the more contentious regions of the country such as the Welsh Marches or the Scottish borders. Many of these themes can be demonstrated at

Stanley Abbey.
Many Cistercian precinct boundaries appear to have been marked by a wall (Robinson 2006, 166); however, this should not necessarily be taken as the norm. At Tilty Abbey (Essex) and Hailes Abbey, for example, there was a combination of stone walling and hedging or paling which, in Hailes's case, survives as an earthen bank (Hall and Strachan 2001, 200; Brown 2006, 27). At Stanley the boundary is mainly marked by a bank and external ditch, the bank was probably surmounted by a hedgerow or paling since there is no evidence of stonework. However, in 1292 the monks were granted the right to dig stone in the king's quarry at Pewsham Forest for 'building the abbey houses and a wall about them' (*Cal Pat R Ed I 1281-92*, 484). Although this implies that the precinct was stone walled, it is not necessarily the case as can be demonstrated at Hailes where a map dating to 1587 shows that the inner court was the only part of the precinct that had a stone wall; it is also noteworthy that in 1550 the 'precinct' at Hailes was said to cover only eight acres, a fraction of what is now considered to be the area and it therefore probably referred to the inner court (TNA: PRO MF1/59; GRO: D2311/T2).

The size of the precinct varied enormously, and although Stanley's measured about 11.4 hectares it was at the smaller end of the scale and similar to Buildwas and Cleeve, but considerably smaller than many others such as Rievaulx, Fountains, Fountains, Bordesley and Meaux (Fig 3:14). Several factors appear to determine the area occupied by the precinct including land-ownership or size of initial endowment; the topography; date of foundation; and previous land-use. Land ownership and topography appear to be the most significant while the date of foundation seems to have had little or no impact. Tintern Abbey provides a useful example of an early Cistercian monastery. Founded in 1138 by Walter Fitz Richard de Clare, who was lord of nearby Chepstow, the abbey occupied a relatively remote position at the foot of the heavily wooded slopes beside the River Wye; thus the monks achieved the seclusion they sought although there was an existing settlement (Robinson 2006, 277). It was endowed with land either side of the river and the precinct covered an area of eleven hectares, which was slightly smaller than Stanley. A much later example is Hailes Abbey that was founded in 1214 by Richard, Earl of Cornwall, it was nevertheless granted the whole manor of Hailes, which enabled the monks to determine the site and size of their precinct unhindered by other landowners. The precinct covered about thirty hectares, which is similar to Meaux Abbey and Fountains Abbey, which were founded in 1151 and 1132 respectively. As far as the topography is concerned, some places were clearly constrained by the landform; at Roche Abbey the precinct was contained between the narrow sides of a steep valley.

Previous land-use seems to have had little effect on the precinct area at Stanley since there is no evidence of cultivation. At Bordesley, there was ridge-and-furrow within the precinct and, significantly, it was also found to underlie the precinct boundary along the northern side implying

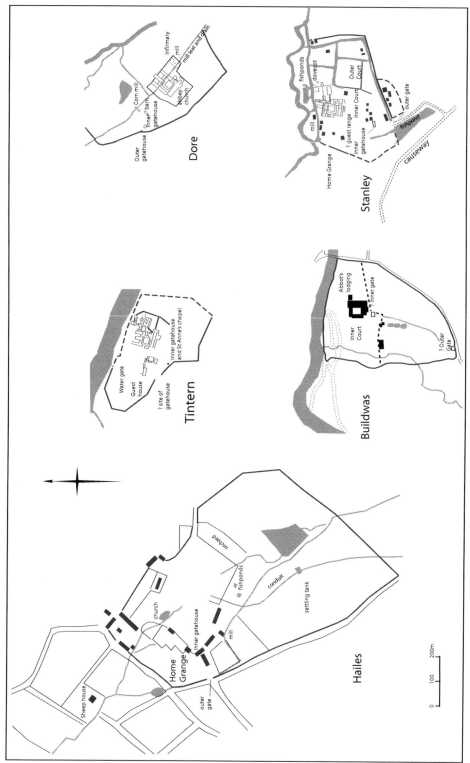

Figure 3:14. Comparative plans of Cistercian precincts (Stanley, Buildwas, and Hailes after Brown 1996; 2002; 2005; Tintern and Dore after Robinson 2006). Tintern, Buildwas, Dore and Stanley all had churches on the south side of the cloister. Hailes provides an example of the aea occupied by one of the larger Cistercian precincts and shows the buildings that survived the suppression until the late sixteenth century.

that the area was cultivated before the establishment of the precinct (Astill *et al* 2004, 130). Perhaps more important would have been the loss of meadow since this resource invariably commanded a higher value, but the incidence of

loss is unquantifiable in the archaeological record.

As we have seen, in seeking their 'desert' the Cistercians were not averse to establishing their monasteries in marsh-land where they quickly became adept at managing this

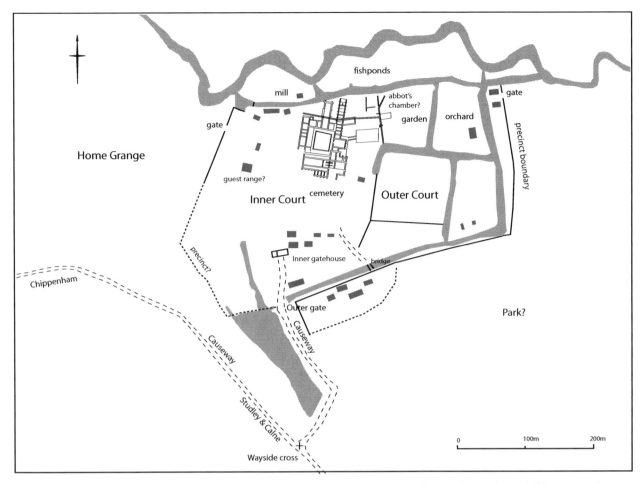

Figure 3:15. Interpretation of the precinct based on the earthwork evidence. The pecked line indicates the probable course of the precinct boundary.

resource. The marshland landscape at Stanley included several braided water channels within the precinct beside the River Marden, one of which they canalised to form the mill leat and water for a fishpond. The remaining braided channels were drained leaving the characteristic meanders as earthworks. This draining of water channels is also evident at Buildwas, but in this case it was to provide additional meadow (Brown 2002, 10). Compared to other sites, Stanley and Buildwas's initial water engineering seems relatively small-scale; at Bordesley it was far more ambitious. The River Arrow was canalised along one side of the valley ensuring a drained landscape for the abbey buildings. At Cleeve Abbey, it has been suggested that the original course of the River Washford flowed around the eastern side of the precinct, but was re-cut so that it flowed along the a channel beside the road to the west (Aston and Munton 1976, 33; Dunning 1985a, 41). Similarly at Rievaulx the acquisition of land in 1147 enabled the monks to divert the river to the south side of the valley. This was accomplished in three phases and effectively more than doubled the size of the precinct (Fergusson and Harrison 1999, 38). However, this interpretation, which is based on documentary evidence, is at variance with on-going field-work, which shows that the river was not diverted and that what has been interpreted as the former course of the river is a leat. The leat lies close to the foot of the escarpment and is higher than the river (Pearson *forthcoming*). At Pon-

tigny, a millrace nearly 3km long and formed by the damming of the river, provided water to three mills and the fishponds. On the higher ground to the south of the abbey two aqueducts allowed seasonal water to drain underneath the millrace into the river. The supply of pure water for the abbey was from two springs or wells located 800 metres to the south of the abbey (Kinder 2001, 43).

Entry to the precinct was through a series of gates, the principal one being the main gatehouse complex and comprised an outer and inner gate. Also in the complex there was probably the porter's lodging, and perhaps stabling and some guest accommodation; it was here that alms would be distributed, visitors, guests, and pilgrims met. The gatehouse complex in Cistercian monasteries was sited in a variety of locations ranging from due west, for example at Bordesley, Boxley, Dunkeswell, and Fountains, to north-west as at Culross, Roche, and Stoneleigh. It seems that the northern side of the precinct was less favoured although it does occur at Neath, and only occasionally was the south-west side preferred as at Hailes, Buildwas and Jervaulx. At Stanley, the earthwork survey would suggest that the outer gate was on the southern side of the precinct at the junction with a causeway (Fig 3:15). A track, cut by a later rectangular depression, led to a rectilinear enclosure, which is probably the location of the inner gate. The gate measures approximately 20m by 10m, which is

47

similar to the extant examples at Cleeve and Kingswood. From this point, the visitor is afforded a view to the west end of the conventual church. The gate was one of the few buildings to survive the Suppression and was still standing in 1619; it had a cottage and garden adjoining it (WSA: 473/246.46). This cottage may well have been the former porter's lodging.

The west front of the conventual church was the main focus for visitors and guests alike when they entered the inner gate, and this presumably played a large part in deciding where the main gatehouse was sited. For example, while the west side of the precinct would seem the most likely location for abbeys that had their conventual churches on the north side of the cloister, a south or south-west position seems to be the preferred location for those whose churches were on the south side of the cloister.

As far as the outer gate at Stanley is concerned, there is little evidence what form it would have taken; indeed, there appears to be little evidence of them throughout the country. In a recent study Fergusson (1990a, 55) found no evidence for Cistercian outer gates in Yorkshire although he did not doubt their existence; however, evidence from Hailes would suggest that they may have been no more than a simple field gate and would probably be the same as others around the precinct providing access to, for example, the home grange (Brown 2006, 29).

Another building that is sometimes associated with gatehouses is the gatehouse chapel. Where such examples have been identified it has been found that they were normally positioned between the inner and outer gates, although some were within the inner court, close to the gate (Hall 2001, 61-92). Hall's research suggests that these chapels fulfilled a variety of needs, with most having a parish function. There is also evidence that some were used as chantries or places of pilgrimage. They were principally used by people who were living or staying outside the precinct, and those who were not allowed within the inner court. As far as Stanley is concerned there is no evidence for such a chapel; however, the possibility of one being located near the gatehouse complex, perhaps the rectangualr depression to the south-east of the main gatehouse, should not be ignored.

Beyond the inner gate lay a series of enclosures, which have been generally termed the outer and inner court, with the spiritual centre, the abbey itself, at the heart of the whole complex. At Stanley it is difficult to ascertain the boundary between the inner and outer courts; however, the earthwork evidence would suggest that the inner court extended north from the gatehouse complex as far as the church and included a large sunken feature, which was probably a substantial building and garden, on the western side. The position of this building, so close to the church, would suggest that it was perhaps a further guest chamber or a monastic official's accommodation.

The remainder of the precinct was taken up by the outer court, and included at least three closes on the eastern side, as well as the mill near the river. In 1612, the mill, which was a combined corn and fulling mill, was two-bays long (WSA: 122/1). The home grange appears to have been a separate entity, occupying land on the western side of the precinct, but nevertheless linked to it by a gate (Chapter Four).

A LANDSCAPE OF LORDSHIP AND SECLUSION

The final topic questions whether we can interpret Stanley Abbey as being a 'designed landscape' or perhaps a 'landscape of lordship and seclusion', which may be apparent in its setting, the expansive fishpond with presumably an abundance of fish, the approach to the abbey, and its little park.

The concept of a designed landscape is more commonly associated with the parks and gardens surrounding post-medieval elite houses and those created by eighteenth-century landscape gardeners. However, this notion of a designed landscape is increasingly being recognised in a medieval context. Houses of the social elite such as castles, episcopal residences and monasteries, as well as being functional edifices could also have symbolic meanings reflecting social expression and visual impressions (Creighton 2009; Johnson 2002, 34). All classes of society would understand the imagery of water, the concept of the Marian *hortus conclusus*, and route-ways in such landscapes. Johnson (2002, 55-92) has shown how access to a castle, for example, could be controlled with perhaps a contrived approach to the inner, private core and how there was restricted access within the castle. In an ecclesiastical context, Taylor has suggested that the Bishop of Ely's parkland and water features at Somersham Palace (Cambs) formed an ambitious scheme of landscape manipulation (Taylor 1989, 211-24). Similarly, at Stow Palace (Lincs), a residence of the Bishop of Lincoln, where access was across a causeway with an expanse of water on either side, and the park, are seen as part of a designed landscape (Everson *et. al.* 1991, 185). Liddiard, in a study of castles, evaluates their functional role as military structures, but also argues that, in landscape terms, their aesthetic setting was a means for displays of lordly status (Liddiard 2005). However, Platt has sounded a note of caution and argues that, while they had many functions, the castle's *raison d'etre* was defence (Platt 2007, 83-102). Caution about the term 'designed landscapes' has also been expressed by Liddiard and Williamson who see that, although medieval elites clearly altered the surroundings of their residences and may have created metaphorical imagery, the term may be inappropriate since it 'essentially implies post-medieval concepts of planning, abstract landscape aesthetics, and perhaps surveying', which did not exist in the medieval period (Liddiard and Williamson 2008, 520). Perhaps a more appropriate term, at least in monastic terms, would be a 'landscape of lordship and seclusion' since it encapsulates attitudes towards religion and status through imagery within the monastic ambit, including the church and conventual buildings, and in the wider landscape.

As we have seen, monasteries did not just have a functional role as places of worship and centres for their grange economy, in some cases there was also a special symbolism in their siting and although their landscape credentials have not had the same attention of scholars as castles and ecclesiastical palaces, in many cases the characteristics in the landscape of lordship are evident in monasteries in a similar manner. Gilchist, for example, in her study of nunneries, has shown how the orientation of their cloisters may have symbolic meaning, and that the high incidence of cloisters in some parts of the country that are positioned to the north of the church may emulate a pre-Conquest foundation in order to 'convey social prestige and royal Saxon piety stemming from the Saxon monastic tradition of abbess-saints' (Gilchist 1994, 138). This 'gender orientation' is also apparent in the north transept of some nunnery churches and its association with the iconography of female saints and the Eucharist, and wall paintings of the Crucifixion and Resurrection. These associations may relate directly to the metaphor of church architecture with its cruciform symbolising the crucified body of Christ with the Blessed Virgin Mary on the right-hand (i.e. north) of Christ (*ibid.*, 140). Other symbols of gender are apparent in the imagery and delineation of space within the nunnery.

As far as the wider landscape is concerned, although there is no contemporary account for Stanley Abbey's setting, a rather poetic and evocative twelfth-century description of the natural beauty at Rievaulx from Walter Daniel's *The Life of Ailred* gives us a sense of how the abbey's landscape was perceived. He describes how:

'High hills surround the valley, encircling it like a crown. These are clothed by trees of various sorts and maintain in pleasant retreats the privacy of the vale, providing the monks a kind of second paradise of wooded delight'. From the loftiest rocks the waters wind and tumble down to the valley below, and as they make their hasty way through the lesser passages and narrower beds and spread themselves in wider rills, they give out a gentle murmur of soft sound and join together in sweet notes of a delicious melody. And when the branches of lovely trees rustle and sing together and the leaves flutter gently to the earth, the happy listener is filled increasingly with a glad jubilee of harmonious sound, as so many various things conspire together in such sweet consent, in music whose every diverse note is equal to the rest. His ears drink in the feast prepared for them, and are satisfied' (Powicke 1950, 12).

Another description, of the precinct at Clairvaux, surely illustrates that as well as having functional characteristics it shows an aesthetic picture and a deeper understanding of its landscape setting. The account describes how the Cistercians managed the River Aube to provide water to various places within the precinct. One area was the 'industrial' zone where water flowed through sluice gates, first to a corn mill and then a brew-house. Next it went to a fulling mill and then the tannery, beyond which it supplied a series of channels that led to other workshops before finally re-joining the river taking with it the 'waste'. Water was also directed around the orchards and gardens that were 'marked out into rectangles, or, more accurately, divided up by a network of streamlets; for, although the water appears asleep, it is in fact slipping slowly away'. From the river, water also 'meander[s] placidly through the meadows, saturating the soil that it may germinate' (Matarasso 1993, 285-91). This graphic account demonstrates how the monks manipulated the landscape, but at the same time saw it as a place of tranquillity and beauty. At Stanley the archaeological and topographic evidence shows that it too displayed elements of such a landscape, but first it is necessary to examine the functional landscape.

A Functional landscape

There were at least two sources of water to the monastery at Stanley. The first was the river, which fed a fishpond and mill, and also acted as a drain for the other parts of the precinct. The second source was the aqueduct that brought fresh water from Loxwell, through a network of water channels bordering the precinct boundary. As we have seen, however, this source may have had special symbolism. The water channels within the precinct appear excessively broad and deep; they also lie within the precinct and, in one place, cut the precinct boundary. In their present form, therefore, they would be more in place in a Tudor or Elizabethan garden setting; however, it is probable, given the topography of the precinct, that they follow, in part, the course of a medieval water channel or conduit (*Chapter Six*). Water features surrounding moated gardens and orchards within precincts were not unknown during the medieval period. A documented case is at Peterborough Abbey where, in 1302, a two-acre *herbarium* was planted and 'surrounded [...] with double moats, with bridges and pear trees and very lovely plants' (Harvey 1981, 13, 85).

Fishponds were as much about status as the monastery itself, and fish were an important part of the monastic diet. At Stanley there were two fishponds and there were also probably fish weirs along the River Marden. The ponds were established by at least the end of the thirteenth century since the monks were required to provide bream and pike to stock the royal fishponds at Marlborough in 1299 (*Cal Close R Ed I 1296-1302*, 287). One of the fishponds, as we have seen, lay beside the millrace along the northern side of the precinct, while the other was a wide pond along the western side of the causeway leading to the outer gate. Brakspear interpreted this latter pond as a millpond (1908, plan facing 548); however, it seems unlikely that a mill was sited in this area since the only source of water would have been from the channel that leads from Abbey Farm, which would have been insufficient and too irregular.

Despite the seeming plethora of water sources at Stanley, how the system functioned remains unclear. For example, was there a conduit house or settling tank for the water from Loxwell; how was the water regulated around the precinct; how were the outbuildings such as the guest range supplied? Although Brakspear's excavation uncovered some evidence of culverts, it is by no means the full extent.

A Landscape of Lordship and Seclusion

As well as having a functional use, there was also a 'landscape of lordship and seclusion' at Stanley. This is perhaps re-enforced by the evidence from sixteenth-century documents, such as an indenture of 1567 that mentions a park (WSA: 1213/20). This is possibly the one on nineteenth-century estate maps shown extending from the southern side of the precinct towards Studley, and while it was part of the post-Suppression landscape, it is probable that its origins lay much earlier, in the medieval period (WSA: 1213/20; Bowood Estate: Stanley maps). Such small parks are relatively common and in this case would form a liminal zone, an area of exclusion and seclusion, between the monastery and the secular world. A similar small park lay beside the precinct at Hailes Abbey and recorded in the mid-sixteenth century (Brown 2006).

The main approach to the abbey displayed symbols of lordship and seclusion. A visitor would first pass a wayside cross from the highway and then approach the abbey along the raised causeway; to the left would be a sheet of water, a fishpond, while on the other side was a park. The gatehouse was the focal point of this approach, its symbolism enhanced since it was the point where alms were given to the poor and pilgrims received. Beyond the gate there would have been a view to the west front of the conventual church – the church being the centre of the spiritual life of the monks and therefore a powerful symbol of Christianity.

Within the monastery there would be further symbolic meanings such as the church, the enclosed cloister and its garden. Although the material evidence does not survive 'above ground' the plan of the church and cloister shows areas with specific symbolic meanings, such as the side chapels along the south side of the nave, and the chapels in the north and south transepts, some of which would presumably have particular saints' dedications. The inclusion of the lane in the west side of the cloister, on the lay-brothers side, provides a further separation with the choir monks. Beyond the cloister there were the orchards and gardens, which would have been places of quietness and contemplation. These were also areas of exclusion to visitors since their access was controlled, but depending on who they were, dictated their degree of access.

The landscape at Stanley can therefore be seen as primarily a functional landscape, one that supplied the needs of the monks, but at the same time we should also recognise it as a landscape of lordship and seclusion that had embedded symbolism which would have been recognised by medieval society.

CHAPTER FOUR

BEYOND THE MONASTIC ENCLOSURE

THE ABBEY ENVIRONS

INTRODUCTION

Stanley Abbey was not only the spiritual heart of a religious community it was also the administrative centre of a network of granges and smaller estates that were essential for its well-being and success. Under the control of the Cellarer, the granges supplied the needs of the monastery and the market. Those close to the abbey, termed the home grange, were generally larger than the outlying examples since they were invariably the earliest to be established and in all probability were endowed by the abbey's patron, or one of his retinue, who had a vested interest in the success of the new foundation.

Much has been written about how the Cistercians reclaimed and cleared land and how they de-populated settlements in order to establish their monasteries or granges. The evidence, however, is largely drawn from the well-documented northern houses and some Welsh houses, but does the evidence from a southern monastery mirror this view? In the north the land was generally sparsely populated and therefore under-utilised; the area of Stanley Abbey was also relatively thinly populated, but nearby were Calne and Chippenham, which were both royal centres with markets and hinterlands of hamlets and farmsteads.

In common with a number of other Cistercian monasteries in England, Stanley Abbey and its home grange lay within a royal forest, which would have had a strong influence on how it developed. The abbey held large tracts of land in Chippenham Forest; in the mid nineteenth century there was a little over 1,481 acres (599ha) of tithe-free land; this was the abbey's land (Christ College, Oxford, mss Estates 93/128). Apart from being a royal hunting reserve, the Forest was exploited for its natural resources such as timber and minerals, and used by animals for pannage and pasture; monastic communities and secular individuals alike cleared land for cultivation.

As well as controlling a large tract of land in the environs of Stanley, the Cistercians were also a great employer, and an economic powerhouse in the region. Although the number of monks and other individuals associated with the abbey at any given time is unclear it must have been large, but perhaps not as many as Rievaulx Abbey (Yorks) where, in the 1167 it was claimed by Walter Daniel, a contemporary biographer of Ailred their most renowned abbot, that there were 140 monks, about 240 lay brothers and about 260 laymen (Powicke 1950, 38). Although this may be an exaggeration it nevertheless points to a large community associated with a monastery. Certainly by 1204, just fifty years after its foundation, the numbers of monks and *conversi* at Stanley was sufficient to enable some to leave and found a daughter house at Graiguenamanagh in Ireland.

Granges and Manors

Economic and social administration during the Middle Ages was centred on the manor and the principal of lordship whereby the inhabitants of the manor owed rents and servile labour to their lord. However, one of the most distinctive features of the Cistercian order was the way in which they managed their landholdings outside this manorial system. This was achieved by organising their estates into a network of demesne farms, or granges, which were ideally consolidated and homogeneous blocks of land, perhaps enclosed and set around its own buildings. This process of consolidation could be a long protracted affair involving grants of land from individuals, purchases or exchanges, and in some cases it was never achieved. It was, however, in many cases a result of conscious economic planning on the part of the monks. Some granges were largely sheep-walks or vaccaries, which could be quite complex when they combined enclosed pasture and rights to graze over a large area, as well as sharing pasture with others. Granges may have fulfilled a variety of other functions such as industrial, agricultural or coastal fishing. Granges were initially staffed by lay brothers under the control of a grange master, or granger, who in turn was answerable to the Cellarer at the monastery. Granges were also initially to be no more than a day's journey from the monastery, which would enable lay brothers to return to the abbey for religious services each Sunday. Another restriction was on the distance from other Cistercian granges, presumably to alleviate over-stocking and disputes.

The establishment of the grange system was a pragmatic solution to the early ideals of the community since one of the Cistercian 'Institutes', as encapsulated in the *Exordium Parvum*, prohibited the monks from profiting from the labour of others, and from manors, mills and churches (Lekai 1977, 282).

Granges were not the prerogative just of the Cistercians but were emulated by some of the other new 'reformed' orders such as the Premonstratensians, the Gilbertines, and Carthusians. Some elements of the system were also adopted by the older orders of Cluniacs and Benedictines but they maintained a largely manorial structure.

In time, particularly with the leasing of land from the thirteenth century, it has been suggested that granges appear to become synonymous with manors and the Cistercians effectively became lords of a manor (Williams 2001, 209). But,

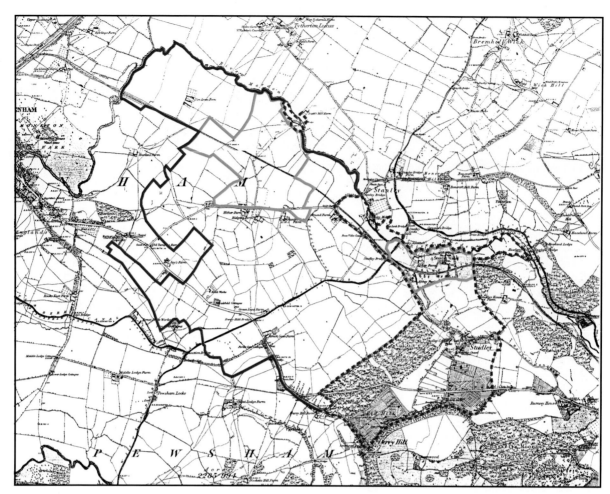

Figure 4:1. The manor of Stanley in the mid-nineteenth century overlain on the 1st edition OS 6-inch map. The pecked area is the manor's land in the parish of Bremhill while the solid red is in Chippenham parish. Titheable land in nineteenth century is shown in green (boundaries re-drawn from maps WSA: 873/350H, BRO: 31965/STG/10, Tithe map Chippenham).

as Alphonso has argued, the Cistercians did not necessarily live outside the manorial system; in her view they exercised some form of seigniorial control of the peasantry from the beginning. The Cistercian domination was exemplified in several ways such as the eviction of peasants to transform settlements into granges or a maintenance and control of a peasant population in their villages (Alphonso 1991).

The Topography of the Home Grange

Bordering the River Marden, the territory of Stanley's home grange extended south-west across the flat plain and beyond the ancient road linking Chippenham and Calne, and south-east from the River Avon to the top of the Corallian ridge at Redhill, later known as Derry Hill (Fig 4:1). The territory spread over two ecclesiastical parishes, those of Chippenham and Bremhill, and included most of the hamlet of Studley. There is no evidence of a church at Stanley and any lay inhabitants presumably attended their respective parish churches, unless they had dispensation to hear Mass in a chapel at the abbey such as a gatehouse chapel, or perhaps another within the precinct. In the late eighteenth century the settlement pattern was one of small hamlets, dispersed farmsteads, mills and what appears to be roadside encroachment. The principal communication

pattern seems to have changed little since the medieval period although several minor routes have been abandoned.

The Outer Granges

Beyond the home grange, deep within Chippenham Forest, lay Loxwell Grange which was also tithe-free in the mid nineteenth century. Two outlying farms, Ash and Nethermore, formed part of the home grange. In addition, there was a grange at Langley Burrell to the north of Chippenham; the tithe-free land here was described on the tithe award schedule as the 'ancient demesne' of Stanley Abbey (WSA: Tithe award schedule and map, Langley Burrell). The abbey also held land at Derriards (later known as Derriards Farm) in the manor of Sheldon and a small amount of land at Tytherton Lucas, although its full extent is unclear (Fig 4:2).

Aim of Chapter

The aim of this chapter is to analyse the abbey environs, the area beyond the precinct wall. It will focus on the home grange as well as the other granges within, or bordering, Chippenham Forest. It is divided into two distinct parts. First, there is an analysis of the forest, its extent, its re-

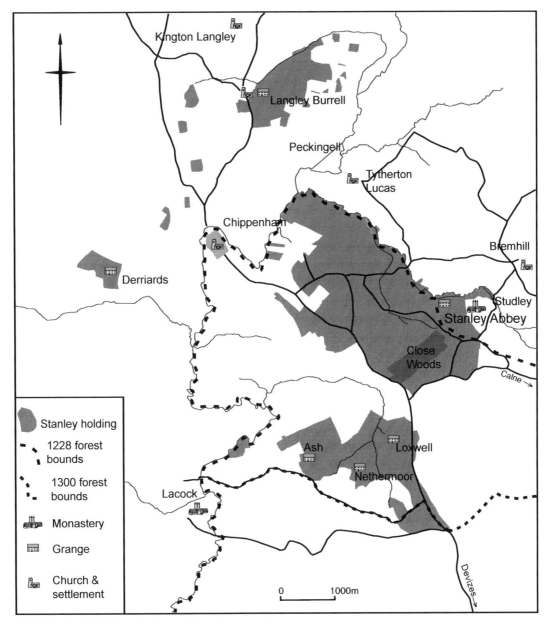

Figure 4:2. Stanley Abbey's territory in the Chippenham region.

sources and land-use by secular and monastic communities alike. The second part addresses four specific themes concerning the Cistercians' attitude to land acquisition in the environs of an abbey and assesses whether they apply to Stanley. First, to what extent did the monks at Stanley clear and colonise the region? In a forest setting, were they able to achieve a viable economic base to support the community but at the same time achieve the seclusion they desired? Secondly, what was the impact on the settlement and agrarian landscape? The third group of questions examines the monks' relationship to secular society and other Orders; were they agents of depopulation, and did they maintain their ideal of not having tenants and manors and therefore not encumbering themselves with 'feudal' connections? Finally, did Stanley differ from other Cistercian monasteries in their choice of site for their home grange and their methods of colonisation?

CHIPPENHAM FOREST

Stanley Abbey and its home grange were established within a royal Forest. The Forest, part of the extensive tracts of royal demesne which included the settlements of Chippenham, Calne, Rowde and Bromham, was part of the former Anglo-Saxon *Selwudu* and was initially administered as a single unit with Melksham Forest from Devizes Castle. However, in 1300 it was divided with Chippenham Forest, also sometimes referred to as Pewsham Forest, in the north covering an area of about eight square miles, and the much larger Melksham Forest in the south (Grant 1959, 407-14; Fig 4:3). There were also two parks in the thirteenth century held by Edmund, Earl of Cornwall, who was lord of the manor of Chippenham (Fry 1908, 268). Their location is unknown, but they presumably lay to the south of Chippenham below the Corallean escarpment.

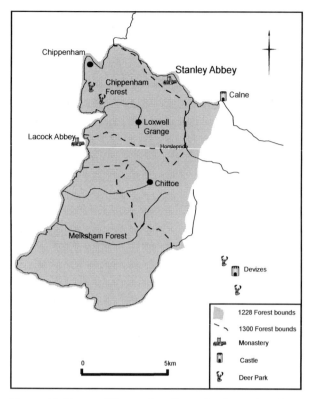

Figure 4:3. Extent of Chippenham Forest (re-drawn from Grant 1959, 447).

Hunting and the provision of venison for the king's table were of prime importance in the economy of the Forest. Fallow deer appear to have been the most common species; these animals were mainly grass-feeders (Rackham 1980, 177) requiring a reasonable amount of pasture, which would imply that parts of the forest contained open glades and pollard trees. Unlike timber, which appears to have been transported only a relatively short distance from Chippenham Forest, deer were moved much further. In 1233, for example, deer for the king were transported to Hereford and Gloucester, and in 1261 seventy deer were sent 'wherever the king is' (*Cal Lib R vol. 1*, 228, 233; *Cal Lib R vol. 5*, 20). They were also sent to re-stock other forests. In 1252, 100 does and fifty bucks were sent to Freemantle in Hampshire and eight years later forty does were sent to Kenilworth (*Cal Lib R vol. 4*, 26; *Cal Lib R vol. 5*, 249). These figures are intriguing since they indicate a high degree of stock management.

Since Chippenham Forest was a royal demesne, the woodland, like the deer, was held directly by the king. Wood was used as a building material as well as for firewood, charcoal, and fencing. There were several grants to the new monastic Orders in the region. Stanley Abbey, for example, received fifty-five oaks in 1222-23, and in 1237 there were further grants of timber for the church tower (Bond 2004, 93; Grant 1959, 409). Six oaks for choir stalls went to Bradenstoke Priory in 1232 (Grant 1959, 409). Fallen oaks were used as firewood; in 1223, Bradenstoke was granted eighteen such trees and another thirty 'dry oaks' were used for the Constable's hearth at Devizes Castle (*ibid.*). The bark of some trees was used for roofing; this material was known as shingles and in 1245, presum-

ably at a time of refurbishment or re-building, 36,000 were sent to the royal castles at Ludgershall and Marlborough (*Cal Lib R vol. 2*, 307). Over the following six years a further 35,000 shingles were sent (*Cal Lib R vol. 3*, 129, 293, 379). Although these figures seem large it was in fact quite modest since, for example, in 1332 over 19,000 shingles were used from another forest to re-roof the refectory at Croxden Abbey (Staffs) and a further 25,500 on its cloister (Lynam 1911, ix). Shingles may also have been the principal roofing material for some of the buildings at Stanley although Brakspear does not mention them in his excavation report. The bark of trees was also used in the tanning of hides. According to Hockey, 'the tannin derived from oak-bark produced the finest leather then known' (Hockey 1970, 55). Although the evidence is lacking, Stanley was probably involved in tanning in a similar manner to other Cistercian houses. The only evidence at Stanley is from a survey in 1612, which shows that there was a bark house 'standing on posts' at one of their former properties in Chippenham (WSRO: 122/1).

One of the consequences of an increasing population during the thirteenth and early fourteenth centuries was the expansion, or intensification, of land-use on to what has been generally termed 'marginal' land such as the downlands, moors and forests. Within Chippenham Forest this expansion took the form of assarting (the clearing of land for cultivation), the draining of the moors and in some cases ditching closes. One individual assarted 145 acres of 'waste' in the forest and, as Payne suggests, this may have been added to Chippenham's existing field system (Payne 1939, 93-96). There were several other assarts but of significantly smaller areas. In 1327, John le Clerk held sixteen acres of waste, and four years later Richard le Tanner was allowed to retain four acres of land that he purchased without licence from the king 'at which land was arrented out of the king's waste in the Forest of Chippenham and Pewsham'. In 1331, Richard Seryven and his wife Alice were allowed to rent out nineteen acres of heath acquired without licence from John Bluet who was the lord of the manor of Lackham near Lacock (*ibid.*, 95). The extent of some assarts can also be seen from the field names such as 'riding' or 'break' and by their distinctive, irregular-shaped fields.

On the Corallean ridge the Forest was exploited for its mineral resources such as ironstone and stone since at least the Romano-British period. Although Chippenham Forest is not as well known for its iron-ore deposits as, for example, the Forest of Dean or Rockingham Forest, it was nevertheless an important resource (Foard 2001 41-95; Meredith 2006). Iron-ore was being processed within the Forest from at least 1229 when the king had the profits from forges from Chippenham and Melksham Forests (*Cal Close R Hen III, 1227-31, 268*; Grant 1959, 409). The processing was done locally, probably by the bloomery method, whereby charcoal-fuelled furnaces were used to produce wrought iron. The bellows of the bloomery were either manual or water-powered (Bowden 2000, 3). The waste material from the process was the slag, which, in the case of Chippenham Forest, is often the only evidence for iron working, although small earthwork depressions and ponds may be the sites of former iron workings as was shown by field-work at Ramsbury and in the Weald (Haslam *et.al.* 1980, 1-68; Cleere and Crossley 1995, 190). The excavation of an iron-smelting site close to the minster church at Ramsbury, which was dated to the late eighth and early ninth century, uncovered several features that were interpreted as smithing hearths and furnaces, the furnaces survived as either slight oval lined depressions measuring about 0.9m diameter and 0.4m deep, as well as a more 'developed elongated bowl' furnace (Haslam *et.al.* 1980, 1-68).

One example of a probable iron-working site lies on the edge of Bowden Park where there are the earthwork remains of a small homestead set within an enclosure (Fig 4:4). The enclosure, which is cut by a narrow ditch near the northern side, contains at least two rectangular stances, probably building platforms, and yards. The first building measures 15m by 10m (Fig 4:4a) and was probably a dwelling since the earthwork is more substantial, while the second lies to the north and measures 20m by 10m; this may have been an outhouse such as an animal shelter, a workshop, or barn. The western side of the enclosure is sub-divided and may have contained either yards or gardens. To the east of the enclosure are several amorphous earthworks, which may have been a work area. The size of the buildings and probable association with the ridge-and-furrow cultivation in the area would suggest a medieval date for the homestead. Although the ridge-and-furrow was not surveyed it can be seen on aerial photographs to the south of the enclosure (NMR: 15584/06 dated 3 Feb 97).

A slight hollow-way extends north-east from the northern side of the enclosure where it appears to be overlain by a flight of three garden terraces that probably date to the eighteenth-century (Fig 4:4b). Small earthen steps in the centre of the upper terrace would suggest that the garden was probably associated with either a detached house or one that was never completed that lay in the area of what is now a coniferous plantation (Fig 4:4c). On the northern side of the enclosure is a long mound, which was probably a 'mount' or viewing platform associated with the garden (Fig 4:4d).

Given the geology of the area and the presence of ironstone, it seems likely that the small ponds to the north and west of the homestead may have been former quarry scoops or hearths and furnaces of the sort identified at Ramsbury and the Weald.

Stone was quarried in a similar manner to ironstone (Parsons 1991, 4) and was extracted from Lower Calcareous Grit, which is more suited for rough walling such as a precinct boundary and as a core in ashlar-faced walls. The better quality stone that was used, for example, as ashlar at the abbeys at Stanley and Lacock, came from their respective quarries at Hazelbury, which lay about 13km to the west (Saunders 1959, 247).

An ample supply of wood and suitable clay, coupled with a source of water and a ready market, also ensured

a flourishing tile and pottery industry within the Forest. Kilns dating to the thirteenth and fourteenth centuries were located a little downhill from the homestead in Bowden Park, on the more disturbed ground at Nash Hill Farm. The site lies on Lower Calcareous Grit associated with Oxford Clays and the excavation uncovered two tile kilns and two pottery kilns (McCarthy 1976, 67-160). The industry probably supplied local demand and the building programmes at Stanley as well as other local monasteries; however, whether the kilns were worked directly by a monastic house is not entirely clear although McCarthy suggests that they were more likely in lay ownership (*ibid.*, 100), despite the area lying on Lacock Abbey's land. Another kiln was excavated in 1992 near Sandy Lane that produced decorated jugs dating to about 1300 (Wilts and Swindon SMR: ST 96NE 451).

Far from being a secluded 'wilderness', which was the Cistercian 'ideal', the monks who settled at Stanley found that the forest was a valued resource that was utilised by the king, secular society and other monastic Orders alike. The Forest was the king's demesne; it was a 'managed' landscape where there was agreement over land that was cleared and cultivated and where there was control over its natural resources. How did the monks adapt into such an environment?

STANLEY'S CLEARANCE AND COLONISATION WITHIN THE FOREST

Having established the extent and resources within Chippenham Forest, this next section will question to what extent the monks at Stanley cleared and colonised the land for their monastery and home grange. Were they able to acquire sufficient land to support the community and at the same time achieve the seclusion they desired?

Forest Exploitation

Although the monks' abbey was in an isolated position on the edge of Chippenham Forest, an 'oasis in a desert', it was still a place where they had to share boundaries and resources with others and with whom they had to negotiate. As with many of the other 'reformed' Orders, the Cistercians appear to have enjoyed special status in the royal forest and were treated differently from secular lords and were often granted exemptions from some forest laws (Young 1979, 44). These may have included the right of free warren, which allowed them to hunt the 'lesser' game, and the use of dogs for hunting. Some Orders also received grants within forests such as the right to enclose and cultivate land, the keeping of sheep, and the use of timber and wood (*ibid.*). Flaxley Abbey (Glos), for example, was given extensive rights within the Forest of Dean including common of pasture and the right to take wood. In 1158, the king also granted them the right to set up an iron forge in the Forest and take two oaks each week for its fuel; however, ten years later this privilege was rescinded because the loss of wood was detrimental to the Forest, in-

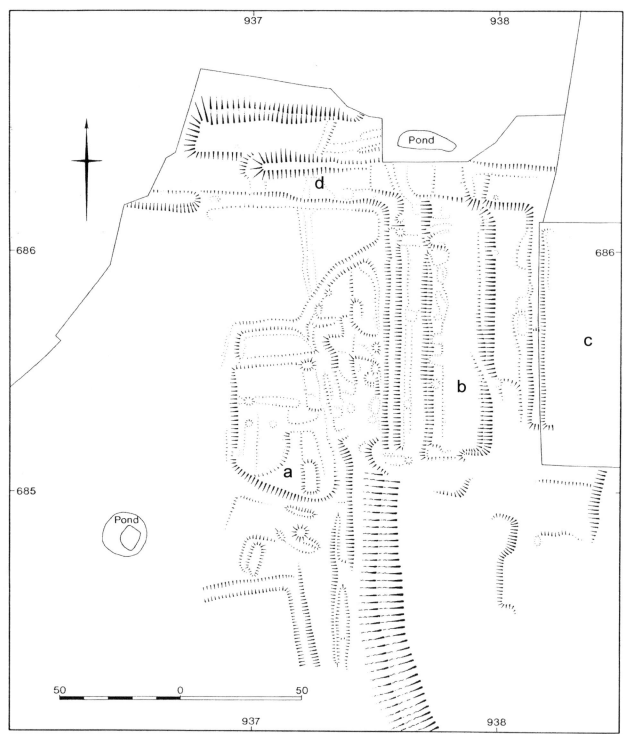

Figure 4:4. The earthworks of a small medieval homestead in Bowden Park.

stead they were given alternative woods (Crawley-Boevey 1845, 31-32; Graham 1907, 94). This change in the grant shows that, although they had special privileges, they were also tightly controlled. Other examples of Cistercian use of forests include Beaulieu Abbey, which held 233 acres (94ha) of waste in the New Forest in 1324 and where the monks could take whatever heath vegetation they needed. Rufford Abbey enjoyed a similar right in Sherwood Forest while, in 1189, Stratford Langthorn Abbey could pasture 960 sheep on the heath at Walthamstow in the Forest of Essex, and Coggeshall Abbey obtained the right to enclose heath and woodland in 1257 (Donkin 1960, 41). The Cis-

tercians were not alone in receiving privileges, the Carthusians at Witham were granted land in Mendip Forest in the late twelfth century for a grange, Hydon Grange, which covered an area of over 1,000 hectares; the Knights Templars had pasture rights for 1,000 sheep and sixty other animals, and the Bishop of Bath, and the Carthusians, had the right to mine lead (Gough 1928, 87-98; Neale 1976, 94; Vellacott 1969, 363).

The Abbot of Stanley was a beneficiary of many of these rights and exemptions in Chippenham Forest and elsewhere. As far as hunting is concerned, in 1304, the abbot was par-

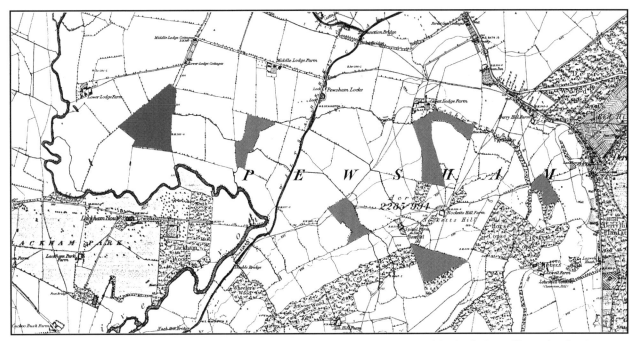

Figure 4:5. The grey areas show the fields with names indicative of woodland clearance while the darker infill are the 'fleet' names in Chippenham Forest (WSA: Pewsham tithe award map). The fields lay to the south-west of Stanley and on the wide flood plain at the foot of the escarpment.

doned retrospectively for taking a hind in Whittlewood Forest (Jones and Page 2006, 122). He was also permitted to keep dogs in Chippenham Forest without their toes being clipped, which was the usual practice to prevent them hunting (WSA: 473/1; Young 1979, 43). Also a document dating to 1253 required the bailiffs and ministers of the forests not to 'charge or fatigue' the abbey's dogs on their land and their granges (*Cal Pat R Hen III, 1247-1256*, 180).

Assarts and Colonisation

The special privileges within the Forest extended to grants of land from the king. One was of a moorland and wood in Le Moor (also known as Flet [or Alflet] Moor) which was close to the gates of the abbey and probably included what later became known as Close Wood. The grant was confirmed in 1189 and was in lieu of the right to timber for building from Chippenham Wood and 3d a day for the farm of Chippenham (WSA: 473/8). This area was formerly common for the manor of Chippenham, and therefore a loss of pasture rights for the tenants. According to the grant the monks were required to enclose it with a low bank and ditch so that the king's deer could enter and leave. The bounds of the wood were given in 1227 as:

'From the road called Wardleghesweye, which divides the said wood from the wood of William Beauvilein, up to the hedge of Wardlegh upon the hill, and thence by ... to Eldeholewey and so by the way called Lamswey and so by the marked oaks to the plain of Pewe and so by the north of the wood to the wood called Wardleghesweye ... '(*Cal Chart R Hen III, 1226-1257*, 37; WSA: 473/40, 62).

Flet Moor extended over much of the low-lying Oxford Clays at the foot of the forest escarpment and as far as the River Avon in the west and the abbey in the east. There is little indication of it today; however, field names such as Long Fleet, Little Fleet and Great Fleet on the tithe map fossilise part of the moorland landscape (WSA Pewsham Tithe Award map; Fig 4:5).

Stanley Abbey clearly needed more land for its growing community and spreading influence. In 1303 they held 211 acres (88ha) of assarted land for which they had to pay an annual rent of 79s 1d (*Cal Pat R Ed 1, 1301-1307*, 205; WSA: 473/11). Although a relatively large amount of land it was not one whole block; however, the nature of the grant, coupled with others, points to a continuing process of consolidation. Apart from three places, 'Wardelay', 'Bycumbe' and 'Ashe', the monks were allowed to enclose the land with a hedge and ditch and cultivate it; however, they were not allowed common of pasture beyond these places thus safeguarding their neighbours' rights and preventing over-grazing. What is clear from the grant is that, since they held the land in severalty and outside the control of a manorial court, they were able to cultivate it as they wished. The grant included:

- 30 acres (12.1ha) 'between the abbey gate and the angle of the abbot's wood in length by 'la Rede Sheepene', deducting 100ft in breadth of the king's soil between the said gate and 'Bradeyate' in length to the highway'
- 8½ acres (3.4ha) 'in a place called 'Bradyate' lying between the abbot's land on both sides'
- 15 acres (6ha) 'in a place without the gate of the house of the abbot's sheepfold'
- 14 acres (5.7ha) 'between the covert of the forest and the stream of the Pewe [Cocklemore Brook], omitting

a plot on the high road leading from Chippenham to Devizes between the said angle of the abbot's close and 'le Wodyate', containing in breadth 100ft';

- 21 acres (8.5ha) 'in a place between the abbot's close and the highway in breadth, and between the stream of the Pewe and the purpresture of Giles de Chiverdon.

- 11 acres (4.5ha) 'in a place called 'Wardelaye' between the covert of 'Bonewode' [Bowood] and the abbot's close' [presumably Close Wood].

All these assarts were close to the abbey and formed part of the home grange; they included pasture for sheep and cattle with a stock enclosure, possibly in the extra-mural earthwork enclosure just outside the abbey gate (Fig 3:11; Fig 4:6). The sheep walks were at 'Wodemanneshulle' and 'Walemersch' since, during the second half of the fourteenth century, the monks received confirmation of a gift of pasture for 300 wethers (castrated sheep) and 300 ewes in these places; this also points to segregation of flocks as witnessed elsewhere (WSA: 473/39). In addition to sheep, in 1415 the monks also had a cattle herd on their demesne of 34-38 cows and produced 750lb of cheese (Hare 2011, 80, quoting TNA: PRO SC6/1054/9).

From the bounds of the wood at 'Flet Moor' and the assarts listed, some place-names can be tentatively identified on later maps; 'Wardleghesweye' for example was probably the road from the abbey to Studley while 'Lamswey' was probably the route between Calne and Chippenham, while 'Wardelaye' was to the south of the Abbot's Wood (Close Wood).'Wodyate' and 'Bradyate' probably refer to gates, 'Wodyate' may be in the area of Forest Gate Farm while Bradyate was south of the abbey near Studley (Fig 4:6).

Two of the assarts account for nearly fifty per cent of the 211 acres: thirty acres were 'in a place called Bycumbe near the grange of Loxwell' and '78½ acres in a place called le Ashe', which was presumably in the area of what later became known as Ash Farm (*Cal Pat R Ed 1 1301-1307*, 205; fig 4:2). In 1263 Ash was described as part of the liberty of the Abbot of Stanley and was exempt from the forest law (Grant 1959, 408n26 quoting TNA: PRO E 32/199/3). Further colonisation in the forest is shown in 1303 when the abbot had to answer for half an acre at Loxwell Grange and twenty-one acres at 'Hedfeld' for which he was able to produce a royal charter as his warrant (TNA: PRO E 32/199/1d).

As well as Stanley Abbey's assarts there were also other parcels of waste that were leased to individuals totalling 184 acres; some were for as little as 1½ rood while one was for forty acres at 'Horslepride' on the southern boundary of Loxwell Grange, with other plots at 'Wardley', 'Bycombe', and Ash (Grant 1959, 412). These grants show that the monks did not have exclusive rights at these places but they nevertheless point to an expansion and consolidation of land at Loxwell Grange itself.

Mineral rights

The monks at Stanley were also active in mineral extraction in the forest, mainly on their grange at Loxwell. In 1222 they were permitted to quarry stone for their church, and in 1292-97 they were allowed to work the king's quarry in Pewsham for further buildings and for the precinct wall (Chettle and Kirby 1953, 271-74). As well as stone, they also quarried ironstone. In 1294 they were granted a licence to dig and smelt the ore on their demesne at Bycombe (*Cal Pat R Ed I, 1292-1301*, 101; Chettle and Kirby 1953, 271). Although the precise location of Bycombe is unclear, the place-name would suggest that it lay at the head of a coombe, probably about 700m to the north of Loxwell where there is evidence of quarrying. The quarry covers an area of about one hectare and consists of a series of cuttings and scoops into the side of the slope.

Location	Evidence	Remarks	Stanley territory
SO 937694	map	Quarr Ground	yes
SO957692	map	Subterranian Cavern	yes
SO940684	earthwork/survey	Bowden Park	
SO937684	earthwork	pond- possible quarry	
SO 937686	earthwork	ponds- possible quarry	
SO 932693	earthwork	extensive quarry	yes
SO 932694	earthwork	extensive quarry	yes
SO 955702	earthwork	quarry	yes
SO 932694	excavation	pottery and tile kilns	

Table 4:1. Industrial activity in the Forest of Chippenham (1300 bounds, but excluding Bowood Park).

Another Stanley quarry may be on Loxwell Heath where a 'subterranean cavern' is marked on an early nineteenth century map (Bowood Estate maps). In an area of arable, there is no longer any surface evidence for this feature and although the 'cavern' may be natural the possibility that it was a mine should not be ignored; it is certainly within the band of Lower Greensand that produces the ironstone nodules.

Further quarries have been identified either through fieldwork or from map evidence, but whether they are medieval is unclear since a chronology in the earthworks has not been determined. In addition, stone was extracted from two of them, Loxwell Quarry and Ash Hill Quarry, in 1868 and 1895 respectively (Table 4:1; WSA: 415/2 and 4). These are the only two areas that were specifically mentioned and, in absence of track-ways, which would have presumably formed from continual and heavy use, or evidence of phasing, it is likely that the others are of some antiquity.

The Home Grange

Land Acquisitions

As well as land grants from the Crown, there were acquisitions from local inhabitants. Unfortunately it is impossible

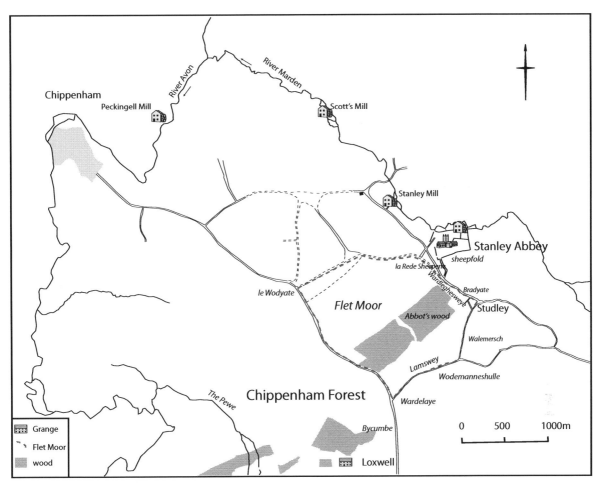

Figure 4:6. Place-names in the area of Stanley Abbey. Flet Moor covered the low-lying land from the abbey to the River Avon. The probable area of this moor granted to the abbey is also shown.

to chart the chronology of endowment since many grants are undated and the only indication is the style of writing; however, analysis of these acquisitions suggests that the Cistercians were not impassive recipients but consciously sought land they wanted by grant, purchase or exchange to create a cohesive block of holdings in the vicinity of the abbey that provided them with the stimulus to develop the region as they chose. This area, along with the Crown grants, was known as the home grange and its composition is shown in the court rolls of 1431-34 where Stanley, Nethermore and Studley are all mentioned (Fig 4:2).

The principal grange buildings lay on the west side of the abbey, presumably including the west range of the abbey and Stanley Mill. In 1596 this mill was described as 'sometime called the grange of the abbey' (WSA: 473/242.32A). The grange also included a detached sheep-house that was recorded in the area of Pound Farm in 1550 (WSA: 473/228.1). This is in addition to the possible sheep-house that lay to the south of the abbey precinct.

Lay patronage and the size of pious benefactions were crucial factors in the success of the monastery. However, a gift was not necessarily a one-way agreement since the monks may have had to offer prayers and intercessions for the donor during their lifetime and masses for the salvation of their souls after death, and even the possibility of

burial within the abbey church. Although the evidence is incomplete it would appear that there were no benefactors of baronial status of lands for the home grange. Apart from a single, large grant of Flet Moor from the king, most of the benefactors were local lords including Sir Edmund Gascelin who was lord of the manors of Chippenham and Sheldon, and several other knights. Prominent amongst them was the Bubbe family who made a number of grants and were witness to several others, and 'Nigel of Stanley' who held land in Stanley and Nethermore and made grants in both places. The size of the grants varied from half an acre to the whole of an individual's holding. Rights of pasture and meadow figure largely in these grants, while the smaller amounts of arable would suggest they were for closes or perhaps strips in an open field. However, there were larger amounts and crofts, which would suggest that some land was held in severalty. The process of consolidation of land is also alluded to; at 'Gosi' meadow, for example, there were grants from two individuals of half an acre each and another two individuals granted half each of the grove known as 'Hulwerta'. There were also ten documents dating to sometime in the late thirteenth or early fourteenth century relinquishing rights of common of pasture, presumably by tenants, in the wood called le More 'beyond the abbey' and 'to the south of the abbey' (WSA: 473/19-28). It is probable that these all occurred at much the same time since the witnesses are similar in each case.

There appears to have been only one gift in free alms, i.e. free of all but royal service, from Joan de Osevilla:

'for her soul's health and that of her late husband William de Rugden [Rowden?] to Stanley Abbey of all that part of his wood in La More between the monks' wood which was of Walter Beavilain from the marsh as far as the hill towards the east and as far as the croft called 'Huppleg' reserving to Joan the upper part of the wood as it extends from the hill to the east' (WSA: 1213/7.

The monks, therefore, acquired extensive land in the Forest; however, it was in two specific landforms and it was this combination that provided the varied resources they needed for a successful foundation. The first was on the higher ground, on the Corallean limestone and lower greensand plateau. This land was acquired from the Crown. Here they had rights to clear, enclose, and cultivate the land; to graze their sheep, cattle, and horses, and where there was pannage for their pigs. They also had the right to extract minerals, although it was not for an indeterminate period. The second landform was on the much lower-lying ground that was composed of Oxford Clays that was susceptible to waterlogging; much of this zone was moorland. It was here that the monastery was founded. The largest single grant was from the Crown of Flet Moor that essentially became the core of the home grange. There were other grants from local lords that were acquired in a more progressive but quite deliberate, piecemeal fashion, leading ultimately to a consolidated block. The monks were therefore certainly well placed to achieve a viable economic base to support the community. As far as having the seclusion they sought, the area was sparsely settled although the few locals and inhabitants of Chippenham exploited its resources, but having acquired their home grange, they achieved a degree of isolation.

IMPACT ON THE SETTLEMENT AND AGRARIAN LANDSCAPE

The second theme examines the impact the abbey had on the agrarian landscape and settlement pattern. It will question to what extent the monks changed the agrarian landscape and the communication pattern in the abbey environs. Following this, it will analyse to what extent the monks exploited the area beyond the forest, which may have formed part of the home grange network.

Arable

The only indication we have of demesne cultivation from the documents is in an account dating to 1415 when there was 149½ acres under the plough. Of this amount oats were the largest crop, amounting to 48.8 per cent; this was followed by wheat and barley with 31.1 and 10.4 per cent respectively. The remainder was made up with peas and other crops (Hare 2011, 61 quoting TNA: PRO SC6/1054/9).

The archaeological evidence is more emphatic for the manor as a whole since an aerial photographic transcription shows that large swathes were cultivated, including areas along the riverbank, which would presumably have been more suitable as meadow (Fig 4:7). The transcription, however, is only an indication of the extent of cultivation since it clearly does not include ploughed out ridge-and-furrow, which may no longer be visible. In addition, the dating is unclear and while the majority of it may be medieval, the possibility that some is later should not be ignored. For example, Codmarsh, which has curving strips, is clearly medieval, as is Great Buddy and Little Buddy where there is also earthwork evidence of ridge-and-furrow; these latter two fields were pasture in 1550 and some others were 'late inclosed' eight years later, which indicates Tudor enclosure and conversion from arable to pasture (WSA: 473/228.1&5).

The best-preserved area of ridge-and-furrow is at Cod Marsh, which lies within the abbey demesne (fig 4:8). Here the remains of five furlongs are evident, with the ridges up to 240m long and c8m apart. Slicing through the strips, but respecting their alignment, is a small stream, or leat, known in the eighteenth century as Pudding Brook. The leat overlies the ridge-and-furrow and a prominent field boundary suggesting that cultivation had ceased before its construction and conversion to pasture. This may have occurred by 1432 when Cod Marsh was enclosed by a ditch (WSA: 2664 box 4).

Meadow

Meadows were a crucial component of the agricultural economy, providing a lush crop of hay and pasture for cattle and sheep. An indication of its value is shown in several *Inquisitions Post-Mortem*; for example, in 1299 a forty-acre meadow in Chippenham was worth 18d per acre, while the arable was a third of this value (Fry 1908, 268). Its value is also implied in the description of the work of customary tenants for the manor of Purford (Surry) in 1331-2, where the work on the demesne water meadows was the first item mentioned in the custumal thus emphasising its importance. The tenant's work included 'damming the water, to overflow the Lord's Meadow ½d'. The meadow was valued at 3s an acre, which was nine times more than the arable (SHC: G 97/4/9). Manors that had little meadow supplemented their crop from elsewhere. The tenants of St Swithun's manor at Enford and Fifield on Salisbury Plain, for example, had to cart hay from another of the monks' estates at Patney, which was eight miles away on the northern foothills of the Plain (Stevenson 1980, 127).

Although it is unclear where all the meadows at Stanley lay during the medieval period, post-medieval and early modern evidence would suggest that it lay principally in small closes or strips along the river alluvium of the River Avon with some along the Marden and to the north of Close Woods. Eastmead, for example, was divided into

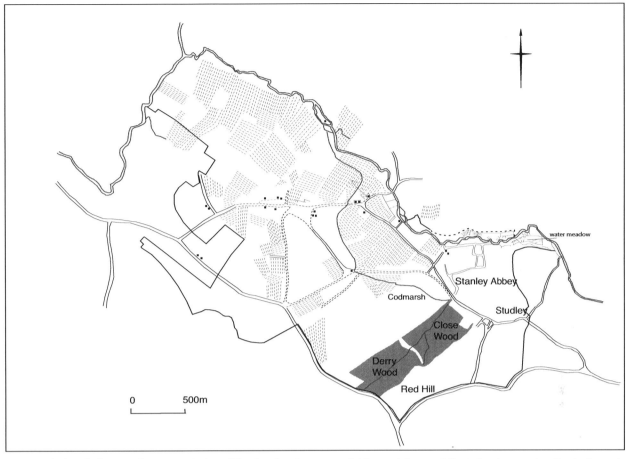

Figure 4:7. Aerial photographic transcription of Stanley showing areas of ridge-and-furrow. A floated water meadow lies to the east of the abbey.

long narrow strips, presumably separated by doles, on the east bank of the Avon and was shared between several tenants including the Wilcox family of Stanley Mill and tenants of neighbouring Langley Burrell. Other meadows such as Goosey Mead, Oxenmead, Milhams and Water-leaze that are mentioned in medieval documents were all small closes along the River Marden.

A Floated Water Meadow?

To the east of the precinct is an extensive meadow; however, this one is unlike any of the others since there are earthworks that are more characteristic of an artificially irrigated, or 'floated', water meadow. This type of meadow, a bedwork, was first recorded elsewhere in Wiltshire in the early seventeenth century and was ubiquitous along the alluvial valleys of the Wessex chalk downlands from that date (Bettey 2007, 8-21). Although the meadow at Stanley is post-medieval or early modern (there is a cast-iron aqueduct spanning a leat on the east side), it may overlie, or 'mask' a much earlier, monastic water meadow. There was one such meadow documented at Stanley in 1189 (Donkin 1978, 120), but its location and what form it took is unknown. Donkin also notes sixteen further examples at other Cistercian monasteries in England (*ibid.*).

As we have seen the Cistercians were adept at water management and they were involved in irrigating their fields

from an early date. A description of the precinct at Clairvaux Abbey (Aube, France) gives a good example. Writing in the twelfth century, a visitor to the monastery described how the monks had managed and directed the River Aube to provide water to various parts of the abbey. In addition:

> the meadow [near the precinct] is refreshed by the floodwaters of the Aube, which runs through it, so that the grass, thanks to the moisture at its roots, can stand the summer heat. Its extent is great enough to tire the community for the space of twenty days when the sun has baked to hay its shorn grassy fleece' (Matarasso 1993, 290).

Irrigation was widely practiced during the medieval period, not just by monastic communities but also by secular lords and communities. In the Al-Andulus region in Spain, there was extensive irrigation in the eleventh century, and in Greenland, at much the same time, artificial irrigation ditches and dams close to farmsteads were used to irrigate the 'home fields' (Arneborg 2005, 137-45). In Italy, the irrigation of grass and arable fields 'was to become, before 1500, the admiration of Europe' (Jones, 1971, 359). It appears to have been first witnessed in Piedmont in the late eleventh century where there are references to partnerships being formed between communities for the maintenance of irrigation channels, but soon after, in 1138, there is the first record in Italy of permanent water meadows, or mar-

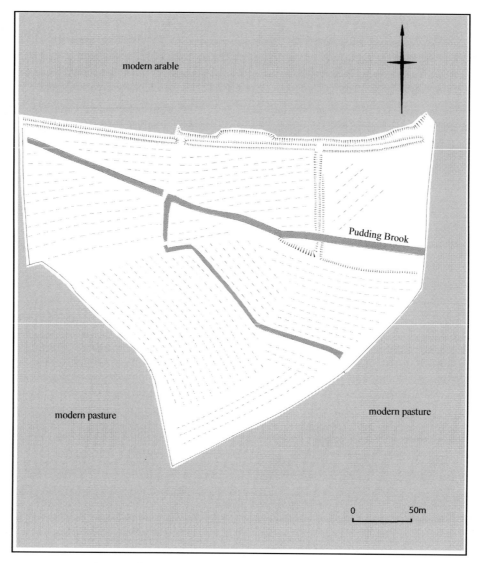

Figure 4:8. Earthwork survey of the ridge-and-furrow at Codmarsh.

cite, on the estates of the Cistercian monastery of Chiara-valle near Milan (*ibid*; Braudel 1992, 46). It seems almost inconceivable that with such a centralised management of the Cistercian community through their General Chapters that an innovation such as this would not have been spread throughout the whole Cistercian network, and where suitable land was available, that it was not managed in this way.

Water meadows were a crucial element in an agricultural regime. Their purpose was to provide an earlier growth of grass so that livestock could gain access to it earlier in the year following the lean winter months, and in some areas it was to supplement the hay crop. As the name implies, water from a river or stream was directed over the meadow thus depositing rich nutrients as well as raising the temperature of the soil slightly. In some cases meadows were also flooded naturally by the seasonal inundation of riverbanks. Buildwas Abbey (Shropshire) is a good example where the meandering River Severn is periodically inundated with floodwater, but where there is also an artificial water meadow (Brown 2002).

The water meadow as we see it today at Stanley was probably in use from the seventeenth century; however, the fragmentary nature of the earthworks would suggest that it was not in use for very long, or that there was an attempt to 'improve' the land by levelling it. Despite this, enough evidence survives to enable an understanding of how it functioned. The meadow comprises several components. First, a main 'carrier', or leat, directed water from a hatch and aqueduct at Hazelbury Mill along the southern, higher end of the meadow. Along the course of this main carrier are several side carriers where the water would flow along narrow channels to a 'stop' at the end of the carrier. The water would then trickle over into a side drain and ultimately back to the river. Although this has all the elements of a classic post medieval 'bedwork' meadow, it may incorporate elements of an earlier, possibly medieval water meadow.

The Abbey Mills, Wool and Cloth Manufacture

According to one of the early Cistercian statutes the possession of mills for anything other than for their own domestic use was forbidden. It was instigated so that they did not profit from the labour of others; however, this rule appears to have been disregarded by many houses from an early date, although there were penalties for those who transgressed (Wardell 1994, 31). Later legislation introduced an important distinction between abbeys that were originally founded as Cistercian and those that were incorporated within the Order such as the Savignacs. Those that were later affiliated to Cîteaux were exempt from the statute and were able to retain their mills while all the others were to abide by it (*ibid.*). This potentially has implications for Stanley since its mother house was Quarr Abbey, a Savignac affiliation and therefore able to retain its mills, and it could be argued that Stanley should be similarly treated despite the Savignacs being absorbed within the Cistercian community before the founding of Stanley. Even if Stanley did not qualify for exemption, it held several mills soon after its foundation, which potentially would bring the monks into dispute with the General Chapter. On their outlying granges and estates they had mills at Codrington, Wadley, Ugford, and Richardson, the latter being a windmill. There were also mills in the Stanley region, three along the River Marden, as well as the moiety of a fourth at Peckingell on the River Avon.

In the sixteenth century two of the mills along the River Marden were fulling mills, one was Scott Mill (presumably after the eponymous clothier who leased it in the sixteenth century) and the other, Wilcox Mill (also later known as Stanley Mill). This latter mill was specifically referred to as part of the home grange in 1545 (WSA: 473/258.5B; 473: 258). The third mill lay within the precinct and was a combined corn and fulling mill. The mill at Peckingell was also a fulling mill and was in existence by at least 1189 when Richard I confirmed the grants made to Stanley Abbey; it is the one identified by Donkin as the earliest documented Cistercian fulling mill in England (Birch 1875, 282; Donkin 1978, 188). Stanley therefore, held a fulling mill within thirty-five years of its foundation and although the dating of the others is unclear, one of those on the Marden may date to at least the thirteenth century since it was mentioned in a dispute between Stanley and Malmesbury Abbey when Stanley diverted the course of the Marden (Brewer 1880, 28-9), presumably to form a mill-race. Also, there is mention of a William Touker (Tucker?) in the court roll in 1431, pointing to a continuing association with fulling (WSA: 2664 box 4).

The field names attached to Wilcox's mill were Shyngley, Rackhaye, Grove, and Coope Field. Rackhaye (also known as Wrack Close) was used for drying the cloth on tenters once it had been fulled; however, there is also ridge-and-furrow extending in a north-west/south-east alignment with the ridges 8m apart across Further Copes and Hither Copes, which would suggest that Wrack Close was the set apart specifically for the fulling process (Fig 4:9).

Much has been written about the Cistercians' involvement in the wool export trade with the Flemish and Italian merchants in the twelfth and thirteenth centuries (e.g.

Jamroziak 2003, 197-218; Williams 2001, 258-9; Donkin 1958, 2-8). In the late thirteenth century the Pegolotti List shows that the Cistercians were providing 85 per cent of the wool from the monastic houses in England that was exported to the Bardi merchants in Italy. Although the figures should be treated with a little caution since they may include wool purchased from other individuals they are nevertheless useful for comparison; Fountains Abbey, for example, provided the largest amount with seventy-six sacks while Rievaulx's total was sixty sacks (Cunningham 1922, 629-34; Burton 1998a, 82). The average for the Yorkshire houses was 38.5 sacks, far higher than for eight of the southern houses whose average was only 13.5 sacks (Hockey 1970, 57). However, it is significant that Stanley's total was forty sacks (although the quality was not high) which, along with Kirkstead and Revesby, was the fourth highest of the Cistercian exports in the country, and the highest in the south of England (Cunningham 1922, 632). This figure shows that Stanley, like other Cistercian houses and major landlords, had considerable sheep flocks in the thirteenth century although the documents are largely silent as regards numbers.

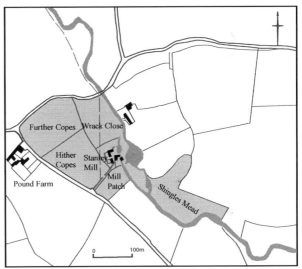

Figure 4:9. Stanley Mill, otherwise known as Wilcox Mill in the sixteenth century. The map has been re-drawn from the OS 1st edition map and the Bowood Estate map of Stanley, which dates to the mid nineteenth century. The pecked lines are trackways.

North-west Wiltshire was renowned as a cloth-producing region during the medieval period and although the Cistercians were not involved, it is probable that Stanley, with its fulling mills, provided a service to the local lay clothmakers, who paid a toll for the use of the mill. In October 1431, for example, the court roll records that the miller, William Greye, 'unjustly took the tolls [of the mill] and he is at mercy' (WSRO: 2664, box 4). According to Donkin, fourteen houses had fulling mills before 1300; the majority were first recorded in the second half of the thirteenth century (Donkin 1978, 188). In Wales and the Borders there were twenty-seven recorded examples, a third of which were held by the Cistercian abbeys at Strata Florida and Whitland (Williams 2001, 253). The mills at Stanley are amongst the earliest fulling mills in the country but, unlike Meaux Abbey where wool was being woven and cloth

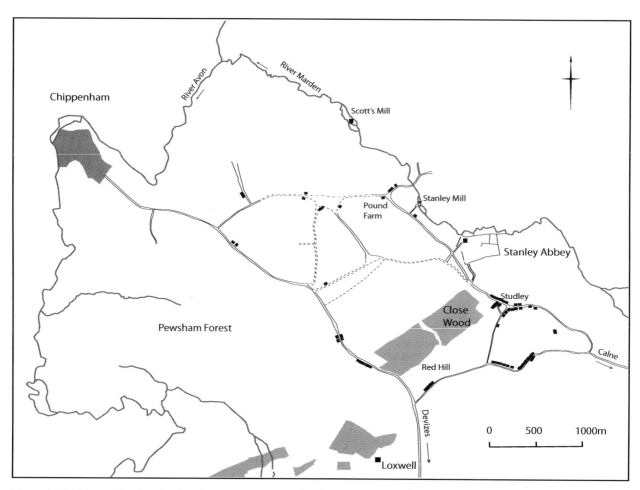

Figure 4:10. Manor of Stanley showing the communication and setlement pattern in the third quarter of the eighteenth century (reconstructed from the Andrews and Dury's map of Wiltshire and WSA 473/256, which dates to 1760).

fulled for the use of 'the monks, *conversi*, and the poor of the neighbourhood' at Wawne Grange (Donkin 1978, 136), there is no evidence that cloth was being produced by the monks themselves at Stanley.

Communications and Settlement Pattern

The post-medieval and early modern communication pattern reflects, in large part, the medieval pattern, but to what extent was it the result of the monks' influence? The principal route was the one linking Chippenham to Devizes and the one that skirts the south-eastern side of Close Wood and Redhill leading towards Calne (Fig 4:10). This latter road was described as an 'ancient' route in the second half of the twelfth century and is also shown as the principal route from London to Bristol via Marlborough and Calne on Ogilby's map of 1675 (Ogilby 1971, plate 11; WSA: 473/32). The Chippenham to Devizes road is also shown on the Ogilby map and may fossilise a much older route since there are several Romano-British villas in the vicinity (*Chapter Two*). These major routes were, therefore, in existence when the monks arrived in the area 1151.

The monks' influence was probably in the by-ways that lead from these two principal routes towards farmsteads and the abbey. They form wide curving routes that converge on areas of settlement thus forming large greens.

These greens, which are on slightly elevated land, were probably the main focus of settlement during the medieval period. Four can be seen; the northerly is an area known as Huttes, which was first documented in 1431 when there were references to the highway as well as a messuage known as 'Swotynges' (WSA: 2664 box 4). By the mid eighteenth century the Huttes landholding lay between a track-way and the Pudding Brook, with closes of meadow, woodland and arable (Fig 4:11). Further east is a much smaller green with Pound Farm on the southern side. Earthwork and aerial photographic evidence show further building stances on the northern side of the track. Part of the present farm building dates to the early sixteenth century (Wilts Building Record: B6358) but, given its position on a green, it may well be on the site of an even earlier building, possibly a sheep house. Another green lies to the south of Huttes; although no buildings survive, earthworks in the area would suggest that there were at least two building stances beside the north-western arm (this area was affected by the construction of a canal in the late eighteenth century). Finally, the junction of the by-ways of the small hamlet of Studley forms a green with the settlement clustering on the roadsides (fig 4:12).

Studley, unlike Stanley, is not recorded in the Domesday Survey. It lies on higher ground above the abbey and the first element, 'Stud', in the place-name would suggest

64

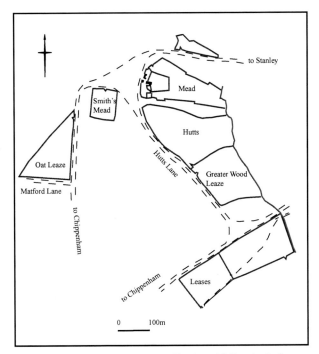

Figure 4:11. Settlement pattern at Hutt's in 1760, which shows one of the farmsteads on the eastern side of the 'green'; however, the Andrews and Dury map (fig 4:9) shows two others on the western side in the area of Smith's Mead (re-drawn from WSA: 473/256).

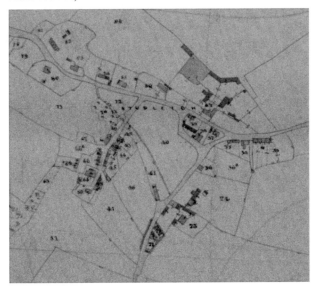

Figure 4:12. The hamlet of Studley (BRO: 31965/STG/10 dated 1862.

that it may have developed as a horse farm (Gelling 1984, 206; Fig 4:12). Indeed, Stanley Abbey had horses within the forests of Melksham, Chippenham and Braydon in 1238 (*Cal Close R Hen III, 1237-1242*, 144). There are also several 'horse' place-names in the vicinity of Loxwell Grange such as 'Horselese' and 'Horselpride', which are mentioned in the 1433 and 1303 respectively (WSA: 2664 box 4; Grant 1959, 447), and Horse Copse, an area of woodland shown on the 1st edition Ordnance Survey map at the northern end of Loxwell Grange. The monks, or more likely their tenants, may therefore have been involved in horse rearing in a similar manner to several other

Cistercian monasteries such as Kirkstall, Holm Cultram, and Quarr (Bond 2004, 66).

There was, perhaps, a change in the road pattern near the abbey during the later post-medieval period. It seems almost inconceivable that the route between Pound Farm and Studley is of medieval date since it lies close to, and almost parallel to, a medieval causeway. Initially it probably went as far as Stanley Mill and only later, perhaps following the Suppression, was the route extended to Studley. This sort of change is not unusual, but what it emphasises is the change in the dominant features in the landscape, the monastic complex, as the landscape was re-fashioned into secular use. At Croxden Abbey (Staffs), for example, the present road, which dates to the eighteenth century, cuts through the ruins of the church. During the medieval period tracks terminated at either end of the precinct boundary, and it was only later that the two were linked when the abbey ruins were little more than a farmstead (Brown 2009). At Hailes the gatehouse was approached via a broad lane, which was abandoned sometime in the eighteenth century (Brown 2006). Other examples include Byland Abbey and Haughmond Abbey in Shropshire (Jecock *et. al.* 2011, 62; Pearson *et. al.* 2003).

Settlement, in the form of dispersed farmsteads and a hamlet, was therefore centred at the wide greens, although there were also mills beside the river. It is noticeable that these 'greenside settlements' were confined to the periphery of the 'core' demesne (Flet Moor) of the home grange.

Outlying Granges

Beyond the immediate area of the home grange, the Cistercians at Stanley acquired further land and its proximity to the monastery would suggest that it may also have been part of the home grange. They settled on this land and exploited it; some was within the Forest, but there was also a substantial amount to the north and west of Chippenham, beyond the forest bounds. This presumably provided a more diverse economic base.

Loxwell Grange and Ash

One of the earliest grants to the Cistercians was in 1150-1151 of land at Loxwell and of a meadow in the Forest for pasture and hay, and 20s worth of land next to the bridge of Lacock and a rent of 3d a day from the farm of Chippenham 'as long as it is inhabited by this religious people' (WSA 473/4). Following the move to Stanley, Loxwell became a grange. The buildings probably occupied the area of the nineteenth century Loxwell Farm, where only two outbuildings survive. The grange estate can be 'reconstructed' from an estate map of Loxwell dating to 1824, which is an area of tithe-free land incorporating Ash Farm (Fig 4:13; WSA: 2454/7).

Field names may suggest land-use. Hazel Coppice, Raspberry Coppice, Horse Coppice and Pigsty Coppice clearly

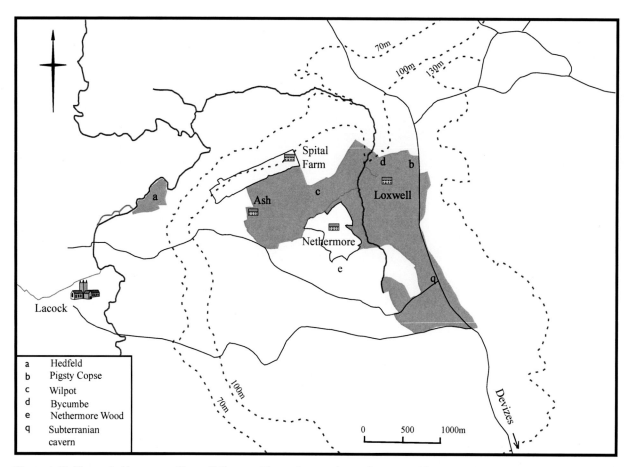

Figure 4:13. The probable extent of Loxwell Grange. The evidence is drawn from a map dating to 1824 which shows Loxwell Farm and Ash Farm (WSA: 2454/7). In addition, a detached portion of Stanley borders the northern side of Ash. In the south is Nethermore Farm with its woodland extending as far south as the road (re-drawn from the OS 1st edition map).

refer to woodland management; however, the latter two may have been the sites of a monastic horse pasture (above) and pigsty. In 1288-1289 there was a dispute between the Abbot of Stanley and Sir Edmund Gacelin, lord of Chippenham, as to the bounds of their respective woods 'and of an oak that Gacelin's men had felled near a pigsty belonging to the abbot' (*Cal Anc Deeds vol. 4,* A6577). Other names, such as Quarr Ground probably indicate a quarry while names such as Great Field and Eight Acres are suggestive of arable cultivation. Hams Close, The Meads were areas of meadow and Great Cow Leaze and Little Cow Leaze refer to pasture. Although it is dangerous to speculate about the medieval landscape from an early nineteenth century map, it at least illustrates the potential exploitation.

Spittle Farm – a detached monastic infirmary?

Research elsewhere would suggest that there were often two infirmaries within monasteries, one for the monks and the other for the lay brothers. This latter infirmary was probably only established when the community was sufficiently large (Dimier 1982, 805). Those infirmaries within the precinct were detached from one another. The lay brothers' infirmary at Roche, for example, was a thirteenth century building situated on the west side of the monastery while the monks' infirmary was earlier, and lay on the east side (Fergusson 1990, 17). Infirmaries were substantial

buildings; at Fountains the lay brothers' infirmary, which was situated on the west side of the monastery measured 37m by 22m while the monks' infirmary, on the east side, was, according to Coppack, 'one of the largest aisled halls ever built in medieval England' (Coppack 1993, 59).

During the thirteenth century the statutes of the General Chapter begin to contain requests from monasteries to establish infirmaries at their granges. These requests appear to have been from continental houses; thus in 1257 and 1259 two Italian monasteries, Casanova Abbey and Fossanova Abbey, were given permission to build an infirmary at one of their granges since the distance to the abbey was too great (Cassidy-Welch 2001, 141). There does not seem to be any similar grants for English houses at this time; however, given the widely distributed land-holdings, particularly of the Yorkshire houses, they may well have had detached infirmaries.

Despite this lack of documentary evidence, place-names may indicate infirmaries at some granges in England and Wales. Spittle Farm, for example, lies within Stanley's territory 2.8km from the abbey and, as the name implies, it could tentatively be interpreted as the site of a former hospital or infirmary, perhaps a monastic infirmary, or perhaps a place of recovery following bloodletting. In 1822 Spittle Farm comprised a little over forty-five acres of titheable land (WSA: 415/8; Fig 4:13); however, there is an earlier

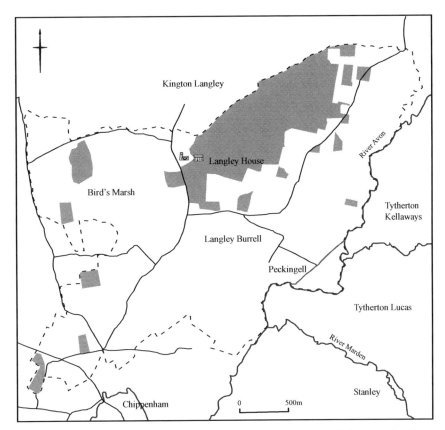

Figure 4:14. Stanley Abbey's holdings in the parish of Langley Burrell (topographical detail re-drawn from OS 1st edition map 1889)

reference to a close of pasture, Spyttle Close, in the Monkton Farley Priory rent roll in 1536 (Seymour papers Vol. 12, f. 131b), which may be in the same area.

In Wales, Williams has identified three examples of infirmaries from place-name evidence: at Strata Florida, Neath and Tintern. He suggests that they may have been 'external' or 'secular' infirmaries for the sick, aged or perhaps used as isolation hospitals (Williams 2001, 152). Tintern and Neath's detached lay infirmaries were situated in hill country about 1.6km from the abbeys, not too dissimilar to Spittle Farm's location.

Langley Burrell

Langley Burrell is not mentioned in the *Taxatio* or *Valor Ecclesiasticus* as a holding of Stanley Abbey; however, the parish's tithe award and map shows that there was over 398 acres (161ha) of tithe-free land that was described as '... containing the demesne of the abbey of Stanley ...' (WSA: Tithe Award map and schedule, Langley Burrell; Fig 4:14). The landholding consists of a large consolidated block on the northern side of the parish with smaller, detached blocks scattered elsewhere. The large block includes what later became the manor house, Langley House, but not the church. It is likely, therefore, that Stanley's grange estate was administered from buildings near, or on the site of the manor house which lay beside the church - a juxtaposition that was considered as an 'ideal' for the success, at least for a Gilbertine grange (Golding 1995, 403).

Derriards

Stanley Abbey held land at Derriards since at least 1198 when it is mentioned in King Richard's wide-ranging confirmation charter (*Cal Chart R Hen III 1226-1257*, 38). The land was a gift from Garnel Manul, or Warneri Mansel, for a rent of 9s 10½d (*ibid*; Birch 1875, 258). This amount implies that the holding was also large, but whether it was a consolidated block is unknown; however, the likely medieval landscape can be gleaned from topographical and documentary sources.

Manul was not the only benefactor during the early years of the abbey since the lords of the manor also granted land. In the early thirteenth century the lord of the manor was Sir William de Beauvilain, and later Sir Walter de Goderville. William de Beauvilain, made a gift of his wood near the abbey and a little close called 'Upleg' and he also confirmed the gift of Derriards (*Cal Chart R Hen III* 1226-1257, 38; Birch 1875, 258), while Walter de Goderville granted land near the abbey and was witness to several other grants.

Derriards lies to the west of Chippenham in the manor of Sheldon (Fig 4:15). An early eighteenth century estate map shows that Derriards Farm lay on the south-eastern extremity of the manor of Sheldon and was one of three isolated farmsteads here during the medieval period (WSA: 740/2/1; Brown 2001a, 209-17). There is however, no evidence of earthworks in the vicinity of the farmstead

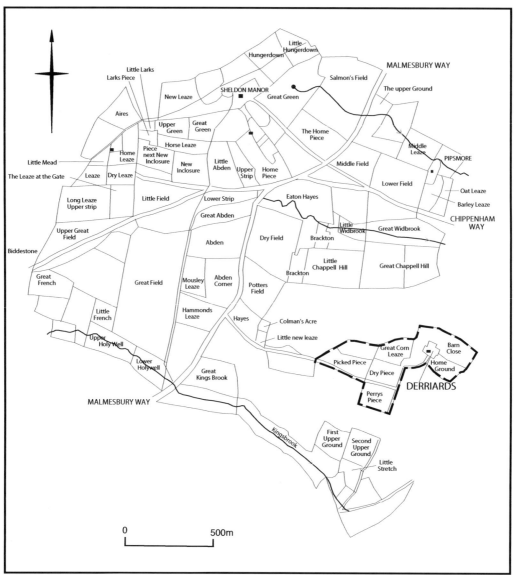

Figure 4:15. An estate map of Sheldon Manor dating to the early eighteenth century (re-drawn from WSA: 740/2/1). Derriards Farm lies on the easter side of the manor; however, Stanley's grange may have extended north to the stream and included Great Chappell Hill and Little Chappell Hill.

indicating, perhaps, that the present farmsteads were built on the sites of their medieval predecessors. Derriards is first recorded in 1167 and the name possibly refers to an animal enclosure (Gover *et. al.* 1939, 90). However, the excavation of sunken-featured building and recovery of grass-tempered ware pottery would indicate settlement in the vicinity during the Anglo-Saxon period (Brown 2001b, 18). The former extent of Derriards is suggested in a charter of John Bobbe [or Bubbe] that describes various fields and meadows, one of which bordered the 'road to Chippenham to the south' (Kirby 2007, 964). A wet, moorland landscape is also implied since, in another grant by John Bubbe in 1327, there is mention of a pasture known as la More and a close which was enclosed by ditches and hedges (Kirby 1994, 313).

Field-names also suggest that Stanley's holding was not just confined to the area of the farmstead. To the north of the farm there are three modern fields known as Priors Field and Vincents; however, the significance is not

readily obvious since they were also known as Chapelhey in 1475, and Great Chappell Hill and Little Chappell Hill in the eighteenth century (TNA: PRO: SC2/209/56; Fig 4:15). There are a number of possible interpretations for the name; it may indicate for example that a chapel was once located here and perhaps formed part of Stanley's grange, or that the rent of these fields was allocated to the upkeep of a chaplain. The field-name, Brackton would also suggest a former settlement.

Derriards is not mentioned in either the *Taxatio* or *Valor Ecclesiasticus* which may simply be an omission or that it had been disposed of, or subsumed with another Stanley holding by the late thirteenth century.

In summary, it is clear that the monks had a profound effect on the abbey environs. They were not passive landlords but adapted the landscape to their own needs along with their tenants. Despite their land being within a forest, they cleared and cultivated it. Some land was already under cultivation when they acquired it, but the archaeological evidence shows that they drained land and extended cultivation over large tracts. Pasture was probably on unimproved moorland and the Corallean ridge where there were two large sheep walks. The abbey was also responsible for harnessing the springs at Loxwell to provide water, via a conduit, to the abbey, as well as possibly creating a water meadow to provide additional hay for their livestock. Mills were established along the Marden, which were used by tenants to process wool and grind corn. Elsewhere, settlement, in the form of dispersed farmsteads and a small hamlet, lay on the elevated land.

STANLEY'S RELATIONSHIP WITH ECCLE-SIASTICAL AND SECULAR SOCIETY

The third section examines how the Cistercians relate to the rest of society. Were they agents of depopulation, and did they maintain their ideal of having no tenants or manors?

As we have seen, Chippenham Forest was an 'exploited' landscape; however, the monks at Stanley were not isolated from society. In addition, they were not the only monastic community that had interests and land in, or near, Stanley and the juxtaposition of some of these were not without their problems. Monkton Farley Priory held some land in Stanley for which they were still receiving rents of 10s, as well as one mark for tithes in Stanley in 1535 (Dugdale 1825 vol. 5, 566; Caley and Hunter 1814, 115). In 1536 the Monkton rent roll records seven of the priory's tenants in Chippenham. One tenant, Richard Apharry, held by copy from 1532 forty acres of pasture at Hardens (presumably in the area of Hardens Farm which is to the west of the Stanley boundary and near the River Avon (Fig 4:1)), and twelve acres in East Mede. The other tenants held smaller amounts of meadow in East Mede and also two acres of arable and two acres of meadow in Stanley Field (Seymour Papers vol. 12, ff.127-132).

The Augustinian priory at Bradenstoke held land in Calne, Chippenham, Langley Burrell and Cocklebury, and a smaller amount in Stanley and Tytherton Lucas. Their earliest grant in Stanley was sometime 1200-1232 when meadow was given to the canons: Godfrey of Stanley gave them an acre in the field known as Goley [Gorsey?], while Matthew Turpin gave them all his land in 'Lotteburn' and 'Brechdych', which lay beside the River Marden. Later, in the mid-thirteenth century, Thomas Bubbe, rather than giving land (which his family had done on several occasions to Stanley), gave the canons 2s annually. There was also an agreement in 1255 between Stanley and Bradenstoke in which the canons surrendered their right of entry into the abbot's wood of 'Afletmore' and the right of firewood there in return for three acres of land in Stanley in a croft called 'Avrehangre', which was near the canons' vaccary (London 1979, 112-4).

Malmesbury Abbey held the manor of Bremhill, which lay opposite Stanley and bordered the River Marden; it was granted to the Benedictines in 937 and was therefore well established by the time the monks arrived at Stanley (Brewer 1879, 349; Fig 4:16). From their home grange they farmed the fertile soils overlying the Corallian limestone outcrop.

Land was not the only possible cause of dispute; the revenue from spiritualities, particularly those of tithes, was also a contentious issue. The Cistercians had been exempted from the payment of tithes to parochial churches on land they tilled by Pope Innocent II in 1132; however, in 1215 this exemption was restricted to land that was newly brought into cultivation (Constable 1964). The effect of this was that churches were denied a valuable source of income and was a cause of disputes between the Cistercians and the episcopal authorities. There were several involving Stanley, even for tithes from their own demesne. In 1214 an agreement was reached whereby the abbey paid compensation of 12d annually to the church at Lacock for tithes of hay on the abbey's demesne meadow at Eland in Loxwell (Birch 1875, 268). Possibly more contentious, however, was a dispute involving Monkton Farleigh Priory, which also hints at their tenurial position within Stanley. The priory held Chippenham church in the twelfth century, together with its five outlying chapels (Pitt 2003, 79), and would therefore have expected to receive tithes within Chippenham parish, which included most of Stanley. In 1314 a dispute between the Prior and Abbot involving the 'new tilled' land of Stanley Abbey in Le Mershe, was settled whereby the monks had to pay a composition of eighty marks in lieu of these tithes (*Cal Anc Deeds vol. 4*, A9366; WSA: 473/9, 37). This is a curious dispute since the Abbot would presumably have still been exempted since, although later than the 1215 tithe exemption changes, it was nevertheless concerned with land that was newly cultivated.

At Studley, although Stanley Abbey held most land, the Cluniac nuns at Kington St Michael also held a small estate (Crowley and Freeman 2002a, 75) and although it is unclear where their grange was located, it was probably in the area of what later became known as Studley Farm, which lies detached from the hamlet and above Stanley Abbey. The present farm buildings date to about 1800; however, they were built on the site of an earlier house, Studley House, which was of at least late seventeenth century date (Cattell 1996). The status of the house as a survival of something more prestigious is confirmed by the earthwork remains of an eighteenth-century formal garden to the east that went with the earlier house and included a small ha ha, avenue and circular pond. Although there is no evidence of a dispute with the nuns, the proximity of their grange, as well as other monastic holdings in and around Stanley, highlights that the Cistercians, although they were clearly the principal lords in the region, were not in a 'wilderness of isolation'; far from it, they were in an exploited landscape albeit in terms of population or arable cultivation it was less so than the valleys of the Wiltshire Chalk country.

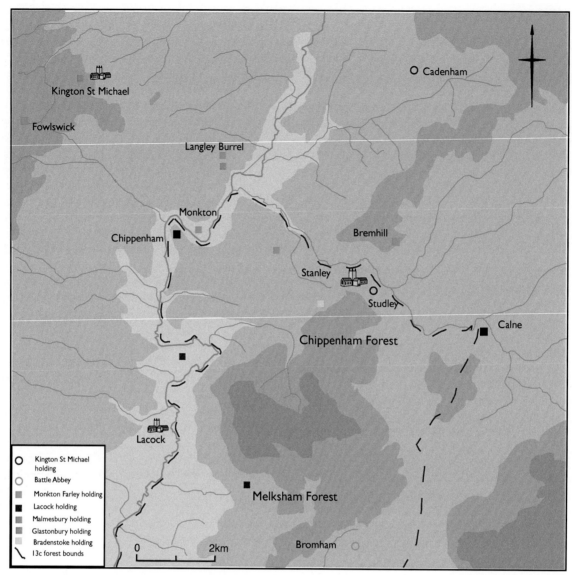

Figure 4:16. Extent of monastic landholding near Stanley by the close of the thirteenth century. In addition, several monastic houses had properies in Chippenham and Calne.

Populating The Landscape

The Cistercians have been perceived by some researchers as agents of colonisation, of land-clearance and depopulation (e.g. Donkin 1978, 39). To take just two examples, at Revesby Abbey (Lincs) the foundation included land at three places and the Earl of Lincoln offered the villagers' alternative land or their freedom. The monks at Rufford (Notts) 'gave money to each of eight men ... in return for a quitclaim of their lands' (*ibid.*, 42). Even contemporary commentators such as Walter Map, writing in the twelfth century at the height of Cistercian foundations, complained that when they failed to find their 'desert' they created one by clearing settlements and displacing the population (Burton 1998a, 54). As far as Stanley is concerned, however, there is no evidence that the monks were involved in depopulation or settlement displacement in the area of their home grange; the initial endowments involved mainly moorland, although tenements and messuages were later mentioned. There is also no earthwork evidence of pre-monastic structures within the precinct.

In Chapter Two the pre-monastic landscape was discussed and it is clear that the population was small at the time of the Domesday Survey when there was only three villagers and three smallholders; this was less than seventy years before the abbey's foundation. What is also clear is that the monks' influence on the settlement and land-use pattern would have been profound.

The next indication we have of population levels is in 1332 when there were fourteen individuals listed in the tax return (Crowley 1989), and since most of the territory was held by the monks it is probable that many were their tenants, although there may also have been a non-monastic presence with some holding land of their own (Table 4:2). Three individuals paid the highest tax, William Berner, John Harding, and William le Brege; these men were clearly individuals of considerable substance with perhaps 200-400 acres of land apiece and may reflect a non-monastic element, perhaps owning the compact block of titheable land shown on the nineteenth-century tithe map (Fig 4:1). An indication of trades is also shown in the names on the tax list, names such as Smith, Hooper, Butcher are self-evident while 'Pistore' was a baker, and Nicholas le Heliare, with the same tax of 12d, was a tiler. Forty-five years later, in 1377, another poll tax levied individuals at a standard rate of 4d on everyone over the age of fourteen. Although they were unnamed, there were sixty-six taxed individuals in Stanley (Fenwick 2005, 10-12). If we assume that the number of individuals per household over fourteen was two or three, this would suggest that there were twenty-two to thirty-three dwellings.

Name	Tax
Peter le Ratelere	3s 4 1/2d
Thomas le Smythe	12d
Nicholas le Hopere	12d
Thomas le Hotte	2s
Reynold Hare	12d
John Pistore	12d
Nicholas le Heliare	12d
Adam Gorwei	2s 8d
William le Brege	7s 2 3/4d
John Pieres	3s
John Hardeyge	8s
Stephen le Bouche	4s 6 3/4d
William Berner	8s 8 3/4d
Roger ate Nelonde	3s 8 3/4d

Table 4:2. The 1332 tax list for Stanley (Crowley 1989)

Manor or Grange?

It is usually the case that the Cistercians favoured demesne farming with lay brothers or hired labour rather than having tenants. However, Stanley does not appear to fit this model, at least not in the fifteenth century, since we have the manorial court rolls for the home grange dating to 1431-1434 (WSA: 2664, box 4). The home grange had a relatively high population and although all the tenants are not listed, there were tithingmen for Stanley and at least thirteen different people mentioned, with Studley and Nethermore listed separately. Many of the offences presented at the court concerned the clearing of ditches and repairing tenements. In October 1431, for example, 'John Touker and John Forthay should scour their ditches, namely John Touker should scour his ditch at Roggescroft and John Forthay his ditch at Huttes by the next court'. In 1433 nine individuals were required to repair their tenements by the next court on the penalty of 20d; and at the same court, in the tithing of Nethermore one of the tenants was brought before the court for agistment and pannage in the forest (*ibid.*). These examples point to the manorial character of the territory, even though it was still termed the home grange. The demesne of the home grange was leased in 1431 since 'the farmer of the manor had his day (i.e. deadline) to scour his existing ditch near le Heward

beside Peverall, Roggescroft and Huttes fully to the grave annoyance of the country'. How long this lease continued is unknown. There are also indications of contact between the home grange and an outlying grange when, John Turnay of Cudrington, one of Stanley's granges, was brought before the court in 1431 (*ibid.*).

Although listed separately in the Domesday Survey, Stanley formed part of the manor of Chippenham in 1154. In addition, the home grange was formed in a piecemeal fashion and some grants entailed the extinguishing of common rights for the tenants of Chippenham on the moor near the abbey gate. However, the home grange was a manor, or had the characteristics of a manor, by at least 1431. This trend towards manorialisation, particularly following leasing, has been witnessed elsewhere (e.g. Williams 2001, 209). In the case of Stanley it may be possible that it had manorial characteristics even earlier than 1431, perhaps by at least 1332 when we see a relatively high population with varying tax burdens.

CISTERCIAN HOME GRANGES

The final theme questions whether Stanley's home grange differed from other Cistercian monasteries in their choice and size of estate; methods of colonisation; and labour.

At Stanley, as we have seen, the home grange was located close to the abbey. The acquisition of land was not a single event but one that took at least fifty years. The single largest acquisition was from the Crown at Flet Moor; this low-lying land became the core of the demesne and although much reduced, remained identifiable in the seventeenth century as we will see in Chapter Six. Significantly, there is no evidence of settlement in this core, although Studley lies on the boundary. Archaeological and topographical evidence shows that it had to be drained before it could be cultivated but even today, despite agricultural improvements, parts are susceptible to waterlogging. Other grants from local landowners were for much smaller amounts that resulted in a compact block of land with tenants and dispersed farmsteads on the elevated land by at least the early fifteenth century. But how does Stanley compare with other Cistercian houses?

First, the grange buildings at Stanley lie to the west of the conventual buildings and cover the western side of the precinct to include the Cellarer's undercroft in the west range. The buildings extend as far as Stanley Mill, and probably incorporated what later became Pound Farm where there was a sheep-house. Although the evidence is lacking at Stanley, evidence from elsewhere shows that there would have been a wide range of agricultural buildings such as barns, cart sheds, and a mill - in other words a farmstead in all but name. This arrangement is mirrored at several other monasteries such as Byland, Hailes, Fountains, Rievaulx and Croxden to name but five. At Byland and Croxden there is also evidence of an enclosed yard against the west range that would have been used by the Cellarer.

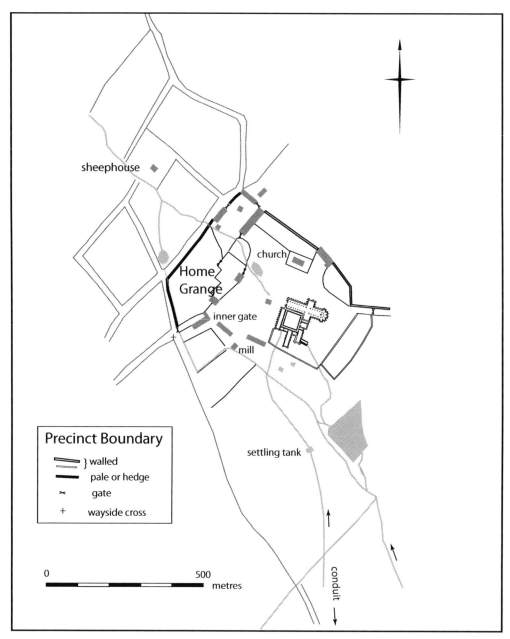

Figure 4:17. The home grange buildings at Hailes Abbey lie on the western side of the precinct amd include the detached sheephouse (after Brown 2006)

There were also mills and orchards within the precincts at Hailes and Croxden as at Stanley (Fig 4:17). Interestingly, although there was a mill within the precinct, Wilcox Mill is outside the precinct despite its close proximity. This may suggest that the mill was acquired, or at least the land was acquired, following the laying out of the precinct.

Turning to the grange estates. Stanley is similar in many respects to other Cistercian home granges in size and the nature of consolidation. In the environs of the Forde Abbey (Dorset), for example, the parishes of Thorncombe, Cricket St Thomas, Winsham and Wayford were all recorded as having large areas of tithe-free land in the nineteenth century and as such they formed the nucleus of the grange estate (Hobbs 1998). Whether this was a single acquisition or, like Stanley, a piecemeal affair, is unclear. When Waverley Abbey was founded in 1128, it was granted land in Waverley as well as a small amount of meadow, pannage

and rights of wood at Farnham. The home grange formed a consolidated block by the abbey amounting to 496 acres (201ha), but there was additional detached land giving an overall area for the home grange of 588 acres (238ha) (Service 2010, 212). Another piecemeal development occurred at Fountains, where it took forty years before one of its three home granges, Sutton, was formed into a compact block of land (Coppack 1993, 87). A similar development occurred, mainly in the thirteenth century, at another of its home granges, Sawley Grange. The grange lay on the northern side of the abbey and in 1535 it covered an area of 144 acres (58ha) and included similar amounts of arable (14ha), pasture (12ha) and meadow (11ha), with woodland making up much of the remainder (*ibid.*).

Some monasteries were endowed with a consolidated block of land from the outset. When Richard, Earl of Cornwall, founded the monastery at Hailes, the monks were

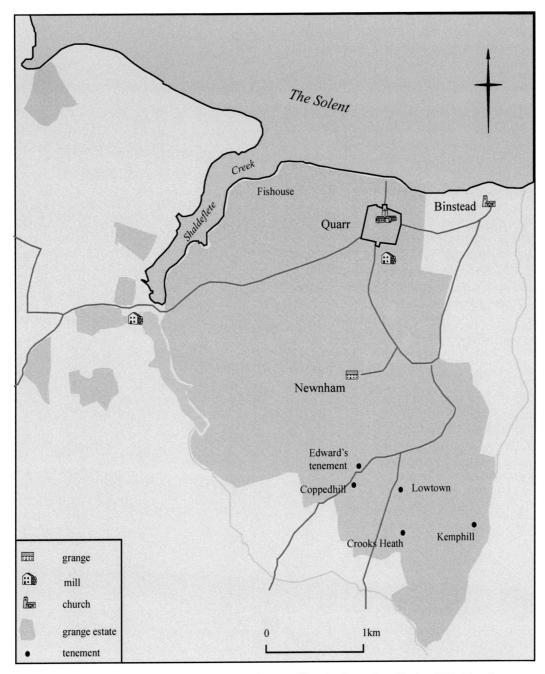

Figure 4:18. Newnham Grange. The home grange of Quarr Abbey (re-drawn from Hockey 1991, Map 1)

granted the whole manor. This clearly had implications for the population, which was relatively high, and they either remained and became tenants of the abbey or, as Winkless has suggested, they may have been moved to a new site at neighbouring Didbrook (Winkless 1990, 9).

The final point concerns the evidence of labour and their status on the home grange (the status of outlying estates, either as granges or manors, is discussed in greater depth in Chapter Five). The traditional view of the Cistercian grange sees its labour being initially provided mainly by lay brothers but later, with their demise, land was leased out and the Cistercians became landlords. Tenants are also evident on several home granges in a similar manner to Stanley, but how early they existed is not always clear. At Strata Florida the area centred on Troed y Rhia formed

part of the home grange and included a sheepcote and dispersed farmsteads. Some of these farmsteads were probably in place prior to the acquisition of the area by the Cistercians (Fleming and Barker 2008, 261-90). As Robinson notes, Strata Florida's granges were unlike the ideal Cistercian model of self-contained farms but more akin to settlements of a still dependent peasantry that had been 'transferred by charter from secular to monastic lordship' (Robinson 2006, 268 quoting Pierce 1950-1, 29).

There were tenants on the Quarr Abbey's home grange in at least the early fourteenth century and probably much earlier. The abbey was founded in 1132 by Baldwin de Reviers (or Redvers), lord of the Isle of Wight on, what Hockey refers to as, 'his manor of Newnham' (Hockey 1970, 84). The reference to 'his manor' presumably implies resident tenants, in a similar way to the manor of Hailes. The home grange was actually centred at what is today Newnham Farm but there were also tenements elsewhere on the grange estate (Fig 4:18). Newnham does not appear to have been leased and an inventory of 1388 lists its contents including household goods and 'the workshop – ploughs, carts, harness, implements – follow the beasts, among which seven mares, seventeen dray-oxen, 224 sheep, pigs, geese, ... corn lying in the granary'. Elsewhere on the grange there was a mill, a sea mill, and a fish house (*ibid.*, 172, 178). With the demise of lay brothers, the monks, like monastic and secular lords elsewhere, would have used wage labour in the form of servants or *famuli* (full time employees hired by the year). In 1420 there were twenty tenants at Newnham paying a total rent of £4 18s 4d, the highest being 8s 5d, which suggests an individual with considerable resources (*ibid.*, 187). This number seems to remain consistent throughout the century since in 1474 there were twenty-two tenants (*ibid.*, 185).

Despite the lack of research into Cistercian home granges, what evidence there is would suggest that Stanley's home grange was similar to those elsewhere. The establishment of a home grange was either piecemeal or a single grant of land. Many of these latter home granges were manors from the outset. In the case of Stanley, the home grange was formed in a piecemeal way; there was a pre-existing population here although their initial status is unclear. The principal grange buildings lay on the west side in the outer court of the precinct, with others beyond the precinct wall.

CHAPTER FIVE

STANLEY ABBEY'S GRANGES AND ESTATES

INTRODUCTION

Zones of Exploitation

The end of the thirteenth century marked the point of maximum expansion for Stanley Abbey. At this time the abbey held land and urban property principally in Wiltshire but also in the neighbouring counties of Berkshire, Somerset and Gloucestershire as well as a small piece of land on the Isle of Wight and the church and tithes of the fishing fleet at Rye in Sussex. Of these holdings only seven are specifically recorded as granges while the remainder were either termed manors or were simply smaller parcels of land. Whatever the case, these territories can usefully be divided into five 'zones of exploitation', which mainly conform to geographical and geological regions (Fig 5:1). The acquisition of land in these zones, however, was not necessarily the result of a conscious policy of land acquisition but more likely a fortunate coincidence, nevertheless they provided the abbey the varied resources they required to prosper.

The first zone was the 'forest zone', which lay around the abbey and formed the central administrative core of the abbey. As well as the home grange, there was a grange at Loxwell and probably one at Langley Burrell with further holdings elsewhere within the zone. Resources such as timber, stone and ironstone were exploited; it was also a cultivated region with meadow and extensive pasture. It was an area of mainly dispersed settlement with three market towns and a few nucleated villages as we have seen in the previous chapter.

The chalklands that extend across much of south Wiltshire from Salisbury Plain and the Marlborough Downs in the west to the Lambourn Downs in Berkshire in the east was the second zone. This region formed a crucial part of the monastery's grange economy to such an extent that two of its granges and a manor were still held directly by the abbey at the Suppression - land elsewhere had long since been leased. The undulating landscape was typical sheep-and-corn husbandry where the higher downs, with its short lush grassland and 'thin' soils, were ideal sheep walks. Cultivation was mainly confined to the more fertile soils near the settlements and extended onto the downs with limited, or temporary, cultivation of the poorer soils on the higher downs. Beside the rivers and streams lay the meadows, which were generally quite small and had to be supplemented with meadow from elsewhere. The settlements on the Chalk were predominantly nucleated and were situated in the valleys, at the foot of the escarpments, or on the flat plain close to spring lines, rivers and streams.

The third zone is the low-lying Clay Vale of Wiltshire and Berkshire, which also incorporated a small part of the Cor-

allian-Gault and Greensand belt at the base of the chalk escarpment of the Marlborough Downs. The area comprised a mainly dispersed settlement pattern. The predominantly heavy clay soils, known as Oxford and Kimmeridge clays, are difficult to cultivate and are prone to waterlogging and as a consequence this was predominantly a pastoral farming region; however, the archaeological evidence of ridge-and-furrow near some settlements attest to cultivation during the medieval period (Lewis 1999, 91). This cultivation is also evident in the documents. For example, William of Colerne, Abbot of Malmesbury (1260-1296), was actively engaged in reclaiming marshland near Chippenham and turning it into enclosed grazing or cultivation. Also an extent in 1360 of a tenement at Lydiard Tregoze stated that it was worth 4d an acre, sown or unsown, while twenty acres in the common fields were only worth 1d an acre (Scott 1959, 11-14). By the later medieval period there is a clear distinction between this area, the 'Cheese', with the emphasis on pastoral farming, enclosed fields and weak manorial control, and the Chalk with its open landscape, cultivated fields and tighter manorial control (*Chapter Six*). It was in this 'Cheese', or 'clayland' zone that Stanley had several territories including one of its earliest, and largest in Wiltshire, at Midgehall and another, Wadley, in Berkshire.

The fourth zone is on the Wiltshire and Gloucestershire Cotswolds. Before enclosure, large areas under cultivation with little permanent pasture dominated this landscape, although there were also areas of extensive pasture on the higher ground. What permanent pasture there was near the mainly nucleated settlements was largely confined to areas inaccessible to the plough such as on the hilltops or steep valley sides. Later, in the fourteenth and fifteenth centuries, the area under cultivation decreased and more land was turned over to pasture.

Finally, the fifth zone is on the Mendip Hills. The western Hills were largely a royal forest and dominated by royal and ecclesiastical estates at the time of the Conquest. Settlement, mainly nucleated villages and hamlets, was largely confined to the valleys at the foot of the hill escarpment with small farmsteads on the upper slopes. Only occasionally, as at Priddy, was there settlement on the higher plateau. On the escarpment are the earthwork remains of a number of farmsteads dating to at least the medieval period, while others from this period may survive as place-names or later farmsteads and field barns. Aston suggests that some may originally have been used as seasonal settlements that later developed into permanent farmsteads (Aston 1994, 228-9). It is also clear that they all lie between the 'zone of cultivation' of the valley settlements and the Royal Forest of Cheddar on what was former marginal or communal land. Large sheep walks extended across the limestone plateau with some arable cultivation; the area

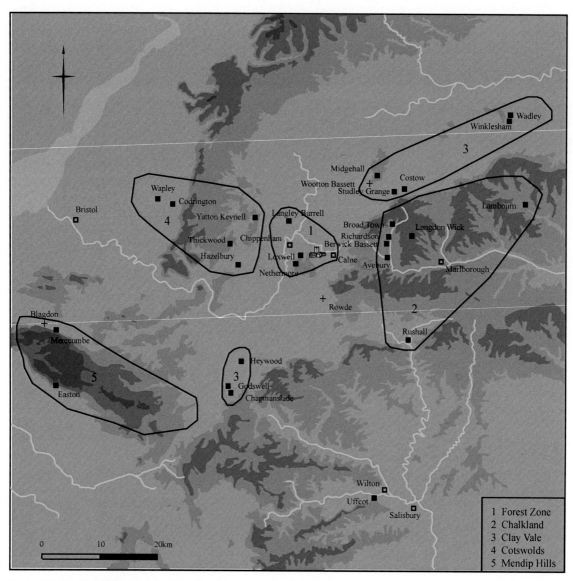

Figure 5:1. Stanley Abbey's zones of exploitation

was also an important source for minerals such as lead and silver that were extracted here since at least the Romano-British period. Woodland and cultivated fields covered the northern and particularly the southern escarpment, while the wetland moors to the south were used for pasture.

These five zones were, therefore, host to Stanley Abbey's lands and provided the resources required for the community with the surplus presumably going to the market.

Aim of Chapter

This chapter analyses Stanley's territories and land-use within their zones of exploitation. It is divided into two distinct, but complimentary parts. First, the location and extent of Stanley's principal land-holdings are identified and an analysis is made of their development and morphology. The second part, the 'Discussion', draws on this evidence and questions some of the traditional views of the Cistercian's predilection to a grange economy that was largely divorced from secular society. It is essentially an extension of Chapter Four, which assessed the impact

of the Cistercian's re-shaping of the landscape of part of Chippenham Forest to form its home grange, but will go further and see if the process of acquisition and management was replicated on its outlying territories.

Five main themes will be addressed in the Discussion and question some of the traditional views about Cistercian settlement and land-use. First, in a region that was more heavily settled and exploited than the north of England, Wales or Scotland, is there any evidence that they depopulated settlements in order to form their granges? Secondly, did they clear and colonise the land? Third, to what extent were the Cistercians manorial; did they have a solely grange economy or, like other monastic institutions, did they also own manors despite the early Statutes of the Order? Fourth, did they separate themselves from secular society by siting their granges in isolated positions devoid of habitation, and farm their land in severalty outside manorial control? Finally, for an Order that rejected the ownership of churches, did the monks at Stanley adhere to this early Statute or did they come to own them along with the benefits they generated?

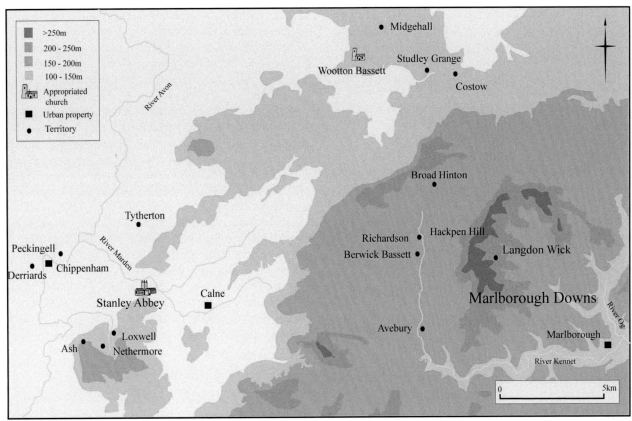

Figure 5:2. Stanley Abbey's granges and holdings on the Marlborough Downs. The map also shows the abbey's land near Stanley and on the Clay Vale

THE CHALKLANDS

The chalklands are arguably the most important of Stanley's zones after the Forest zone. It was here that the White Monks had a couple of small estates on Salisbury Plain, at Rushall where they had pasture for 150 sheep, and Stapleford, and a mill at Ugford near Wilton, but more importantly were their holdings on the Marlborough Downs and the Lambourn Downs (Birch 1875, 239-307; Fig 5:1).

The Marlborough Downs

Throughout much of the later Middle Ages Stanley Abbey held large tracts of land on the Marlborough Downs. This land lay principally on the Lower Chalk bench to the north of Avebury and included an estate at Berwick Bassett; a grange at neighbouring Richardson; land at Broad Hinton; tenements and meadow at Avebury; as well as an extensive sheep walk on Hackpen Hill. To the east of Hackpen Hill, in an area of largely Middle Chalk, the monks also had a grange at Langdon Wick, and further east a burgage and house in the market town of Marlborough (Birch 1875, 239-307; Fig 5:2).

Settlements on the Downs are largely confined to the river terrace that cuts through the Lower Chalk although there were a few isolated farmsteads of the higher downs. The River Kennet, which rises near Broad Hinton, flows south and then east towards Marlborough and the confluence with the River Og. In common with chalk downland regions elsewhere in Wessex the tithing and parish bound-

aries extend either side of the settlements with meadow confined to an area near the settlement, arable extending from the settlements onto the higher downland and to the west, and pasture on the escarpment and plateau beyond. This tripartite division of land ensured that each settlement had a proportionate share in the available land resources and appears to have its origins by at least the Anglo-Saxon period (Hooke 1994, 88-90).

When Stanley Abbey acquired land on the Downs it was already an 'exploited' landscape. Several pre-Conquest monasteries held land here including Glastonbury Abbey, which had three estates: Winterbourne Monkton, Mildenhall to the east of Marlborough, and Badbury on the northern escarpment. The nuns at Amesbury Abbey held Rabson in Winterbourne Bassett and there were further estates belonging to two of Winchester's monastic houses: the cathedral priory of St. Swithun's, and Old Minster. Wilton Abbey held land along the Kennet valley near Marlborough. In addition, large tracts of the downs were a royal estate centred on Marlborough Castle (Brown 2005a, 181-90).

Following the Norman Conquest there were further grants to the new 'reformed' orders at much the same time that Stanley was acquiring land. These included the Gilbertines, who had a priory at Marlborough by 1199 with estates along the Kennet valley. The Knights Templars had three estates, all outlying farms of Sandford Preceptory at Oxford. By far the largest estate, however, belonged to the Norman abbey at Bec Hellouin, which held Ogbourne St

Andrew and Ogbourne St George; their land extended onto the higher downs either side of the River Og. Ogbourne was the administrative centre of a bailiwick that included twenty-four manors across the south of England (Morgan 1946, 38). There were also two other smaller alien priories at Clatford and Avebury (Brown 2005a, 181-90). But it is to an analysis of Stanley's territory that we now turn.

Richardson

Richardson is situated 4km north of Avebury at 170m OD and, apart from a couple of cottages and a chicken farm, there is no other settlement; however, extending across much of the western side of the River Kennet as far as the farmstead are well-preserved earthworks, which represent a settlement and a later garden landscape, and include slight traces of ridge-and-furrow beyond the surveyed area. Analysis of these earthworks, together with the cartographic evidence, enables the grange landscape to be 'reconstructed'.

The Earthworks

The earthworks lie on the southern edge of the parish of Winterbourne Bassett bordering Berwick Bassett and cover an area of about 12ha (Fig 5:3; Fig 5:4). They appear to be in two distinct parts that are separated by a hollow-way. Along the northern side there are a series of rectilinear closes, terraces and platforms that can be interpreted as mainly garden earthworks, although they may well overlie medieval features (*Chapter Six*). In their present form these are probably associated with a post-medieval house, which was situated on a level platform (5:4a).

On the southern side of the hollow-way there are several rectilinear platforms and enclosures that are characteristic of settlement earthworks. They comprise at least fifteen building platforms, most of which are set within their own yards. At (5:4b), for example, a ditched building platform lies on the north-western side of a wedge-shaped enclosure or yard. To the east is another building platform (5:4c) with its yard to the east; the building measures about 22m by 15m overall with an entrance placed centrally on its eastern side. The size of the building would suggest it was either a two or, more likely, a three-bay structure. To the east of this building is another wedge-shaped platform with two building stances on the western side (5:4d). The southern stance is a level platform and is similar in size to (5:4c) while the one to the north is smaller and probably an outbuilding. Other homesteads can be seen in the earthworks to the north and east.

On the eastern side of the settlement is an L-shaped bank with an internal ditch truncated in the south by a field boundary beyond which is woodland. At the northern end is a square enclosure measuring 35m by 35m (5:4e). This enclosure is separated from the settlement and is dissimilar in form to their earthworks. However, it is similar to some enclosures on the Marlborough Downs, on Hackpen Hill and at Newton Farm, that have been interpreted as sheep enclosures (Smith 2005, 195-7, figs 18.3 and 18.5) and it is possible the one at Richardson is yet a further example.

In the wood to the south of the farm are the fragmentary remains of a moated site (5:4f) with the remainder underlying the modern farm buildings. The moat platform meas-

Figure 5:3. Settlement and garden earthworks at Richardson viewed from the north. The probable site of the grange is in the woodland (top right). A hollow-way, partly waterlogged, defines the edge of the settlement and garden earthworks (NMR: 15208/37 © English Heritage).

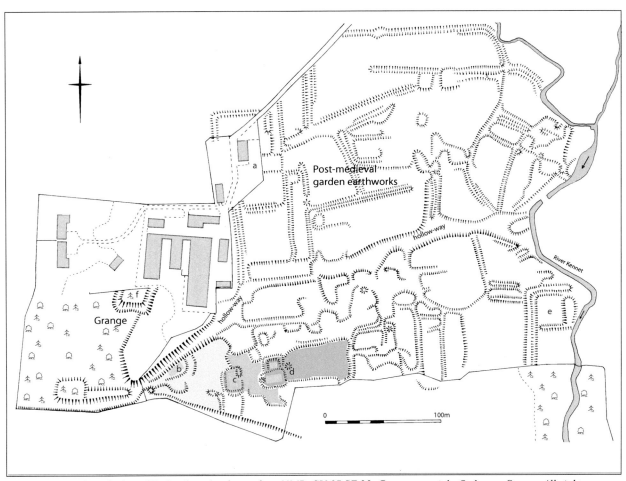

Figure 5:4. Earthwork plan of Richardson (re-drawn from NMR: SU 07 SE 23, Crown copyright Ordnance Survey. All rights re-served). The shaded areas represent the probable extent of three homesteads.

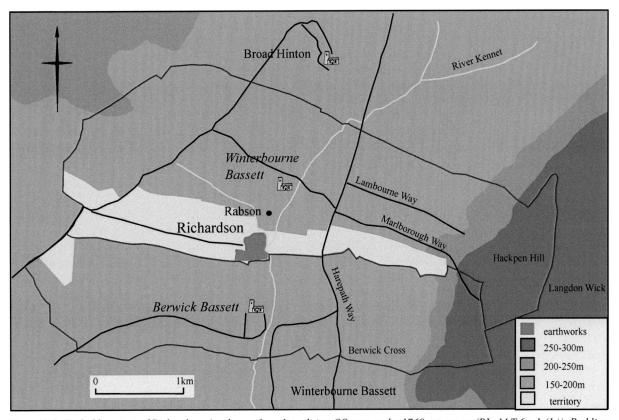

Figure 5:5. Probable extent of Richardson (re-drawn from 1st edition OS map and a 1760 estat map (BL: M.T.6.e.1.(1.)). Red lines are the parish boundaries of Berwick Bassett and Winterbourne Bassett.

ures about 35m by 40m and stands up to 0.6m high, but was originally larger. The moat is linked to the hollow-way and settlement nucleus by a curving scarp and is therefore an access route. The size of the moat and its position at the extremity of the settlement indicates that it was a demesne residence, and therefore probably the centre of Stanley's grange. Although the archaeological evidence is absent, it is likely that there were further grange buildings in the wood and underlying the modern farm.

The earthwork evidence, therefore, shows that the grange buildings were 'attached' to the end of the nucleated settlement; land does not appear to have been cleared nor does there appear to be any depopulation when Stanley acquired land here in the thirteenth century. Sherds of medieval pottery dating to the twelfth and thirteenth century found during the survey of the site and the poll tax return point to an inhabited grange and village at this time. Significantly, the poll tax return of 1377, about 150 years after the formation of the grange, records thirty-one taxpayers (Beresford 1959, 310; Fenwick 2005, 18), giving a population of 65-70 people inhabiting perhaps fourteen or fifteen households, which equates well with the earthwork evidence.

The Grange Landscape

A survey was undertaken in 1536 for Lord Seymour who had acquired five of Stanley's estates following the Suppression: Richardson, Langdon Wyke, Berwick Bassett, Midgehall, Studley Grange, and a tenement at Broad Hinton. Richardson was surveyed along with Berwick Bassett and Langdon Wick and they were described as 'sometyme part of the abbey of Stanley' (Seymour Papers: Vol. 12, f172).

It is clear from the Seymour survey that the grange had a two-field system, an East Field with seventy-eight acres and a West Field with seventy-nine acres giving a total of 157 acres (63ha). These fields were presumably located on either side of the settlement. The size of the furlongs varied from 2-32 acres. For example, eighteen acres lay in 'Grange Pece' in the East Field, and there was seven acres in 'Mylbarough' [Marlborough] Furlong. There was also a windmill in East Field 'against Botern Furlong'. In the West Field there were twenty-two acres in 'Crobarowe Furlong' and only two acres in 'the furlong next Richardson Hedge' (Seymour Papers: Vol. 12, f172). Meadow was confined to the river gravels and amounted to a mere 1.75 acres (Fig 5:5). Pasture was mainly on the escarpment and plateau, on the upper and middle chalk beyond the open fields; however, there were two small closes, one of which was called 'The Grange' and presumably lay beside the grange and contained seven acres. On the downs there was extensive pasture for nearly 2,000 sheep and fifty wain loads of hay at Wick. Pasture on Fore Down amounted to seventy-six acres (31ha) and was sufficient for 350 sheep, while a sheep walk at Wick extended for 180 acres (73ha). There was also pasture on Cow Down, which was held in severalty (Seymour Papers Vol. 12, f.171).

Cutting through the estate was Harepath Way, presumably the course of a herepath from the Anglo-Saxon settlement at Avebury. Two tracks led from Harepath Way onto the downs and the sheep pastures on Hackpen Hill. Marlborough Way was probably a main route to Marlborough while Lambourne Way was another sheep drove. In the west lies a wide track-way leading to Broad Hinton with branches off to Richardson and Winterbourne Bassett. Although this is now a minor track it would appear that this was one of the principal route-ways in the medieval period.

Brief Historical Background

Stanley Abbey held land at Richardson in or before the thirteenth century when the monks received a yardland from Theobald of Winterbourne and smaller amounts from other individuals. Further grants followed in 1227 including the holdings of the Hospital of St Bartholomew, Bristol, which they acquired for rent (Freeman 1983b, 188-9). The amounts granted show that the process of grange formation was piecemeal, by grant, purchase or exchange in a similar manner to many other Cistercian granges. However, what is significant is that the grange was established within an existing settlement and manorial framework.

The manor of Richardson is recorded in 1242-1243 when ¼ of a knight's fee was held of the honor of Hereford. The overlordship of the manor descended with the earldom of Hereford until 1383 when it passed to Mary, wife of the future Henry IV. In 1242-3, William Quinton held Richardson of the honor and in 1368 it was held by William Wroughton; it remained in his family until 1604 (ibid., 188). Walter Marshal, earl of Pembroke, also held ½ knight's fee in Richardson in 1242-3 and in 1316 it was probably held by Ralph Mauduit. Rents and services from Richardson were settled on Sir John Roches and his wife in 1399, and it later passed to their daughter (ibid.)

There was, therefore, a manor and grange at Richardson and the grange was 'attached' to the settlement. Little is known of the agrarian landscape here, but in 1392 the demesne of the manor amounted to six yardlands (Freeman 1983b, 189).

Berwick Bassett

Berwick Bassett lies to the south of Richardson on the west bank of the River Kennet. There is little in the way of earthworks here apart from a small area to the north of the church where there is a hollow-way leading towards Richardson and several closes defined by banks and slight ditches.

During the medieval period there were two manors, one of which was held by Stanley Abbey and the Crown held the other (Freeman 2002, 10), but there may well have been a grange here within Staneley's manor (Discussion).

By at least the early sixteenth century, Stanley's manor appears to be a 'mixed farming' regime with three copyhold tenants as well as demesne land (Seymour Papers Vol.

Copyholder	Date of Copy	Holding	Arable		Meadow (acres)	Pasture
			East	West		
Richard Towers	1510	Messuage, garden, orchard	48	40	3	21 beasts and 100 sheep in the comon field West Lees, and Hackpen Hill
Thomas Crytt	1518	Tenement and curtiledge	12	13		11 beasts, 40 sheep and 2 horses
John Browne	1513	Messuage, garden, orchard	21.5	22	2	100 sheep and 2 horses
Total			81.5	75	5.5	

Table 5:1. Stanley Abbey's copyhold three tenants at Berwick Bassett

12, f.172). The land was cultivated, like Richardson, in a two-field system with a total of 403.5 acres (163ha) of arable land. The tenants' land was divided almost equally between the East and West Fields, but the demesne, which amounted to 247 acres (100ha), had 70 acres in the West Field with the remainder in East Field (Table 5:1). This imbalance of about 100 acres is intriguing and may be due to greater acquisitions in East Field, alternatively there may have been a separate field perhaps held in severalty that was brought into East Field - possibly a grange. On the downs there was a close of ten acres on Cow Down that was also held in severalty for part of the year. There was only a small amount of meadow amounting to 5½ acres (Seymour Papers Vol. 12, f.173).

Langdon Wick

The third of Stanley Abbey's major holdings on the Marlborough Downs was at Langdon Wick where there are well-preserved earthworks. The landform here is undulating and varies in height from 185m OD on the lower downs to 270m OD. It lies principally on Middle Chalk with a narrow band of Upper Chalk, overlain in places by small pockets of Clay with Flints, across the higher ground on Hackpen Hill. A 'finger-like' projection of Upper Chalk extends south-east from Hackpen Hill, centrally across the grange estate, dividing it between two distinct areas of downland.

The grange lies at the head of a dry stream defined by a narrow band of valley gravels. It was in an area that had already been exploited during the prehistoric period with large tracts of 'Celtic' fields evident on Preshute Down. There was also a barrow cemetery on Rough Down that defines the southern extremity of the estate.

The Earthworks

The grange lies within a polygonal enclosure that overlies a 'Celtic' field system and covers an area of c1ha. It is defined by a bank and partial external ditch (Brown 2005b, 35-48; Fig 5:6). In the north-west there is a grouping of four compounds each with one or two buildings and a yard; all have sarsen stones in their banks. The largest compound measures c20m by 15m and consists of an L-shaped platform, which may have held a couple of buildings, set above a rectangular yard (5:6a). This yard has entrances on the northern and eastern sides. To the east of this compound, and separated from it by a narrow entrance gap, is another building platform with a slight cross division (5:6b). Again, a yard occupies a lower level to the east. The third compound (5:6c) comprises a building platform with an internal cross division that suggests a two-bay structure, which is set along the northern perimeter bank with a yard occupying the area to the south. The fourth compound (5:6d) lies to the north-west of (5:6a) and has a small building platform in the west contained within a walled enclosure and another to the south. The buildings in this area vary in size from 12 by 6m to 10 by 4m and were probably either one or two-bay structures.

To the east of the four compounds is a large rectangular enclosure, or yard (5:6e), which is cut by a diagonal scarp. This enclosure was probably a stockyard; it is defined on three sides by a bank with sarsen stones protruding while the fourth side is left open. A gap (5:6f) along the western bank provides access to the compounds.

To the east of the yard (5:6e) is a platform (5:6g) measuring 25m by 15m and defined in the south by an L-shaped bank and by a shallow scarp on the other two sides. The northern side is parallel to the diagonal scarp in (5:6e), suggesting that the two are contemporary.

To the south of (5:6g) is another, larger embanked enclosure (5:6h) measuring 40m by 20m with an entrance on the northern side. Internally there are two slight L-shaped scarps, which probably define building platforms. This enclosure, together with the platform (5:6g), is set apart from the others and may form the principal homestead of the grange. What the four compounds represent, however, is not entirely clear. They are smaller than the homesteads at Richardson, which may suggest differing status or occupations; they may have been dwellings for the grange servants or perhaps the re-used remains of a pre-grange settlement. There were, therefore, two distinct habitation areas within the grange. A ministers' account dating to 1292 provides evidence of structures and functions within the grange. It lists, for example, wages paid to servants and mentions payments for women milking ewes, and the roofing a building, presumably for the granger and other monastic staff, is specifically mentioned. Elsewhere on the grange there would have been barns for storing the grain that was mentioned in the account as well as a dairy for the cheese and milk (*p. 84*).

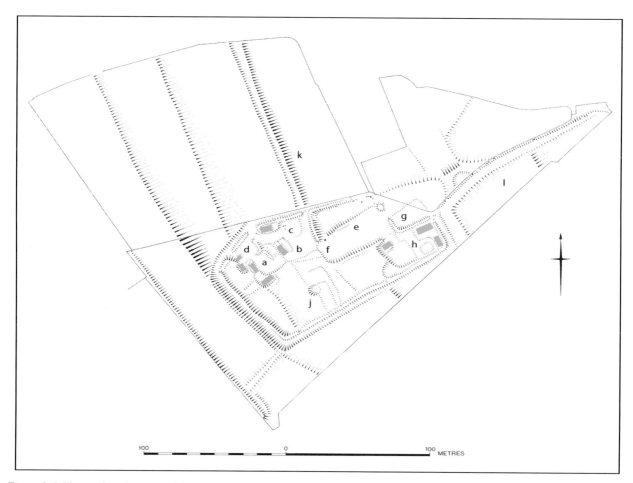

Figure 5:6. The earthwork survey of the grange at Langdon Wick (after Brown 2005b).

The south-western quarter of the grange enclosure contains a series of slight linear scarps, at least one of which is the remains of a 'Celtic' field lynchet, while others may represent small stock enclosures. A circular depression (5:6j) is probably the site of a well. Extending in a northerly direction from the entrance gap along the northern side of the grange is a double-lynchet track-way (5:6k), which utilises a former 'Celtic' field lynchet, while on the eastern side of the grange is a broad, slightly curving earthen and sarsen bank (5:6l).

The Grange Landscape

At Langdon Wick there is archaeological evidence for an inner and outer enclosure (Fig 5:7). The outer enclosure covers an area of about fifteen hectares and is defined on three sides by a bank and a steep natural escarpment along its northern side. An east/west bank slicing through the area to the east of the inner enclosure effectively divides the outer enclosure into two large closes, with perhaps further close boundaries marked by some of the 'Celtic' field lynchets. It is unclear what these closes would have been used for, but given the evidence from granges elsewhere, it is probable that they were used as sheep or other stock enclosures with perhaps some agricultural buildings such as sheep houses (Platt 1969, 42). Two tracks lead from the inner enclosure to the outer enclosure.

An estate map shows that it covered an area of 743 acres (c300ha) and apart from one small area, was tithe-free (WSA: 1780/4). Pasture covered much of the northern part of the estate. At the time of the Suppression it amounted to at least 227 hectares (560a) and included land sufficient for nearly 2,000 sheep (Seymour papers, Vol. 12, f174). On Preshute Down, the survival of extensive tracts of 'Celtic' fields, coupled with the apparent absence of any ridge-and-furrow, suggests this area was pasture; however, the north-western side of Preshute Down was under cultivation in the late-eighteenth century, which may have resulted in the levelling of any field systems here. As far as meadow is concerned, its extent in the medieval period is unknown but it is likely that it was in much the same area as in the late-eighteenth century when it was confined to the area of the valley gravels, along Long Mead and Little Mead, and within the grange's outer enclosure (Fig 5:8). Arable cultivation is more evident, with traces of ridge-and-furrow surviving to the north and east of the grange.

Although the grange contained a range of agricultural buildings, other sheep enclosures, including shelters for the shepherds, may have existed further afield. Smith (2005, 194) suggests that most sheep enclosures on the Marlborough Downs were 'typically sub-square or sub-rectangular' in plan and surrounded by a bank and external ditch. There are two possible examples, the first is sub-

82

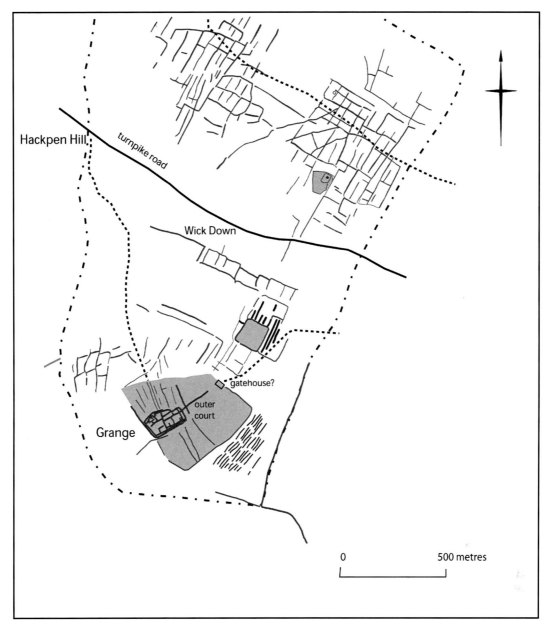

Figure 5:7. The grange lies within the shaded area and comprises the inner (the surveyed area) and the outer enclosure. The other two grey areas are probable sheep enclosures. The grange estate is outlined by the pecked line, which was tithe-free. In the north there is an extensive 'Celtic' field system, while the small continuous lines to the east of the grange denote ridge-and-furrow (after Brown 2005b, 42).

square in plan and lies to the north of the grange while the second lies on the southern side of Preshute Down, in the prime area for pasture, where a Bronze Age enclosure, with what was termed by Piggott as an 'ancient' pond close-by (1942, 48-61). It is conceivable that this enclosure was re-used as a small sheep enclosure, particularly given its juxtaposition to the pond, which in form appears to be earlier than the sub-square examples built elsewhere on the downs during the eighteenth and nineteenth centuries.

When compared to some other granges elsewhere, the inner enclosure at Langdon Wick is relatively small whereas its outer enclosure, at c15ha, is considerably larger. At Monknash, a grange of Neath Abbey in Glamorgan, the inner enclosure covered an area of c2.4ha (c6a). The outer

enclosure was c8.3ha (c20a) and included a large barn and dovecote (RCHM (Wales) 1982, 262-65). Another of Neath Abbey's granges, Gelligarn, had an inner enclosure of similar size to Monknash's, but its outer enclosure, at c11.6ha (c28a), was larger, but still smaller than Langdon Wick (ibid., 260-62). Nevertheless, some granges were similar in size to Langdon Wick. The inner enclosure of Tewkesbury Abbey's grange at Llantwit, for example, measured c1.2ha (c3a); here the remains of a gatehouse, barn, dovecote, and other buildings have been identified (*ibid.*, 299-303). At Griff, a grange of Rievaulx Abbey, the inner enclosure was much smaller, covering c1.6ha and containing a dwelling, outhouses, and a large barn-like structure with opposing entrances along the longer sides (Hunt and Stone 2003, 31-32).

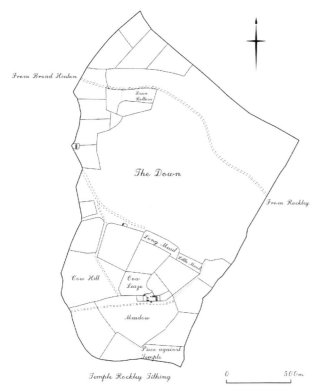

Figure 5:8. Estate map of Langdon Wick. The grange buildings lay in the area of meadow to the south of the farmstead. Titheable land was in the south and know as 'Piece against Temple' (re-drawn from WSA: 1780/4).

The Ministers' Account of 1292

A tantalising insight into the economy of this downland estate is revealed in the only surviving ministers' account for 'Langeden' (TNA: PRO SC 6/1054/18; Hobbs 2005, 47-8 in Brown 2005b, 35-48). Dating to 1292 (a year after the *Taxatio*), it shows that its economy was based on sheep-and-corn husbandry, similar to other chalk downland estates. The account covers two dates, 3 April 1292 and 25 November 1292. The first gives an account of receipts and expenses from Langdon, presumably the manor, while the second gives receipts and expenses as well as profits of the grange. This implies there were two elements: a general account, presumably of the demesne, as well as details for the grange.

The grange account shows the profits and that it had an annual value of £8 5s 10d. There was 2qtr of wheat, which were destined for the abbey, as well as maslin and oats. Unfortunately there is little detail of the staff although allowances for servants and milkmaids are mentioned. In the dairy there were ten weys of cheese, eight of which were for the abbey while the other two were for the grange; there was also twenty-one gallons of butter for the abbey. The cheeses and butter were worth £3 12s, which was 43 per cent of the annual value of the grange. There is mention of the cellarer's cart as well as the abbot's horse and a mare and its foal.

The other account shows that there were paid servants and milkmaids in the same way as the grange account; a roofer was also paid to repair a building, the *domus*. Presuma-

bly this was roofed in reeds since 14d was spent on their purchase. Although there was clearly pasture, there were also arable fields where oats, maslin, barley and dredge (a mixture of barley and oats) were the main crops grown along with a smaller amount of wheat, a third of which was supplied directly to the abbey. The fertility of the soil was supplemented by the purchase of dung. Sheep are not enumerated; however, women were paid to milk the ewes and oil was purchased for the lambs, which would have been used to protect them from disease. Wax and honey were also sold for 6s. There was also a receipt from Marlborough suggesting that the estate also administered the abbey's property in Marlborough.

The evidence from the account is perhaps too slight to draw any firm conclusions, but it nevertheless shows that Langdon Wick was more complex than the 'standard' or 'ideal' Cistercian grange, and that there were servants rather than tenants working on the demesne and grange.

THE CLAY VALE

Stanley Abbey had seven estates in the clay vale: in Wiltshire these were Midgehall, Studley Grange, Costow, Heywood Grange, and Godswell with land in Chapmanslade, while in Berkshire they held Wadley and a grange at Winklesham (Fig 5:1). There is little archaeological evidence for these estates apart from aerial photographs; however, supplementing these with the map and limited documentary evidence enables the extent and land-use of most to be determined.

Midgehall

Midgehall was the largest of Stanley Abbey's estates in Wiltshire. There is little documentary evidence for it prior to the mid-sixteenth century; however, its importance to the abbey is reflected in the *Taxatio* in 1291 when, with an assessment of £20, it was their second highest valued estate, and in 1535 it was valued at £40, which was still the highest assessment after the home grange (Astle *et.al.* 1802, 193).

The grange buildings lay centrally within its estate at 125m OD on the southern edge of Braydon Forest. It was first specifically known as a grange in 1228 when there was a dispute between the Abbot of Stanley and the rector of Lydiard Tregoze over tithes (Story Makelyne 1909, 334). The landscape is gently undulating and ranges in height from 100 to 140m OD. Several streams rise to the east of the grange and flow east and north-east to Lydiard Tregoze before emptying into the River Ray. The estate forms the southern side of the parish of Lydiard Tregoze and is on the foothills of the Marlborough Downs; its extent can be seen from the large swathe of tithe-free land (WSA: Tithe map Lydiard Tregoze; Fig 5:9).

To the south of Midgehall lies Studley Grange, which is also in the parish of Lydiard Tregoze. This grange was probably established following the acquisition of Midgehall (*Discus-*

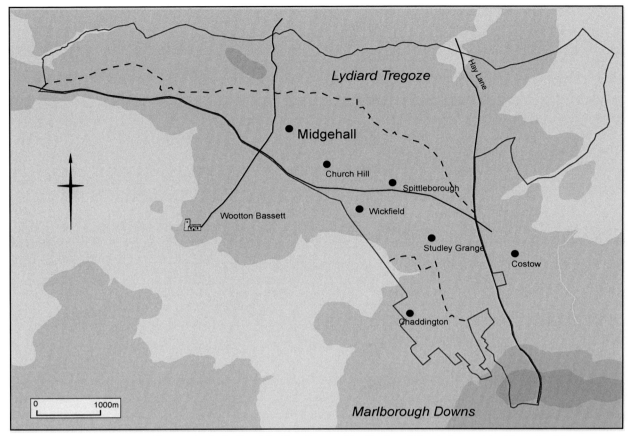

Figure 5:9. Stanley Abbey's holdings at Midgehall and Studley Grange. The black peck line is the combined bounds of the two estates.

sion). To the east of Midgehall, Stanley held a small amount of land at Costow, which, by the sixteenth century, was linked to Studley Grange (Seymour Papers Vol. 12, f. 154). In addition to the Cistercians, the Augustinians at Bradenstoke Priory also held land in Lydiard Tregoze at Chaddington in 1213 (London 1979, 61-4; Fig 5:9).

Midgehall is a moated site, although it has now been largely backfilled and is occupied by an eighteenth or nineteenth-century house (NMR: SU 08 SE 10). Seven hundred metres to the south is the site of a probable post-mill (NMR: SU 08 SE 35). The mill lies on relatively high ground, on Church Hill, where analysis of aerial photographs also shows cropmark evidence of a possible medieval settlement; however, its form and extent is unrecorded (NMR: SU 08 SE 26). The toponymn, Church Hill, is intriguing and may refer to the site of a former church or chapel. Chapels are not unknown on some of the larger Cistercian granges; indeed, there was one at Codrington and although the General Chapter initially banned them, they became increasingly common in the thirteenth and fourteenth centuries (Platt 1969, 25).

A couple of hundred metres to the north of Church Hill is a pillow mound, which is probably post-medieval (NMR: SU 08 SE 41). Elsewhere on the estate there is evidence of ridge-and-furrow cultivation near Spittleborough Farm (Wilts SMR: SU 08 SE 610).

A survey dating to 1534, on the eve of the abbey's suppression, gives a clear indication of the landscape and economy of Midgehall (Seymour Papers Vol. 12, f.148-152). At this time the demesne amounted to 1,031 acres (417ha), with 600½ acres pasture, 126 acres meadow, 178 acres arable and 124 acres of wood. By this time it was an enclosed landscape with closes varying in size from 240 acres at Wyke Fyld and one of 120 acres at Bryre Fyld, to twelve acres at the Grove. Wyke Fyld probably lay in the area of the present Wickfield Farm near the estate's south-western boundary. As well as giving the acreages the survey specifies the number of cattle that could be pastured in the summer in each close and the number of wethers or ewes in the winter. Thus, Wyke Fyld was large enough for 300 cattle in the summer and 500 ewes in the winter, while in Hill Close there was a hundred acres of pasture for 100 cattle in summer and 102 wethers in winter, and the 12 acres of Grove Close could support ten cattle in the summer and twenty ewes in the winter. In total, the demesne was sufficient for 702 cattle and 1,132 sheep. This may suggest movement of livestock between the abbey's granges.

Meadow, which presumably lay close to a stream and the grange, amounted to 126 acres, which was also in closes. Stock levels were also prescribed for each close in a similar manner to pasture. There was 178 acres of arable land and field names such as Breche, Middle Breche, Little Breche and Clay Brech, indicate assarted land. Managed woodland covered an area of 120 acres. At Wyke Field Coppice, for example, there was 20 acres of wood which 'is of two years growthe' (*ibid.*).

Copyhold	Date	Holding	Orchard/ garden	Pasture	Meadow	Arable	Wood	Total land	Animals	Tenant's meadow
1	1521	cottage and barn		6a	4a			10a	6 horses	
2	1494	messuage	0.5a	1.5a	13.5a	14.25a		30.25a		
3	1519	cottage	1a		12a			13a		as many beasts
4	1518	cottage		3a	1a			4a		as many beasts
5	1520	messuage	1a garden		14a	4a		18a		3a
6	1540	messuage		3.75a	2.5a			6.25a		5a
7	1498	cottage			3a			3a		0.25a
8	1496	messuage		8a	20.5a			26.5a		5.5a
Total				22.25a	70.5a	18.25a		111a		
Percentage				20%	64%	16%		100%		
		Farm of manor		963a	103a	178a		1244a		24a
Total				985.25a	173.5a	196.25a		1355a		
Percentage				73%	13%	14%		100%		

Table 5:2. Tenantry land at Midgehall in the late-fifteenth and early-sixteenth century (Seymour papers vol. 12. f.148-150).

In addition to the demesne, there were also eight copyholders (Table 5:2). Their holdings varied from 3 – 30¼ acres, most of which was pasture or meadow. Most had access to the Tenantry Meadow, presumably a common meadow where they were either allocated an area or the number of beasts they could pasture was stipulated.

Studley Grange and Costow

Studley Grange lies to the south of Midgehall in the parish of Lydiard Tregoze. The earliest form of the name is Stodlegh and, as with Midgehall, it is probably a pre-Conquest name (Gover *et al* 1939, 276). The first element may refer to a stud, while the second element is a *lēah* name, meaning a clearing or glade in a wood, and later 'pasture and meadow' (Gelling 1984, 198). Studley, therefore, was probably a settlement prior to the acquisition of Stanley, which was probably by 1189 at much the same time as Midgehall, and remained in Stanley's hands until the Suppression although it had been leased since 1460 (*Cal Pat R 1452-1461*, 640). In 1505 the grange comprised 244 acres (c99ha), with thirty-three acres meadow, 161 acres pasture and fifty acres of arable. Analysis of aerial photographs shows ridge-and-furrow extended over much of the grange.

It is not entirely clear when Stanley first acquired land at Costow, but it was probably sometime before 1227 when there was a confirmation of a grant of land here (*Cal Chart R Hen III 1226-57*, 38). At the Suppression, Stanley still held two tenements amounting to 129½ acres (c52ha) of which 49½ acres was pasture, 29½ acres was meadow and 50 acres arable (Story Makelyne 1909, 336).

Wadley

At the time of the Domesday Survey, Wadley was part of an already exploited landscape; there were thirty-one hides of land, which, for the most part were royal demesne (Ragg 1906, 334). In the twelfth century it was referred to as a member of Faringdon, and was granted by king Stephen to Thame Abbey (Garbett and Clapham 1924, 489-99). It would seem that Wadley was a manor by the late twelfth century when a deed transferring it to Stanley describes it as: '… of all the land which they [Thame] have of the grant of King Henry, son of Matilda, in the manor of Word [Wadley], which was formerly a member of Faringdon' (*Cal. Anc Deeds vol. 3*, A4864).

Wadley lies on slightly rising ground on the south side of the River Thames. Although its extent in the later medieval period is not entirely clear, it may well be coterminous with the bounds on a mid-nineteenth century estate map (Fig 5:10). In 1657 the covered an area of a little over 1,621 acres (656ha) with land and tenants in Littleworth and Thrupp and a mill on the River Thames; the total area for the estate was 2,339 acres (947ha) (Oriel College archive).

Wadley was in an area that was heavily exploited by ecclesiastical institutions. In Littleworth, the Knights Hospitallers held a small estate, but the main concentration was in Faringdon manor where the Benedictine monastery at Reading, the canons of Llanthony, the bishop of Winchester, and the Norman monasteries of Bec and Cluny all held land (Hockey 1974, xxxiv, 13). More importantly, in 1203, Faringdon became the temporary site of another Cistercian monastery but the following year the community moved to Beaulieu and Faringdon became the centre of a network of six granges and two mills (Fig 5:11).

In 1212, Stanley held thirty-two librates of land in Faringdon manor; presumably this was their Wadley estate. Wadley paid an important part in abbey's economic fortunes; in 1291 it was valued at £47 3s 4d, their highest valued estate

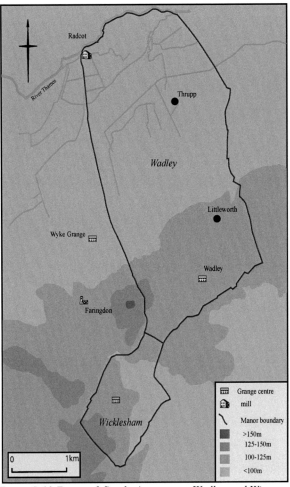

Figure 5:10 Extent of Stanley's manor at Wadley and Win-klesham Grange (re-drawn from estate map of manor held by Oriel College archives).

and more than twice as much as Midgehall (Chettle and Kirby 1956, 270).

In 1317 the manor was leased for three years 'in aid of the acquittance of his [the abbot's] debts due to the king' (*Cal Pat R Ed II, 1317-21*, 658). There followed further short-term leases until 1363 when the monks sold it, describing it as 'sterile and unprofitable', but the main reason was to re-pay debts (Chettle and Kirby 1956, 271; *Cal Anc Deeds vol. 1,* A165). The manor remained in secular hands and in 1440, Henry VI granted it to Oriel College, Oxford (Garbett and Clapham 1924, 494).

A custumal and survey dating to the seventeenth century lists the freehold land and copyhold tenements in Little-worth and Thrupp as well as a mill on the Thames that 'stood of the time that the manor fell into Oriel College hands' i.e. 1440 (Oriel College archive). The tenants' land lay principally in Thrupp and Littleworth, while the de-mesne was largely at Wadley. In 1596, the demesne was mainly pasture and there were 900 lambs, 700 ewes, twen-ty-four rams, twenty-four cows, a bull and three mares at Wadley and Wincklesham (Nichols 1841, xli).

Tenants and Settlements

Eighteen copyholders are listed in the custumal at Little-worth each occupying either a messuage or cottage, and most held either one or two yardlands although two indi-viduals held three yardlands and another held only a cot-tage and garden. In Thrupp there were five copyholders: two holding 0.5 a messuage and two yardlands (presum-ably half of the same messuage), another a messuage and a yardland, while the fifth held a cottage at Thrupp Marsh.

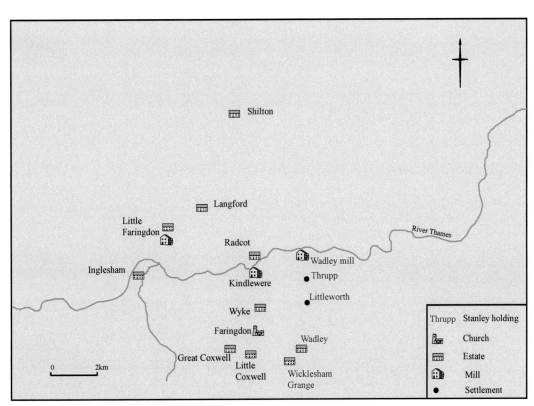

Figure 5:11 Prox-imity of Beaulieu Abbey's estates to Stanley's in the Farringdon region.

There were a further twenty-two yardlands elsewhere in the manor (Oriel College archive).

In the mid-nineteenth century Littleworth was a small hamlet with most houses bordering the south side of a curving road. There are sixteen properties; some of the larger plots had outbuildings. Some of the property boundaries on the south side appear to be agglomerated holdings while on the north side of the road settlement is more interrupted and there appears to be a 'green' further north with several empty plots. Given the number of copyholders and the plots, it is tempting to see this settlement pattern fossilising the medieval pattern. By contrast, Thrupp was much smaller in the mid-nineteenth century and appears to comprise a couple of large farmsteads and five smaller homesteads (Oriel College archive).

Winklesham Grange

Winklesham Grange lay to the south of Wadley and amounted to 276 acres (112ha) in the seventeenth century (Oriel College estate maps). Little is known about the economy of this grange, and the only indication that it was a grange was in 1246 when one of the lay brothers was mentioned in a court case (Clanchy 1973, 351). In 1291 it was valued at £10 (Astle *et al* 1802, 191b). In 1363 it was leased along with Wadley when it was referred to as the 'manors of Wadley and Winklesham' (*Cal Anc Deeds vol. 1*, A165).

Heywood Grange and Godswell

Heywood Grange and Godswell lie close to the western boundary of Wiltshire within Selwood Forest. Godswell was in the possession of the abbey by 1189 (Birch 1875, 281). Several individuals had granted land here including a pasture for 400 sheep at 'Walemerse', and in 1242-3 the estate amounted to a carucate, including small parcels of land in Chapmanslade (*ibid.*, 259; Crittall 1965, 161). In 1291 the *Taxatio* valuation was £5 10s (Astle *et. al.*, 1802, 192). Although Godswell is referred to as a manor when it was first leased in 1324, it was known as a 'grange or manor' in 1539 when the rent of the farm was £4 16s 8d (*ibid.* 162; WSA: 473/40.99).

Heywood lies 7km north-east of Godswell on the clay vale near Salisbury Plain. Stanley was granted land at Heywood sometime at the beginning of the thirteenth century, and further grants were made in a piecemeal fashion to form the grange. In 1291 it was valued at only 10s. In c.1327 the grange was first leased, however, it remained a possession of the abbey until the suppression by which time it had been annexed to Godswell (Crittall 1965, 162). In 1536 the grange was valued at £2 13s 4d, which was half the value of Godswell (Caley and Hunter 1814, 114).

COTSWOLDS

Stanley Abbey held several estates on the Cotswolds. In Wiltshire these included parcels of land at Colerne and Thickwood, a small estate at Clopcote, a quarry at Hazelbury, and a probable grange and the advowson of the church at Yatton Keynell. In Gloucestershire, the abbey had land at Codrington and Wapley.

Codrington and Wapley

Stanley's land at Wapley and Codrington is an example of the abbey holding a manor, which included a separate grange.

Land at Codrington, along with the village or hamlet of Wapley and land in neighbouring Winterbourne, were held in 1163-1164 by Ralph Fitz-Stephen who granted them to Stanley Abbey sometime before 1191 (Rudder 1779, 787; Birch 1875, 283). Malmesbury Abbey and St Augustine's Abbey, Bristol, also held smaller amounts of land here in the twelfth century, but in 1230 Malmesbury's land, with two tenements, was transferred to Stanley (Moore 1990, 123). In 1291, Stanley held seven carucates at Codrington with a mill and rents of assize at 40s and 40s from free tenants; however, in later documents Codrington and Wapley are interchangeable suggesting that the two manors were a single unit (Astle *et. al.* 1802, 236; Moore 1990, 123).

Figure 5:12. Codrington Court. This is a fifteenth century house, much altered in later centuries. The chapel is situated on the right of the house.

Although a grange is not specifically mentioned at Codrington, its existence is indicated by the Abbot of Stanley's desire to erect a chapel, presumably to serve the lay brothers; however, this was opposed by St Augustine's since they held the advowson of the church at Wapley (Fig 5:12). The dispute was finally settled in 1280 when Stanley was granted permission to build a chapel provided it was for the sole use of the capital messuage at Codrington, and no other individuals were to use it without the permission of the minister of Wapley (Rudder 1779, 788).

The monks did not retain direct control of Codrington for long since it was leased in 1323 (*Cal Pat R Ed II 1321-24*, 284). The abbey's interests here declined in the mid-

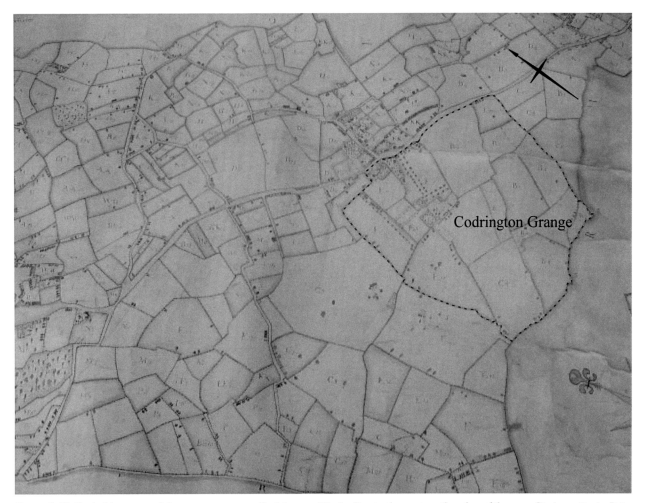

Figure 5:13. Probable extent of the grange estate at Codrington. Wapley lies to the west on the edge of the map. St. Augustine's, Bristol, had a fifteenth centiury 'infirmarium' on the northern side of the road from Codrington (GRO: D 1610/P43; NMR: ST 77 NW 20).

fifteenth century and in 1455 the abbot requested a licence to lease the manor to John Codyngton for £11 because 'the manor had gone to waste'. Codryngton agreed to repair and rebuild the manor house if it could be granted to him and his heirs (TNA: PRO: SC 8/251/12533; *Cal Pat R Hen VI 1452-61*, 252). The amount for the lease is of significance in defining the area of the abbey's demesne since it was the same value mentioned in an inquisition for the manors of Wapley and Codrington in 1471 and the same as at the Suppression (Codrington 1898, 308; Caley and Hunter 1814, 114). In 1510 the manors of Wapley and Codrington comprised seven messuages, three tofts, 300 acres of arable, sixty acres of meadow, 200 acres of pasture and twenty acres of woodland; therefore the demesne, the area of the former grange, amounted to 580 acres (235ha) (Codrington 1898, 311).

The grange was centred at Codrington Court on the east side of the parish (Fig 5:13). A map of the manor dating to 1762 shows a largely enclosed landscape. At Wapley there is a large green with the church on the eastern side and seven dwellings on the other sides. These dwellings may be on the site of those referred to in 1471. However, further dispersed farmsteads lie along the tracks. There is no settlement between the two manors (GRO: D 1610/P43).

Yatton Keynell

Stanley Abbey held three small blocks of land at Yatton Keynell. The initial grant in 1247 amounted to 50½ acres, with pasture for eight oxen and 100 sheep at an annual rent of a pair of white gloves. In 1259 there were further grants of one third of a messuage for a life rent of ten quarters of good corn, and of 123 acres of land in Easton and Yatton Keynell. This was followed three years later by the advowson of the church (Chettle and Kirby 1956, 270). The tithe map of Yatton Keynell shows an area of tithe-free land lying to the north and south of West Yatton Farm, which was probably the extent of Stanley's grange (Fig 5:14). Crucially West Yatton is not specifically named in any grant, but in an area of predominantly nucleated settlement it would suggest that it was uninhabited prior to the monks' acquisition. The 'West' in the place-name also suggests a secondary or later settlement.

The tithe-free area covers 197 acres (80ha) and probably represents the grange estate. It is sited in a typical Cistercian position - on the parish boundary - remote from any other settlement. This area is much larger than the initial grant, which suggests that most of the grant of 123 acres were in Yatton Keynell and not Easton. The grants were also generous since the grange was slightly larger than

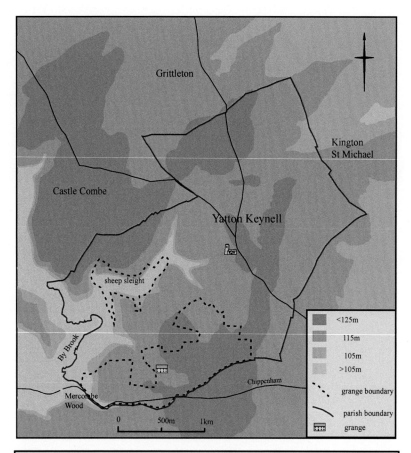

Figure 5:14. The grange at Yatton Keynell. The pecked black line represents the tithe-free land and the probable grange territory (WSA: Yatton Keynell Tithe Map).

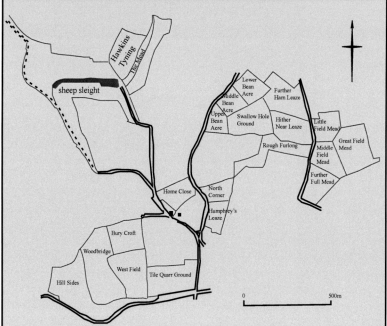

Figure 5:15. Field names at Yatton Grange. Fields that are not named did not form part of the grange territory.

the Yatton Keynell capital messuage in 1633, when there was 183 acres (74ha) (Fry and Fry 1901, 435). The grange buildings were presumably sited in the small enclosure in the same area as the present farm. The grange comprises three distinct blocks of land. First there was the sheep pasture on the steep slopes to the north. The second block lies to the south and comprises sixty-five acres (26ha). The third block is to the east of the grange. Field names, albeit late, in these latter two blocks such as Upper Bean Acre, West Field, and Rough Furlong, indicate that the land was

suitable for cultivation, while names such as Full Mead on the eastern side shows areas of meadow (Fig 5:15).

MENDIP HILLS

Stanley held land on the northern and southern escarpments of the Mendip Hills. On the northern escarpment it had a grange at Merecumbe in the parish of Blagdon and the church and temporalities of Blagdon, while in the south they had another grange at Easton, which lay to the west of Wells. There was, however, already considerable church land on the Hills mainly belonging to the cathedral church at Wells, which they acquired in the eleventh century. In addition, Glastonbury Abbey held land at Wrington on the northern foothills. The cathedral priory of St. Swithun's, Winchester also held land at Bleadon, Priddy and West Harptree. Following the Norman Conquest there were further grants to other monasteries, the largest being to the Carthusian monks at the Witham and Hinton Charterhouses who held large tracts of land and mineral rights on the high plateau. Other Cistercian abbeys also had a number of granges on the Hills; in Blagdon, for example, there were three granges and smaller parcels of land belonging to Stanley, Flaxley Abbey and St. Mary Graces Abbey in London. In addition, the Augustinians from St Augustine's, Bristol held pasturing rights and land at West Harptree, East Harptree and Rowberrow, and the Knight's Templar had a couple of estates on the plateau near Witham's Hydon Grange. The Mendip Hills were, therefore, an exploited region, not only for its vast sheep walks, but also for pannage in the woodland and arable cultivation, but more importantly for its minerals.

Merecumbe Grange

The grange at Merecumbe lay on the eastern boundary of Blagdon. Although the area of the grange is unclear, it is probably represented by the area of old enclosures on a 1787 map (SRO: D\P\blag/20/1/1; Fig 5:16). The modern farmstead lies at the foot of a narrow coombe that extends up the escarpment towards the plateau. The irregular field pattern here would suggest that the grange was established from assarted land.

Merecumbe was given in free alms to Stanley sometime between 1151-1166 and therefore amongst the earliest of its acquisitions. The grant included customary rights in Blachedune [Blagdon] wood and for ten pigs without pannage (WSA: 1213/2). There was a further gift in the first half of the thirteenth century when they were granted common of pasture for 500 sheep and other animals in Blagdon, and ten pigs without pannage 'in my Forest of Blakedon' (WSA: 473/14).

Easton

As well as land on the northern escarpment, Stanley also held a hide of land in the twelfth century in the south, at Easton (Birch 1875, 243). From the documentary evidence we can see the piecemeal and fragmentary nature of acquisition of land to form a grange since some grants were for the whole of an individual's holding while at least one was for as little as ¼ of an acre. There is also a reference to a mill and the wall of a grange (ibid., 258). In 1291 the estate was valued at £3 5s, but by the sixteenth century this had been reduced to £2 (Astle et al 1802; TNA: PRO SC6/Hen VIII/3958).

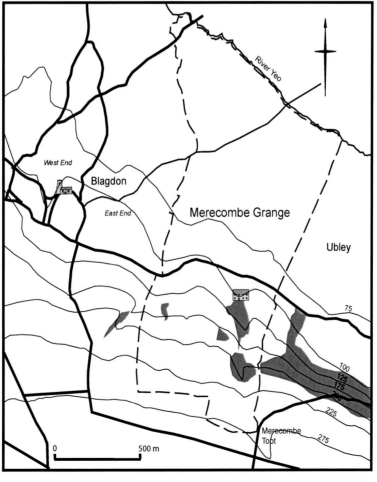

Figure 5:16. Probable extent of Merecumbe Grange (re-drawn from SRO: D\P\blag/1/1).

Figure 5:17. Field pattern on the escarpment and plateau at Easton. The black pecked line represents the possible extent of Stanley's grange estate (adapted from Brown 2008).

In the medieval period there were three estates at Easton: Stanley Abbey, Milton, and the Vicars Choral from Wells Cathedral. The area of the estate can be 'reconstructed' from eighteenth-century maps which shows that Stanley's grange probably lay to the west of the tithing (Brown 2008, 6).

Despite the lack of documentary evidence, archaeological field investigation and aerial photograph transcription shows that cultivation terraces, or strip lynchets, and field banks extend over much of the escarpment as far as the plateau where they give way to common pasture (Fig 5:17). This cultivation is confined to the Keuper Marl soils, which are ideally suited to the plough. On the low-lying land to the south of the settlement the moors would have provided good pasture and wildfowl.

CHURCHES AND URBAN PROPERTIES

Churches

Amongst the revenues specifically rejected by the first fathers of the Cistercian Order was the ownership of churches, altars and tithes. However, despite these restrictions and the frequent admonitions of the General Chapter the Cistercians appropriated churches from an early date, and Stanley was no exception (Desmond 1976, 250-1).

Stanley's Churches

Stanley Abbey held five churches at varying times and an analysis of them shows that there were two methods of

acquisition. The first was a grant from a lay lord, and in Stanley's case this could be seen as gaining a foothold in a region from where they could acquire more land. The church at Blagdon on the Mendip Hills, for example, was acquired by the monks soon after the abbey's foundation, and as well as holding the advowson they would have held the glebe, which amounted to 23¼ acres in 1613. The monks later established a grange within the parish, at Merecumbe. The church was a valuable asset although the abbey was the patron for a little over 150 years; in 1291 its tax assessment was £8 but by 1317 Sir William Martyn was the patron (Astle *et.al.* 1802, 197b; Weaver 1889, 28). Similarly at Yatton Keynell the monks held the advowson of the church, but also acquired land elsewhere in the parish to form a grange. The church was granted to the abbey in 1262 and included a ½ virgate of land, but thirty-eight years later it was leased along with the grange (*Cal F of F Wilts 1195-1272*, 52, 54; *Cal Pat R Ed III 1327-1330*, 484). As with Blagdon, a later glebe terrier shows that the church was a valuable asset with thirty acres in the common fields, fourteen acres of meadow, and thirty-five acres of pasture. There was also another sixteen acres of arable or pasture held in severalty (Hobbs 2003, 493).

The other method of acquisition was in the fourteenth century when three churches (Wootton Bassett, Rowde, and Rye) were granted to the abbey with the specific aim of alleviating the monks' financial difficulties (*Cal Pat R Ed III 1361-4*, 351; *Cal Anc Deeds vol. 1*, A165, A169). The monks were granted their advowsons with leave to appropriate in 1362. Thus this phase of acquisition is quite distinct since it occurred a hundred years after Yatton Keynell and for a totally different reason. It was a means of acquiring an immediate financial benefit, rather than a means of developing landed property. The glebe from these three churches was a valuable source of income; Wootton Bassett had ninety-three acres and common of pasture for cattle at Wotton Bassett and in the Forest of Braydon (Hobbs 2003, 482). The granting of churches to help the finances of a monastery appears to have been a fairly regular occurrence. For example, Croxden Abbey's finances were aided by the appropriation of Alton church in 1398, and Tintern appropriated Woolaston church due 'to the heavy burden of charity and hospitality' (Duggan and Greenslade 1974, 228; Williams 2001, 272).

During the medieval period the upkeep of the chancel was the responsibility of the patron while the nave was the responsibility of the parish. Analysis of the fabric of churches can sometimes show what interest and involvement the patron had in the church. Unfortunately all the churches that were held by Stanley have undergone extensive repair and rebuilding and it is unclear, without further detailed work, if they maintained an interest.

Urban Properties

Many monastic houses held properties in cities, market towns and ports since they provided access for trade and a source of income from leasing. In some cases the development by some monastic houses resulted in their markets acquiring borough status, but as far as the Cistercians were concerned their early statutes forbade income from markets and fairs, although this was soon ignored. In the first half of the thirteenth century, for example, they had acquired four markets and six fairs and by the mid sixteenth century thirty-five of their monasteries had markets and fairs. These included nine boroughs such as the planned borough of Charmouth, which was created by the Abbot of Forde in 1320 when regular burgage plots on either side of the main street were laid out and rented (Bond 2004, 277, 288).

Although Stanley did not hold any boroughs, it was nevertheless heavily involved in the acquisition of urban property, particularly in the local market towns of Chippenham, Calne and Marlborough, but also at Wilton and Salisbury and further afield in Bristol and London. These properties were a source of revenue but also a base for the abbey's business transactions. In Chippenham, Stanley held several properties along the High Street and St Mary's Street near the church; the earliest recorded in the town was a burgage for a rent of 12d in the early thirteenth century. In Calne they held a burgage and four messuages, and by 1227 they had been given a further four messuages. By the Suppression they had eleven tenements (WSA: 1213/3; 473/10; Hobbs 2003, 89; Crowley and Freeman 2002a, 68). In Marlborough the abbey also held a house and land (*Cal. Anc. Deeds vol. 4*, A9375; Birch 1875, 268, 276-7). In Bristol, where Stanley presumably exported its wool,

the abbey was free of tolls and in 1385 the monks held a tenement near the market and a burgage 'beneath the gate' (BRO: GWB/5163/120).

DISCUSSION

The two hundred years following the Norman Conquest was a period of dramatic change in the English countryside as the population grew, more land was brought into cultivation and settlements expanded. It was also a time when land was acquired by new lords, including those of the new 'reformed' religious Orders. Foremost, and arguably the most successful, were the Cistercians who established about seventy-five monasteries in England and Wales during this period. Supporting these monasteries was a network of estates that were quite distinct from those of other landlords. The traditional view is that the Cistercians managed their estates differently; that they depopulated settlements in order to establish their granges; that they cleared wasteland and cultivated 'new land' from consolidated blocks; and that they rejected the rents and income from manors, churches, and mills. However, analysis of the evidence from Stanley Abbey points to a more complex situation.

First, there is no evidence that the Cistercians at Stanley actually depopulated settlements. Indeed, there is some evidence to the contrary, that they were incorporated into an existing nucleated settlement at Richardson. In at least two cases, Merecumbe and Yatton Keynell, it is likely that granges were established on new sites on the boundaries of parishes and remote from other settlements. The first element in the place-name, Merecumbe, probably refers to a settlement on a boundary while the second element refers to a combe, an apt description for this particular grange. At Yatton Keynell, Stanley's landholding was in an area of largely nucleated settlement and it is likely that the grange was newly established.

Sites that were already occupied include Langdon Wick, Lambourn, Up-Lambourn, Midgehall, Wapley, Codrington, Richardson, and Berwick Bassett. The grants for the majority of these sites indicate that there was some form of community prior to Stanley's acquisition, and place-names are a further indicator. At Clopcote the second element in the toponymn is 'cot', which would suggest that it was a pre-Conquest farmstead. The evidence for Langdon Wick is, however, more complex. Although much of the settlement on the Marlborough Downs was in the valleys and along watercourses, there was some downland settlement by at least the twelfth century at places such as Raddun and Barbury, and Langdon Wick is yet another example (Brown 2005a, 186). Prior to Stanley's acquisition of Langdon Wick in 1189, it was part of the barton of the royal castle at Marlborough. The 'wick' element in the place-name suggests some form of outlying settlement, which is apt since it lies at the furthest extremity from the castle. It may, however, have its origins as as a bercaria (sheep farm) in much the same way as Raddun, a grange of St. Swithun's Priory (Winchester), which lies a couple of kilometres to the south of Langdon Wick. The earthworks at Raddun have been surveyed and an excavation by Fowler revealed that it comprised six buildings, one of which dated to the sixteenth-century while the others were thirteenth and fourteenth century. From the subsequent research, it was concluded that Raddun was a sheepcote in about 1220 and later developed into a farmstead. However, there were also four sherds of seventh-eighth century pottery pointing to an even earlier origin (Fowler 2000, 121-35). Langdon Wick may have developed in a similar manner, and it is tempting to see it as an outlying bercaria or dairy farm of Marlborough Castle, which later developed into a grange of Stanley.

The second point is that the Cistercians cleared and reclaimed wasteland. This has received much attention by researchers (e.g. Knowles 1950, 349; Donkin 1978, 103-34, Williams, 2001, 225). In Wales, Williams believes that '[…] very often, that much preparatory work [i.e. assarting] was necessary before intensive agriculture could be undertaken'. He goes on to cite Gerald of Wales, a well-known contemporary critic of the Cistercians, who commented: 'Give them a wilderness or forest, and in a few years you will find a dignified abbey in the midst of smiling plenty' (Williams 2001, 24). However, Donkin concedes that:

'the extent to which the Cistercians developed arable and pasture at the expense of 'waste' and woodland varied from region to region and even between neighbouring houses. While many studies stress their contribution, others have produced conclusions that are less in accord with the general reputation of the order' (Donkin 1978, 109).

This accords with Alphonso, who points out that, 'many local studies have revealed that their [Cistercian] settlements were almost entirely located in previously inhabited areas, where much of the reclamation and clearance had already taken place' thus agreeing with Donkin's second point (Alphonso 1991, 133). An example is Bordesley Abbey where research by Price showed that reclamation was severely limited on some of its territories and in some cases the monks were forced to adapt within existing settlement patterns. Much of the land given to them was already being cultivated and clearance was therefore unnecessary (Price 1971, 61). The situation is therefore clearly more complex and clearance was by no means ubiquitous. It was the topography and soils of a specific area that determined whether clearance was appropriate, regardless of the monastic Order that held the land. Previous research is also often biased since it tends to concentrate on new clearance with little consideration of previous cultivation. Stanley Abbey provides a good example of this complexity and by using the landscape evidence it is clear that in some areas there was reclamation and clearance while in others it was unnecessary.

Let us begin with the chalklands of south Wiltshire and Berkshire. The archaeological evidence shows that land did not require clearing; land that was suitable for cultivation was already cultivated while much of the higher downlands was used for grazing since at least the Anglo-Saxon period.

Apart from Langdon Wick, settlements on the Marlborough Downs were principally on the lower chalk bench beside a river. As has been shown, it was an exploited landscape with large areas already in the possession of some of the late Anglo-Saxon monasteries or the Crown. For instance Richardson Grange and Berwick Bassett were sandwiched between the estates of Malmesbury Abbey and Amesbury Abbey. The land that Stanley acquired was neither poor quality wasteland, nor uncultivated. The thin soils on the lower chalk were easily cultivated and an ideal arable zone, while the escarpment and higher downs provided suitable grazing for sheep and cattle. The grants for Richardson show that land was in cultivation when Stanley acquired it; for example, a furlong known as Akerfurlong is mentioned in a grant, and in another '1½ acres in the territory of Ricardeston, in the tillage called 'la Woremfurlong' between their land and his [Richard Thebaul]' (*Cal. Anc Deeds vol. 5*, A12128; *vol. 4*, 6492). The arable land was close to the settlement and extended towards the base of the escarpment. The aerial photographic evidence shows that on this flat, fertile area there are only fragmentary remains of ridge-and-furrow (NMR: SU07SE23). It is an area that Bonney (1980, 41) referred to as 'permanent arable', i.e., the most fertile soils that successive generations cultivate, thus destroying evidence of earlier cultivation. This contrasts with the chalk escarpment and downs beyond the lower chalk bench which is less fertile; however, the extensive tracts of 'Celtic' fields clearly show that they were cultivated during the prehistoric period but subsequently abandoned and used for grazing livestock. These pastures were far from being 'marginal' or wastelands but were valuable in supporting large flocks and, incidentally, keeping the ground clear. John Aubrey described the downlands as:

'the turfe is of a short sweet grasse, good for the sheep, and delightful to the eye, for its smoothnesse like a bowling green, and pleasant to the traveller; who wants here only variety of objects to make his journey less tedious for here nil nisi campus et aër, not a tree, or rarely a bush to shelter from a shower' (Britton 1847, 107).

Although Aubrey was writing in the mid seventeenth century his remarks apply equally to the medieval period.

In some places, however, there was occasional temporary expansion of arable onto the downs. On the Lambourn Downs, at Upper Lambourn (known as Up-Lambourn in the medieval period), where Stanley held at least a hide of land in 1151, an aerial photographic transcription shows extensive 'Celtic' field systems to the north-west of the settlement showing that this area has not been ploughed to any great extent since the prehistoric or Romano-British period and was therefore used as pasture during the medieval period (NMR: NMP SU 2878-SU3584; Fig 5:18).

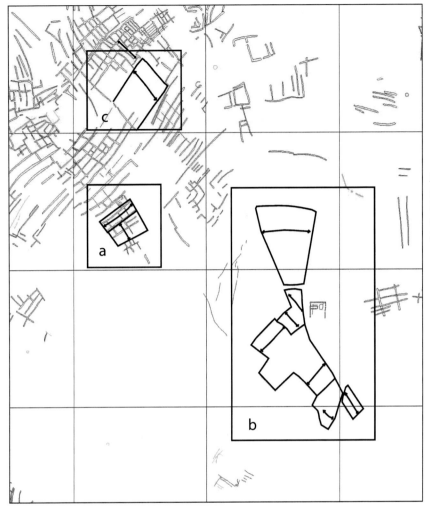

Figure 5:18. Simplified transcription of area to north-west of Upper Lambourn. The red lines denote 'Celtic' fields and the black areas are ridge-and-furrow (NMR: NMP SU 2878-SU3584, © English Heritage)

However, there is evidence of ridge-and-furrow in three specific places. In one area medieval cultivation overlies a 'Celtic' field system but does not destroy it, indicating that this was a temporary expansion of cultivation onto the downs (Fig 5:18a). The second area shows an extensive area of ridge-and-furrow but with no evidence of prehistoric cultivation, suggesting that this was more intensively cultivated and destroyed any earlier evidence of fields (Fig 5:18b). In the third area the ridge-and-furrow is bounded by a 'Celtic' field system, which suggests that the intensification of agriculture in this small area has destroyed evidence of the prehistoric fields (Fig 5:18c).

These cases are not unique but occur elsewhere on the chalk downlands. On Salisbury Plain, for example, ridge-and-furrow overlies large swathes of 'Celtic' fields on Thornham Down, (McOmish *et.al.* 2002, 112). The archaeological evidence is supported by documentary evidence; an inquisition at Erlestoke on Salisbury Plain in 1308 states: 'on the hill there were 300 acres of land on the downs worth 2d an acre, when sown, otherwise nothing', implying an intermittent cultivation of an outfield or 'up-and-down' husbandry (Fry 1908, 139). On the Marlborough Downs there is also evidence of ridge-and-furrow on the higher downland, including Langdon Wick and Raddun (Fowler 2000, 17, transcription in fig 15.3(a))

On the Clay Vale, unlike the Chalk, there is evidence of reclamation and clearance on some of Stanley's estates: at places such as Midgehall, Studley Grange, and Wadley. Midgehall is first mentioned in 983 when it was known as *micghaema gemaere*, which Gover interprets as a 'corner of land frequented by midges' from the OE *mycg*. The second element is OE *haeme* denoting the inhabitants of the place, the 'boundary of the people of Midgehall' (Gover *et.al.* 1939, 275). The landscape evidence accords well with this interpretation of a predominantly marshland region where there are several marsh field names and where the fields are largely enclosed by ditched boundaries. The grange was centred on a moated site. Midgehall is not mentioned in the Domesday Survey and presumably formed part of Lydiard Tregoze where there was land for seven ploughs, forty acres of meadow, thirty acres of pasture and a substantial amount of woodland, presumably on the western side of the parish where there is still extensive tracts on the edge of the former Braydon Forest. To the south and east of Midgehall lay Studley Grange and the small estate of Costow. Costow is in a similar area to Midgehall with the fields contained within ditched boundaries; however, the second element in the place name 'Studley' is the OE *lēah*, which in this case indicates 'pasture', and when linked to the first element would suggest a horse pasture (Gelling 1984, 206). However, the aerial photographic evidence would suggest an expansion of cultivation with ridge-and-furrow here and on the rising ground, which may well have been the result of assarting. Wadley is another *lēah* place-name where the first element is probably a personal name and where the low-lying ground has ditched field boundaries and canalised water channels suggesting landscape drainage. The Cistercians of Stanley, however, were not unique in clearing land; for example, in the mid-thirteenth century the Abbot of Malmesbury made extensive enclosures to the west of Chippenham and near Yatton Keynell he drained a large area of land and surrounded it with hedges (Watkin 1956, 221).

On the Mendip Hills the large number of barrows and the fragmentary remains of field systems on the higher plateau point to extensive settlement during the prehistoric period, but during the medieval period the plateau was a royal forest and used largely for sheep-walks and mineral extraction (Aston 1994, 228). Stanley's grange at Easton lay at the foot of the Hills with cultivation, in the form of strip lynchets and field banks, confined to the lower slopes and extending towards the top of the escarpment. Woodland is quite widespread along the southern Mendip escarpment, which would suggest that the cultivation at Easton was the result of assarting. On the Moors to the south of the Hills the area had been drained in the Romano-British period, with further draining during the medieval period. At Merecumbe Grange the shape of some of the field boundaries would suggest that there was some assarting near the plateau.

The third main theme to emerge from the analysis of Stanley's estates is the recognition that some estates were manors, or at least had some manorial characteristics. As has been noted, one of the most distinctive features of the Cistercian economy was the way they managed their estates from a network of granges that were unencumbered by the manorial system whereby land was divided between lords and tenants with lords having, for example, to collect rents, organise labour services, and hold courts. In addition, rights over the land were shared between the lord and tenant; however, this did not persist and the Cistercians soon came to be lords of their own manors. According to Williams (2001, 209), the gradual modification and transformation of a grange caused by leasing was the most common method of this change to manors, and that by the Suppression the lands of several Welsh monasteries were organised into manors. There are cases, however, where an abbey was granted manors from the outset. Hailes Abbey, for example, was granted five manors in 1254 by their patron, Richard, Earl of Cornwall (Baddeley 1908, 56). The abbey also held the manor of Hailes and it was here that the abbey was founded and from which the home grange estate was formed. In addition, both Stoneleigh Abbey and Bordesley Abbey were founded within royal manors and granted the lordship of the respective manors (*p. 97*).

The date when, or if, a grange became a manor is not an issue here, nor how they were formed; the significance of the Stanley research is the recognition that, as well as be-

ing lords of manors they also held granges adjacent to, or within the manor. The manors concerned were at Wapley, Wadley, Midgehall and Berwick Bassett where each had an adjacent grange at Codrington, Wicklesham, Studley and Richardson respectively. Apart from Richardson, the granges may initially have formed part of the manors, but were detached from the parent estate so that they could be farmed independently from the manor. Thus the Cistercians at Stanley maintained their special character that was emphasised by the demesne (their grange), but they also held a manor with its own demesne and tenants' land.

The most compelling example is at Wadley, which was in Stanley's possession in the late twelfth century and described as a manor at this time. A seventeenth century manorial survey and custumal, which reflected the situation in 1440 when Oriel College acquired the manor, shows that the demesne was centred at Wadley with tenants holding land at Littleworth and Thrupp. There was also a mill on the River Thames that was leased to a tenant. The grange at Wicklesham is not mentioned until 1246 although it had been established by this date since a lay brother 'of Wicklesham' is specifically mentioned (Clanchy 1973, 351). Forty-five years later, Wadley and Wicklesham were assessed separately in the *Taxatio*; Wadley was valued at £47 3s 4d and Wicklesham £10 5s (Astle *et. al.* 1802, 191-191b). However, it is clear that they were formerly one manor and therefore administered together since a grant in 1363-1364 states that: '[…] their manor [Stanley Abbey] lately called 'Worda' but now called the manors of Wadele and Wykynlesham […]' (*Cal Anc Deeds vol. 1*, A165).

A similar case can be made for Wapley and Codrington where both were described as manors in 1490 (Codrington 1898, 308). The demesne was centred at Codrington Court and the building of a chapel in 1290 here would suggest a Cistercian grange, while the tenants' messuages and land were at Wapley. As for Midgehall and Studley Grange, both were initially granges and lay adjacent to one another within the parish of Lydiard Tregoze. However, in 1324 Midgehall was known as a manor when it was first leased, and it is probable that the two terms, grange and manor, were synonymous by this time (*Cal Pat R. Ed II, 1324-27*, 11). Eight years later, in 1332, there were nine taxpayers on the estate (Crowley 1989, 73). These individuals may have been in place much earlier, which would suggest that although a grange, Midgehall, with its lay population, had some of the characteristics of a manor with another grange at Studley.

Berwick Bassett is a more complex example. Stanley claimed to have been granted the manor in the late twelfth century, but in 1328, following a dispute, the manor was divided into two, one being held by the Crown and the other by Stanley (Freeman 2002, 10). Thus the manors had their own tenants who owed customary dues, services and rents to Stanley and the Crown. However, there may well have been a grange within Stanley's manor since, although there was a two-field system, the demesne in one field was much larger than the other, implying that there was a separate holding of about 100 acres, perhaps a grange, which became absorbed into the overall demesne by the sixteenth century.

Stanley's manor at Berwick Bassett may have controlled a much larger area; certainly it had another grange, Richardson, on the parish boundary with some of its land actually in Berwick Bassett. In 1535 Stanley's holdings here were described as 'Berwick Bassett, cum Richardson et Langdon Wick', which may imply that they were jointly administered by this date (Caley and Hunter 1814, 114). There was also a lay manor at Richardson albeit with an absentee landlord, but Stanley's grange, with its hall, barns and other outbuildings, was probably centred on and around the moated site at the western end of the settlement of Richardson where there were 65-70 individuals in 1377. Some of these individuals may have worked for the grange, possibly in a similar manner to Kingswood Abbey's grange at Hazleton, which developed as a nucleated settlement and where there were seventeen slaves recorded in the Domesday Survey. In 1240, Hazleton had a staff of seventeen who appear to be 'living-in servants rather than tenants' (Dyer 2002, 26). There is no mention of any individuals at Richardson in the 1536 Seymour survey despite the listing the three tenants at Berwick Bassett. This would suggest that either the grange was abandoned, which seems unlikely since the land is described in some detail, or that it was still staffed by the monastic servants. In 1560 there was still a link between Berwick Bassett and Richardson when there was a grant of 'the manor of Berwick Bassett with Richardson' (*Cal Pat R Eliz I, 1558-1560*, 437).

The Cistercians at Stanley were not unique in England in having granges within their manors; there are parallels elsewhere in the country. For example, at Stoneleigh, the Cistercians were granted the whole of the soke of Stoneleigh. At the time of the abbey's foundation there were probably six settlement nuclei, but in addition, there were later eight granges within the manor: the home grange, Stoneleigh, Bockyndene, Cryfield, Milburn, Helenhull, Stareton, and Horewelle (Hilton 1985, 90). Another example is Bordesley, which was founded within the large royal manor of Tardebigge in Feckenham Forest where the thirteenth century court roll shows that the Abbot was lord of the manor as well as holding land. A grange was also established, its home grange, at Hewell (Wright 1976, 20; Price 1971, 51).

The fourth theme that has emerged in this study of Stanley's granges is the extent to which the Cistercians consciously separated themselves from the local economy. It has been assumed that they were in some way on their own, that they farmed their land irrespective of what others were doing; in other words they were able to separate themselves from the local agricultural practices and do things as they pleased. They could, for example, have a pastoral grange in an area that was otherwise primarily arable, or that they could combine industrial activities on predominantly arable granges.

The evidence from Stanley shows that, while it is true that they sought the ideal, to farm their granges from consolidated blocks, they were also involved in farming in common as far as pasture was concerned. This is manifested in several grants that stipulate their rights to the common pastures with, in some cases, the number of sheep specified. Thus, at Lambourn in 1198, Stanley was granted pasture for a hundred sheep 'in the common pasture', while at Codrington they had common of pasture 'in the places where the other tenants of the manor have it'; and at Merecumbe in 1227 the Abbot had the 'right to common for all his animals of all sorts from his grange of Merecumbe' (*Cal Chart R Hen III, 1226-1257*, 38; *Cal Pat R Ed III, 1327-1330*, 486; Green 1892, 66). This clearly shows that the Cistercians would have had to negotiate and deal with secular society, although they also held pasture in severalty. At Richardson, for example, they held seventy-six acres in severalty on Forehill Down as well as land on Cowe Down (Seymour Papers Vol. 12, f.173).

Contact with secular society through common rights is also evident at other Cistercian monasteries. At Stoneleigh Abbey the tenants of the manor had common pasture rights in the fourteenth century at Hazelwood, in return the tenants of Coventry had similar rights in the north of Stoneleigh. There were other inter-commoning rights with tenants of Kenilworth (Hilton 1985, 90).

On the Wessex chalklands, research by Hare shows that the White Monks leased their arable lands earlier than their sheep walks (Hare 1985, 82-94). This would be advantageous since lay landowners would have to negotiate with the monks about 'folding' their sheep on the arable fields. Other contacts with the agrarian society would be manifested in the farming of the monks' land that was not consolidated; in other words, land that was in the open fields, which was controlled by manorial courts.

Finally, the actual morphology and function of a grange should be compared to secular farmsteads. There appears, as one would expect, to be no major difference in form or function between a grange and a lay manorial centre or smaller farmstead; the range of agricultural activities of granges was just as wide as their lay counterparts. Most granges also have the same physical features as lay manorial sites; features such as dwellings, barns and out-houses, mills, and perhaps moats are evident on both types of site. Although granges may be seen as the 'model' farms of the period because of their method of agriculture, there was clearly no standard layout; the form and size of their landholding depended to a large extent on the type and availability of land and the function of the grange. Some of Stanley's granges were sited in isolated positions and developed a distinct morphology, others were 'integrated' within an existing settlement nucleus or a settlement developed around it. The evidence also suggests that some granges, far from being sited in uninhabited areas, lay within a fully developed landscape. It is also a myth that the Cistercians accepted poor quality land, or were fobbed off with 'cheaper' endowments by secular benefactors who were keen to secure a hasty passage to heaven. They secured the best land available. True, the land they acquired varied enormously, but nevertheless each estate contributed to the overall economic requirements of the monastery.

Some granges, however, were quite distinctive. Both Richardson and Midgehall were moated sites in a similar way to lay manorial centres. At Richardson the earthwork evidence would suggest that the grange buildings were appended to an existing village and centred on the moated area. In contrast, Langdon Wick was situated in an isolated position and the earthworks would suggest that the grange buildings were 'contained' within an enclosure that overlay a 'Celtic' field system. There appears to be two distinct settlement nuclei within the enclosure, one of four homesteads, presumably for the servants, while the other may have been the principal grange buildings and included a dairy. The earthworks would also suggest that the buildings at Richardson were larger than those at Langdon Wick, presumably emphasising different roles. In addition, this enclosure was set within a larger, outer enclosure with lynchets forming closes for grazing and stock. Although the area was ideally suited as sheep pasture, arable cultivation also took place and ridge-and-furrow is apparent on aerial photographs beyond the outer enclosure.

The final theme assesses the impact on the community from the monks' ownership of churches by comparing the value of the churches, the extent of glebe, and whether the monks were involved in the maintenance of their churches.

Despite the early statutes of the Cistercian Order it is clear that Stanley held churches from its foundation, but three of them were acquired during a period of financial hardship. The appropriation of a church or chapel provided a good source of income for the monastery since it meant that the monks held the great tithes of corn, hay and wood, as well as the glebe land. One example of their value of several cited by Desmond is that of Whalley Abbey, which, in 1296, appropriated the local church and its chapels yielding an annual income of £173 (Desmond 1976, 253-4). Whether this amount was atypical is unclear, but even a cursory trawl of the evidence from some other monasteries shows that it varied greatly. For example, Quarr Abbey held three churches, two of which for only a short period of time, and in 1535 the spiritualities amounted to £21 2s 6d (Hockey 1970, 36, 240). By contrast in Wales, although the majority of Cistercian monasteries had less than four appropriated churches, those of Vallis Crucis, Margam and Aberconwy had eight, nine, and six respectively, and Whitland had twelve including one that had five pilgrimage stones in the cemetery (Williams 2001, 300-14), which would presumably have attracted additional income. As for Stanley, its three appropriated churches were worth seven per cent of its income in 1535 (Table 5:3).

Glebe was land that was granted by the lord of an estate for the support of a priest. Although it is impossible in many cases, and certainly in the case of Stanley, to disentangle the revenue derived from tithes and glebe, the extent of glebe can be ascertained from seventeenth-century glebe terriers and, although there may have been small additions, particularly to monastic glebe, Blair nevertheless contends that for Surrey and Sussex at least they are the most stable of small land units and correspond to peasant Domesday holdings of a virgate or half virgate (Blair 1991, 139-40). If the monastery held the advowson, which normally preceded appropriation, it entitled them to appoint the vicar who in some cases obtained the small tithes, which may include income from the altar and perhaps a portion of the glebe.

	Appropriation	Taxatio valuation	1535 valuation
Blagdon	1154	£8	
Wootton Bassett	1363	£16	£7
Rowde	1363	£8	£5 13s 4d
Rye	1363		£3
Yatton Keynell	1262 (advowson)	£8	

Table 5:3. Value of Stanley's appropraited churches

The ownership of a church by a monastic community had implications for the church fabric. During the thirteenth century there was significant building or re-building of churches caused by a rising population and prosperity as well as changes in religious practice, which led to changes in the Mass whereby the clergy were segregated from the congregation in the chancel. This resulted in many chancels being replaced by larger, longer and lighter east ends. At much the same time, and in succeeding centuries, naves also underwent changes with aisles, porches and towers being built and side chapels and chantries inserted (Cross and Barnwell 2005, 14-16).

The responsibility for church maintenance was divided between the patron and parishioners in the thirteenth century whereby the patron was responsible for the upkeep of the chancel and the parishioners took on the maintenance of the nave. This division of responsibility may be manifested in the differences in building styles, which may, in part, reflect the interest of the two parties in a particular church. However, whether Stanley was conscientious in the maintenance of the chancel of their churches is unclear since they have all undergone major re-building in the nineteenth century.

CHAPTER SIX

RE-FORMING THE LANDSCAPE:

THE SUPPRESSION OF THE MONASTERY AND THE AFTERMATH

INTRODUCTION

The dissolution of the monasteries in the 1530s was the largest transfer of land since the Norman Conquest over 450 years earlier. However, it occurred at a time when there were other major changes in the English landscape and society. These included major upheavals and a division in the Church that witnessed a break with Rome and the abandonment of many traditional beliefs, which were supplanted by other practices. It was also a time of continuing agricultural innovation and change in the rural landscape. Buildings were transformed as living standards improved and people's perceptions of privacy changed. Finally, this period witnessed the polarisation of cultural differences in the Wiltshire regions.

During this period there were massive changes in the agrarian landscape as fields on the clay vale, which included Stanley, continued to be enclosed and turned over to pasture (Thirsk 1967, 67). In addition, although the artificial floating of water meadows from the early seventeenth century is more associated with the chalk downland streams, there is earthwork evidence that some meadows were also floated along the River Marden at Stanley and Bremhill. It was also a time that witnessed the disafforestation of the royal forests and extinction of common rights, which led to social unrest in the region (Kerridge 1958-60, 64-75). Parks were also created at Bowood, Bowden and Spye, all within the former Forest region, and as well as being statements of power and exclusivity, they had a restrictive effect on communities leading to tension and resentment.

Cultural distinctions between what John Aubrey called the 'Chalk' and 'Cheese' districts of Wiltshire became noticeable during the sixteenth and seventeenth centuries. On the Chalk, the downlands of south Wiltshire, men '[…] being weary after hard labour, they have not leisure to read or contemplate of religion'. By contrast, those in the Cheese region, the clayland, '[…] hereabout is but little tillage or hard labour, they only milk the cows and make cheese; they feed chiefly on milk meats, which cools their brains too much, and hurts their inventions', they were 'addicted to Puritanism, witchcraft beliefs, and compulsive litigiousness' (Britton 1847, 11-12; Underdown 1985, 73). Although Aubrey's remarks may seem rather stark and uncompromising, there were nevertheless major cultural differences that were manifested in several ways (Underdown 1985, 73-105). For example, there was a strong loyalty to the community in the Chalk regions as opposed to the individualism that was more prevalent in the Cheese region; this is perhaps best exemplified by the preference to sports where football was mainly played in the Chalk

and cricket, or its variants, which was more about individual skill, in the Cheese areas (*ibid.*, 75).

The Reformation heralded significant upheavals in religious practices with Catholicism being ultimately supplanted by Protestantism, which had a profound effect on the fabric of churches and their congregations. Within the churches, altars were replaced by communion tables and moved nearer the nave, images of saints were defaced or destroyed, wall paintings white-washed, processions banned, and services were conducted in the vernacular language. In addition, the liturgical calendar and festivities were largely abandoned and some feast days prohibited (Duffy 1992). Puritanism, which had strong roots in the clothing areas in the north of the county, was promoted by such leading gentry as the Bayntuns, who were the new owner's of Stanley and many of its estates, and the Hungerfords, who held a considerable territory in the west of the county. In the Cheese country the divisiveness of Puritanism and the frequent failure to maintain collective displays, such as the Rogationtide perambulations, led to a decline in parish identity and unity. This process was much slower on the Chalk (Underdown 1985, 78-89).

This period was also one that Hoskins has termed 'the rebuilding of rural England', in 1570-1640 (Hoskins 1953, 44-59). Although more recent research would suggest a much wider time-span his central premise, that of a transformation in rural housing, still stands (Howard 2007, 2; Johnson 2010, 87-88). Hoskins identified three major changes: the building of new houses, the modernisation of existing houses, and an increase in furnishings and equipment in houses (Hoskins 1953, 44). It was a time when the medieval open hall began to disappear as ceilings and stone chimneys were inserted and new houses were invariably built with them from the outset. These changes, although absent in most of the present buildings, are manifested at Stanley in the hearth tax returns, household inventories, and a manorial survey from the beginning of the seventeenth century.

All these changes had a profound effect on communities and their landscape throughout the country - not least at Stanley. Although a detailed analysis is beyond the scope of this study they should nevertheless be borne in mind when considering the Suppression. In addition, the history, reasons, and consequences of the Suppression have been well documented and will therefore not be considered in any great detail here (e.g. Knowles 1976; Woodward 1966; Youings 1971b). Suffice to say that it not only ensured the ruination of monastic houses but also saw the destruction of monastic culture, of hospitality and almsgiving, all of which had a profound effect on the local communities. In the words of Joyce Youings the Dissolution was '[...] a restoration to secular uses of land and other endowments provided over many centuries, very largely by laymen, for the support of houses of regular clergy and nuns' (Youings 1971b, 1).

Aim of Chapter

This chapter analyses the post-Suppression landscape of Stanley Abbey and its territories. It spans a period of a little over one-hundred years and falls within two quite distinct episodes in our history: the first was the 1530s and 1540s when England's religious institutions were overturned, and the second was the 1640s, specifically the English Civil Wars when there was further political change leading to the temporary demise of the Crown and accompanied by division of communities and much destruction. This end-point, therefore, is a historical as well as an archaeological end-point; it has been chosen since it was during this time that the status of Stanley appears to decline, spurred on by the financial problems of the Bayntuns and a move from their principal residence at Bromham following its destruction.

The theme of this chapter, therefore, is the 'secularisation of the landscape'. It analyses the changes in the landscape wrought by the Suppression of Stanley. Given all the other changes that were occurring at this time, it is perhaps difficult to filter out the effects of one specific cause (i.e. the Suppression), nevertheless it is argued here that several changes can be identified that were directly attributable to the Suppression. First, and most significant in landscape terms, it is manifested in the destruction and transformation of the monastic buildings to a 'secondary' or 'minor' mansion house with its attendant gardens and parkland; this new enterprise existed alongside an evolving farming landscape and culture. Second, there were clear consequences for the manorial tenants as the number of copyholds decreased with a consequent increase in leaseholds; their dwellings and outhouses were also transformed, some using material from the monastery. The Suppression also afforded opportunities for the lords and tenants alike with some becoming more entrepreneurial. Finally, the fortunes of the abbey's estates were mainly a consequence of their size, their value, and the new lords that acquired them.

THE FINAL YEARS OF THE MONASTERY

The final decades of Stanley Abbey can be gleaned from the rather scant documentary sources such as the evidence of leasing, an account of the abbey's lands in 1528, and the valuations for the *Valor Ecclesiasticus,* but also by comparing it with other monasteries in the south of England.

Leasing of Land

The leasing of Stanley's granges first occurred during the early fourteenth century and continued into the fifteenth and early sixteenth centuries, thus leading to a gradual secularisation of their territories. Initially the leases were short-term, but in the sixteenth century they were for con-

siderably longer periods. However, leasing should not necessarily be seen as an inevitable, irreversible development since even where demesne had been leased the monks were sometimes prepared to resume cultivation whenever it suited them. Thus at Stanley, in 1528, all the abbey's demesnes had been leased, although part of the rent for the lease of the home grange and four other properties was not received because the abbot had 'occupied them for his greater profit' (Hare 1985, 91; Hare 2011, 80; TNA, PRO: SC6/Hen. VIII/3958). This land was at Richardson, Berwick Bassett, Langdon Wick and the extensive sheep-walk on Hackpen Hill. It is significant that these holdings all lie on the chalk downland where direct cultivation by monasteries continued longer than elsewhere, and even when the arable was leased the sheep walks continued to be held by the monks for some time (Hare 1985, 82-94). This continuation of large-scale sheep farming by the monks shows that they clearly understood the value of wool for cloth manufacture and the meat and milk of the animals. But perhaps more importantly they understood the value of the sheep fold to maintain the fertility of the thin chalk soils from which there was a financial gain when their flocks were put onto tenants' land. Although folding was not as systematic or large-scale as in the eighteenth and nineteenth centuries, it nevertheless took place. There are no figures for the value of the sheep fold at Stanley but the return for one of Netley Abbey's chalkland estates, at Kingston Deverill, illustrates its value; in 1436 and 1448 the abbey received about half as much for renting out its flock for manure as it received from its whole wool sales and it is probable that Stanley was similar (*ibid.,* 90).

As for the home granges some, such as at Stanley, appear to have been held directly by the monastery up to the closing days of the suppression while others were retained into the last decade (Hare 1985, 87). Although much of Stanley's home grange was held in demesne since at least 1528 small, 'specialist' areas had been leased; Stanley Mill, for example, which lay close to the abbey precinct and described as 'near the grange of Stanley', i.e. the home grange, was leased to a yeoman/clothier in 1521 for forty-one years; and two years later Scott's Mill was also leased (WSA: 473/258; WSA: 1259/22). This left just the combined fulling and corn mill within the bounds of the precinct in the hands of the monks thus ensuring that they retained a part in the lucrative fulling process and ensured that tenants were still obliged to pay for their corn to be ground and cloth to be fulled. Hiving off of small parts of home granges can also be seen at Cleeve Abbey (Som.) where a new park at its grange at Stout, which lay close to the abbey, was divided and let in small closes in 1507; by the Suppression, four of the five granges that probably constitute the home grange had been leased. One of them was let on very favourable terms for a period of ninety-nine years, the first fourteen were rent-free (Dunning 1985b, 60-61).

As for Stanley's other estates, new leases were issued in the early sixteenth century. Thus Studley Grange was leased in 1505 and in 1534, the latter just eighteen months before the abbey's suppression. The manor of Midgehall was leased to William Pleydell, one of the rising local county gentry, for ninety-six years on the payment of £40, and it became his principal residence (Seymour Papers Vol. 12, fol. 136, 154). Pleydell also held several estates from Beaulieu Abbey, becoming the largest single farmer of abbey lands in the region. He acquired large tracts of land in the Faringdon region, at places such as Inglesham, Wyke and Kindlewere (Hockey 1976, 174-5).

The leasing of land to relatives or the friends of the abbot was also widespread in the closing years of a monastery suggesting that the monks may have been aware of the way things were going and that they endeavoured, wherever possible, to ensure the most favourable conditions and terms in such uncertain times. Stanley was not immune to this nepotism since an individual named William Morley, who held Loxwell Grange in 1539 and was bailiff of the manor and woods of Stanley and Loxwell, was probably the brother of the last abbot (Caley and Hunter 1817, 115; WSA: 473/40.99).

The situation at Stanley was that only a small part of its land was held by the monks in the 1530s, while the remainder was leased, which means that laymen already managed most of the land and the Suppression appears not to have been such a revolution.

The Suppression of Stanley

Stanley was a relatively small monastery, although it appears to have been well maintained. An account of the abbey's lands by its receiver general in 1528 shows the income from rents and land held in demesne. Its total receipts were £175 11s 4d with £39 17s 6½d in expenses, and £133 6s 6d that were termed 'cash expenses' (TNA: PRO SC6/Hen VIII/3958).

Seven years later, in 1535, the *Valor Ecclesiasticus* shows that Stanley was valued slightly higher at £177 0s 8d. A year later, the king's commissioner's report for Stanley was favourable and it was valued at £204 8s 6.5d with £32 9s for the demesne and mills of the demesne. Its buildings were 'large and strong [...]'. They were all 'in a very good state, part new built'. The value of the lead and bells was estimated at £65 10s. There were nine monks and a novice, who all wanted to continue in the religious life. There were also forty-three servants and a schoolmaster, four waiting servants, ten officers of the house, eighteen hinds (servants in husbandry who would have been hired by the year rather than day labourers) in various granges, three dairywomen, and seven corrodians (TNA. PRO: SC12/33/37; Bettey 1989, 62). On its lands the abbey had 400 sheep at Berwick Bassett and 400 on other manors (Bettey 1989, 34 quoting PRO: E315/398, f.90). However, with an income at the time of the *Valor Ecclesiasticus* of less than £200, Stanley was suppressed in February 1536 along with the other 'smaller monasteries'. The abbot received a pension and was appointed suffragan bishop of

Marlborough; as for the monks, some apparently went to Beaulieu Abbey as well as other Cistercian houses where they remained until the suppression of the greater houses (Baskerville 1937, 148; Bettey 1989, 64).

RE-USE OF MONASTIC BUILDINGS

The most dramatic change to the landscape at Stanley following its suppression was the ruination of much of the monastery's buildings and the establishment of a new secular lordship. However, the traditional view that the Dissolution led to the immediate destruction of the buildings has been the subject of extensive reappraisal in recent years, most notably those studies that culminated in the publication of a series of papers on the subject in 2003 (Gaimster and Gilchrist 2003). What is clear is that the fortunes of the abbey buildings throughout the country varied greatly and that changes were not always immediate, or necessarily permanent.

Many monastic houses were converted into secular mansions; their buildings, which generally followed a formulaic layout, could be relatively easily adapted to a secular use. Howard (2003, 221-34) suggests that there were four phases of change and while some were altered soon after their suppression, it was perhaps several decades before others underwent any change. In many cases there was also further alteration and modification to take account of new social and architectural ideas of the time. At Neath, for example, a residence was established soon after its suppression but there was further work from 1545, including changing the orientation of the residence (Robinson 2006, 264).

Some of these monastic conversions are prominent in the landscape today as great country houses; places such as Lacock, Longleat, Bindon and Forde to name but four in the south of England are a testament to these changes; however, the fortunes of others was not so assured and for various reasons they may have been totally abandoned, but more frequently they were converted into farmsteads. Sometimes this demise occurred within perhaps a couple of generations of the Suppression while at others their decline was far more protracted and, although the ruins of some became 'eye-catchers' in a Romantic setting, in many cases little survives to suggest their former status apart from perhaps a few earthworks or cropmarks and the occasional fragment of masonry. Stanley Abbey is one such place where all that survives is a farmstead, and it is only by analytical survey and investigation of the earthworks that the monastic layout and later adaptations can be understood.

Most discussion of the conversion of monasteries tends to overlook the area around the buildings where there were gardens and perhaps parkland; but gardens are an integral part of any residence and should not be ignored. These gardens were distinctive, reflecting both their aesthetic qualities and functions but also, as will be discussed later, in many cases they may reflect the religious and political sympathies of the landowner.

As well as being converted into mansions, several monasteries became the focus for industrial activity. At Malmesbury, the nave of the church became the parish church and the new owner took up residence in the former abbot's house and converted the conventual buildings into a workshop for cloth manufacture (Bettey 1989, 129; Howard 2003, 229). At Tintern, although there is evidence that it was used as a residence, an iron foundry lay elsewhere within the precinct (Courtney and Gray 1991, 149). Iron was also being produced at Rievaulx and Whitland while at Neath, although a mansion house was built soon after its suppression, it was unoccupied by 1699 and copper smelting and forging later took place (McDonnell 1963, 176-79; Barnwell et al 2005; Robinson 2006, 267, 296).

Another use for monastic buildings was as a ready quarry for its stone. For those monasteries, such as Quarr, Netley and Beaulieu, which lay along the south coast of England this meant that some were used for Henry VIII's programme of coastal fortifications.

As for Stanley, there is compelling evidence that, although virtually nothing survives 'above ground', there was a mansion house soon after the suppression.

THE NEW LANDLORDS AND BENEFICIARIES

Recipients of former monastic land fall into two categories. The first were those closely associated with the king's household, while the second were the gentry families, merchants and lawyers, many of whom were already leasing monastic lands or acting in some administrative capacity for the monastic houses (Bettey 1989, 133). Sir Edward Seymour was the principal beneficiary of monastic lands in Wiltshire. Following the suppression of the smaller houses in 1536 he acquired land from Stanley Abbey and Maiden Bradley Priory, and later he was granted lands of Amesbury Abbey, Easton Priory and Monkton Farleigh Priory (*ibid.*).

Another courtier was Sir Edward Bayntun who was a prominent landowner in north Wiltshire. He was vice-chancellor to all but the first of Henry VIII's wives and therefore in a good position to take advantage of the plight of the monasteries in the 1530s. As well as holding a position in the royal household he was also elected to parliament. He was associated with Thomas Cromwell and he became a staunch Protestant (ODNB web entry). His principal residence was at Bromham on the south-eastern edge of Chippenham Forest. Prior to the Suppression he was steward of Battle Abbey's Bromham estate as well as being involved in the administration of Bradenstoke Abbey and Malmesbury Abbey and as a result acquired Malmesbury's large estate at Bremhill as well as Bromham following the Suppression; however, his largest acquisition was when he bought all but six of Stanley Abbey's estates (Chew 1956, 313; Chettle and Kirby 1956, 274). Thus Bayntun's power-base was a consolidated block of land to the east and south-east of Chippenham as well as detached holdings elsewhere in neighbouring counties (Fig 6:1).

The second group of beneficiaries of monastic land included those individuals who were engaged in the management of the monastery or had leased land prior to the Suppression, these included Sir Henry Long who was the Chief Steward, Thomas Semayn, the Under Steward, Thomas Buryman the receiver general, and William Morley, John Biggs and John Stratton were bailiffs. Sir Henry Long's importance nationally is reflected by the fact that he attended Henry VIII at the Field of Cloth of Gold. His principal residence was at Wraxell, which was a former holding of Shaftesbury Abbey, but as far as can be ascertained he does not seem to have had an interest in Stanley's lands (Pugh 1953, 22).

STANLEY ABBEY

Little is known about the ruination of Stanley's buildings and the disposal of its fixtures and fittings following its suppression, but presumably it followed a similar fate to many other monastic houses where local people were quick to take advantage of their abandonment. Typical examples are the accounts of the pilfering and the degradation at Roche Abbey, Whitland Abbey, and Hailes Abbey. At Hailes the spoliation was on such a scale that a commission was convened to enquire as to where and by whom the materials had been taken. It would appear that everything that could be re-used was taken including small items such as iron hooks, door locks, paving stones and floorboards. Larger items were also removed and even trees and beehives (Shagan 2003, 162-96). Another enquiry was convened at Whitland where there had been the wholesale plunder; only the 'grett chamber and two little other chambers' were spared since they were locked. Men were found to be busy 'digginge and hewinge out the free stones' and carrying them away for the conversion of Laugharne Castle (Robinson 2006, 296). In Yorkshire, Michael Sherbrook, writing in his old age in about 1591, described the 'momentous events of his youth' - the dissolution of Roche Abbey. He wrote: '[…] all things of price were either spoiled, plucked away or defaced to the uttermost […]. It seems that every person bent himself to filch or spoil what he could […] nothing was spared except the oxhouses and swinecotts' (Sherbrook 1959, 123-5). This sort of spoliation was, however, not ubiquitous, particularly those such as Lacock and Titchfield, which were occupied as soon as the abbey was dissolved.

Following Stanley's suppression in February 1536 its estates were quickly broken up, six manors going to Sir Edward Seymour, Viscount Beauchamp; however, it was not until June the following year that Sir Edward Bayntun purchased the abbey and the remainder of its estates for £1,200 (*L & P Hen VIII vol. 10*, 526; *vol. 12*, pt.1, 143). It was therefore over a year before the abbey was sold and during this time it was presumably in the hands of one of the king's officials. There is no account of the transformation or destruction of the church and conventual buildings, nor indeed which buildings survived, but it probably followed the fate of other monasteries. In some

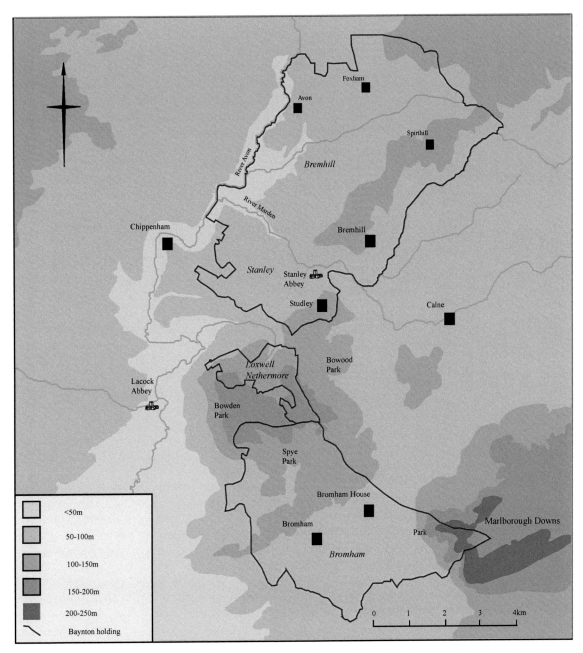

Figure 6:1. Extent of the Baynton landholding in the environs of Stanley Abbey. The Baynton's lived at Bromham House until its destruction during the English Civil Wars when they moved to Spye. The River Marden separates Stanley from Bremhill

cases the process began even before the monks had left the monastery. Plate and jewels were sent to the royal treasury or local receiver's strong room, and books of any value went to the royal library. All church furniture and domestic items were then sold by auction at the abbey. The official instructions were that the commissioners were to 'pull down to the ground all the walls of the churches, stepulls, cloysters, fraterys, dorters, chapter howsys' (Knowles 1976, 267); however, this did not happen in many cases and some buildings were retained to form the nucleus of a new residence. Those that were deemed superfluous were stripped of everything saleable or plundered by the locals. The destruction was an expensive undertaking, in Lincolnshire, for example, it was estimated that it would cost £1,000 to destroy all the churches. As a result it was proposed that they should be 'defaced' and left uninhabit-

able by removing stairs and roofs (*ibid.*). Similar methods were employed elsewhere. The lead from the roofs, as well as the bells, was particularly valuable and it was melted down into pigs. The amount of lead retrieved from Stanley was sixteen fothers, which was far less than Malmesbury's 127.5 fothers, or Hailes's 119 fothers, but similar to Maiden Bradley, which had eighteen fothers (Bettey 1989, 126). Much of the lead from the north Wiltshire houses was sent to Bristol, although some of Malmesbury's went to roof a building in Poole. It is also tempting to see, however, Stanley's lead going to Edward Bayntun since he purchased 133 fodders for Bromham House (*ibid.*).

Brakspear's excavation of the site in 1905 gives a flavour of what may have occurred at Stanley, albeit scant. The excavation showed that two columns of the east wall of the church were detached from their base or foundations, which, as far as Brakspear was concerned, showed that this part of the building had been destroyed by the use of props and mining. A skeleton was also found, which Brakspear suggested was one of the workmen (Brakspear 1908, 554). This method of undermining the foundations of a building appears extreme but it was also used at Lewes and Chertsey (Knowles 1976, 267).

Figure 6:2. Extract of Speed's map of Wiltshire dating to the early seventeenth century showing the location of Bromham House and its park. Spye Park lies to the north-west of the House and Stanley on the northern edge of Pewsham Forest and to the west of Calne.

The destruction and subsequent transformation of the buildings at Stanley occurred, or at least gained momentum, sometime after June 1537 presumably under the direction of Sir Edward Bayntun when he purchased the abbey site. He was also involved in building a new mansion house at Bromham using stone from Devizes Castle and Corsham Court, and although the house would probably have been largely complete by the Suppression he may have used some stone from Stanley either for his mansion house or his hunting lodge at Spye Park (Fig 6:2). The house at Bromham, which lay close to the London road, appears to have been a spectacular building, described as nearly as large as Whitehall and 'fit to entertain a king' as well as being 'one of the famousest buildings in the Western parts'; Catherine of Aragon was a frequent visitor as was Henry VIII and Ann Boleyn in 1535. James I also visited on three occasions (Anon 1902, 129-37; Baynton-Coward 1977, 2). Bromham House was largely destroyed in 1645 during the English Civil Wars and only a fragment survives (NMR: ST 96 NE 13).

With such a prestigious building only 10km from Stanley it is clear that the former abbey was never intended to be Bayntun's principal residence, but rather it was tenanted and used as a 'secondary' residence. Members of the family lived here on occasions; in 1555, Henry Bayntun, brother of Andrew Bayntun and the new lord of the manor, leased Stanley and in 1584, another Edward Bayntun held a moiety of a house and other facilities (WSA: 473/228.26).

But even following the destruction of his mansion in 1645 Bayntun still did not move to Stanley and instead established himself at his hunting lodge at Spye Park. The choice of Spye over Stanley may have been because it lay close to the London road, in a more prestigious position, whereas Stanley was more isolated. According to John Aubrey, who was writing sometime between 1659 and 1670, Stanley was situated in 'very rich land, and lies by the river's side, but in a place in the winter altogether unpleasant. Here is now scarce left any vestigum of Church or house' (Jackson 1862, 112-3). The buildings were clearly not as spacious as Bromham House, and in any case had been reduced to a farmstead and therefore it was perhaps unsuitable for further alteration into a grand mansion.

The Archaeological and Architectural Evidence for Re-use of Abbey and Precinct

The years' following the Suppression of Stanley was a period of great change as the abbey and its environs were transformed to a new, secular use that had little regard for its former sanctity. This was also a time when the new secular owners 'moulded' the landscape to their own ideals and beliefs and reflect trends seen elsewhere in the country. Although there was clearly much destruction with some buildings left to decay or used as a ready quarry, there were parts that were retained and incorporated into a secular house and garden set within a wider parkland landscape. The period of use as a residence for the middling echelons of county society was relatively short-lived, perhaps for as little as two or three generations and presumably before the mid seventeenth century when it was a tenanted farmstead; however, this initial period of change can be seen in the archaeological and documentary record.

All we can see today are two farmsteads, one dating to the nineteenth century while at the other, Old Abbey Farm, one of its buildings dates to the sixteenth century. Elsewhere, the site of the former monastery is reflected, in part, by Brakspear's excavation, but analysis of the earthworks reveals elements of a post-suppression landscape as well as the monastic landscape.

The house

Firstly, what is the evidence for the buildings? An indication of what building became the mansion house can be seen from a series of leases and surveys dating from the mid sixteenth century. The earliest reference dates to 1555 when the Abbot's lodging was searched for counterfeit coin-making equipment (Bettey 1989, 124). In 1567, thirty-one years after the abbey's suppression, there is mention of the 'site of the late monastery of Stanley, the church, belfry and churchyard, houses, dovehouses, mills, and ponds [...], together with the park of Stanley and various closes' (WSA: 1213.20). Although it is not particularly detailed, it would suggest that the church and tower, or at least the remains of it, was still standing at this time, a theme that will be explored later. A lease of 1600 is unequivocal; it mentions the 'mansion house and all other buildings commonly called by the name of the Abbot's Lodging' (WSA 473/245).

The limited documentary evidence therefore indicates that the mansion house was a conversion of the Abbot's lodging and was known by that name in 1555. The archaeological evidence supports this and places it at the west range of the conventual buildings. Brakspear's excavation plan shows that the west range was a nine-bay building with a central entrance thus making it ten bays - the same length as the mansion house described in the 1612 survey. This central passage in the west range was a link between the outside court and the inner court and cloister garden. In addition, although much of the range was tentatively dated to the twelfth century, there were three internal walls in the west range dating to the fifteenth century or later and, according to Brakspear, this range was 'less destroyed than the rest of the work' (Brakspear 1908, 572), which may suggest that it was demolished later than the rest of the abbey. Although there is no archaeological evidence it is probable that the monastic kitchen along the north range was also retained; as Howard says 'a working kitchen [in any converted monastery] would hardly be abandoned' (Howard 2007, 16).

An alternative location for the mansion house, but unlikely, would be the east range, in the former novice's lodging, which was dated to the twelfth century although the date for some of the internal cross-divisions was far from clear and Brakspear thought that 'it is uncertain if all the cross walls are of monastic date'; however, his remark appears confusing since he goes on to say: 'there was no direct evidence that any post-Suppression alternations had been made in this part of the building' (Brakspear 1908, 566). The building, at twelve bays long, was also larger than the mansion house mentioned in 1612. It is quite conceivable that more of the conventual buildings were retained after the Suppression; indeed at some monasteries, such as Neath and Lacock, most of the conventual buildings were converted into secular residences (Robinson 2006, 266; Howard 2007, 35). Examples of alterations of the east range can be seen at Jervaulx and Quarr. At Jervaulx there was evidence of later sub-division of part of the east range while at Quarr the range was divided by cross walls into at least four chambers; however, it is unclear for what purpose or when this alteration occurred (Brakspear 1908, 566).

Brakspear noted several small finds from his excavation, including a shilling from the reign of Elizabeth and other post-medieval artefacts; however, their provenance was not recorded nor their association with other features and therefore they cannot be used to suggest post-medieval occupation in any particular part of the conventual buildings.

What form the post-Suppression house took is unknown but evidence from elsewhere would suggest that the upper floor was possibly used as the residence. The adaptation of an upper floor to create what Rosalyn Coope calls a 'corridor-gallery' serving the rooms off the gallery can be seen at places such as at Lacock and Newstead, and a similar thing may have happened at Stanley (Coope 1986, 43-72). At Hailes where the upper floor of the west range, which was also the former abbot's lodging, was similarly converted into the mansion house and described by Celia Fiennes as:

'...a good old house and there is a pretty Chappel with a gallery for people of quality to sit in which goes out of the hall, that is a lofty large roome; good parlour and severall good lodging roomes, you ascend into the house by severall stone steppes' (Morris 1947, 30).

The Abbot's lodging at Stanley may not have been such a grand scale as Hailes but nevertheless the accommodation may have been at first floor-level giving views over the gardens and parkland.

Apart from the Abbot's lodging, the documents indicate that several other monastic buildings were retained within the precinct such as a fulling mill, a corn mill, barn, brew-house and bake-house, malt-house, the abbey gate, and the Porter's Lodge and adjoining stable (WSA: 122/1; 473/245; 473/246.46). As Howard observed 'it was expected these [the domestic buildings in monasteries] would continue to be used from the beginning' (Howard 1987, 139). Although there is no excavated evidence for these buildings the location of some can be tentatively identified from the earthwork survey plan (Fig 6:3; Fig 6:5). By 1612, there was a fulling mill with one pair of stocks, a corn mill of two bays, a two-bay ox-house and a four-bay hay barn, which was lofted and had a stone chimney (WSA: 122/1). This latter building was presumably an adaptation of a monastic dwelling in a similar manner to a barn in Chippenham that was converted to a dwelling (*p. 112*)

The Gardens

An integral part of the setting of any house would be its gardens, and possibly associated with them there may have been a park. In England, during the mid and later sixteenth century, gardens invariably incorporated features such as 'compartments', terraces, mounts, ponds, rabbit warrens, water gardens and wilderness gardens (Henderson 2005, 122-41). These typically Tudor and Elizabethan gardens emphasise the status of the lord and in some cases their political or religious tendencies.

At Stanley some of the earthworks are associated with a post-Dissolution layout suggestive of not only the house but also garden features. The most striking is the suite of big 'canals' that divide compartments with different, distinctive indications of function, which are characteristic of a post-dissolution garden. Although some of these 'canals' may, in part, mark the course of the monastic culverts, in their present form they probably reflect a post-dissolution 'water garden'. Evidence for this is apparent in several places: first, and most significantly, all the 'canals' lie wholly within the precinct and one of them, the long north/

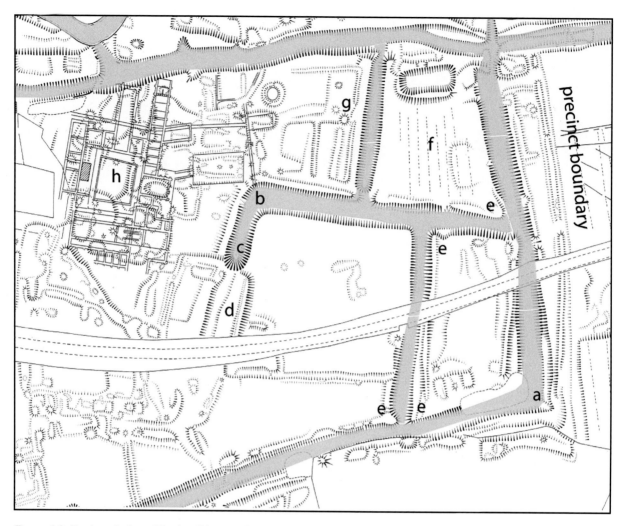

Figure 6:3. Earthwork plan of Stanley Abbey overlain with Brakspear's excavation plan and showing the post-medieval garden layout. The mansion house was the west range wih the kitchen in the north-west corner of the north range.

south 'canal' on the eastern side of the precinct, cuts the precinct boundary bank in the south-eastern corner (Fig 6:3a); secondly, a monastic culvert that was excavated by Brakspear enters the deep central east/west 'canal' on its northern side at an acute angle, which suggests that the culvert has been cut or deepened and widened (Fig 6:3b). Also, in a monastic context, there seems no reason why there is a central north/south 'canal' (Fig 6:3b-c) given that it is leading away from where the water would be required, i.e. the north range 'service' area of the monastery and reredorter. The 'canals' have sloping sides and none are stone-lined as can be seen at places such as Roche, Cleeve, and Hailes. There also appears to be an association between the 'canals' and other parts of the garden layout such as the terracing that lies at right-angles to the south end of the central 'canal' along the south side of the church site (Fig 6:3d). Also notable are the bastion-like corners of three of the compartments that have connotations of military display and symbolism that is characteristic in some sixteenth and seventeenth century gardens (Fig 6:3e).

The earthworks, and the documents, suggest that there were other gardens within the precinct apart from the water garden. On the northern compartment, to the east of the Abbot's

Lodging, there is slight ridging indicative of orchard planting (Fig 6:3f). The large, rectangular pond on the northern side of this compartment is clearly a later pond, but the ridging overlies a rectangular feature on the eastern side, which was probably a building. To the west, there is the earthen bank of a small walled garden. This enclosed garden is compartmentalised giving a formal arrangement with a small mound, possibly a seat or prospect, on the eastern side (Fig 6:3g). Another small enclosed garden lies within the earthworks of the church and conventual buildings (Fig 6:3h). Here there is a square, level platform, which was probably a privy, or cloister garden, with elements of the monastery forming a suitable backdrop when viewed from the Abbot's lodging. Such a garden is mentioned in 1617 when Robert Tyncker leased the fulling mill, the corn mill, 'the Abbey orchard, the Cloyster Garden and House orchard and garden [...]' (WSA: 473/258.45).

Rabbit warrens, or conegre, were an integral feature of a sixteenth and seventeenth century garden. As well as providing meat and fur, in a post-medieval context they may also have had ritual symbolism (Stocker and Stocker 1998, 265-72), particularly in a garden setting such as here at Stanley. In 1584 there is mention of a 'clapper of cumyes',

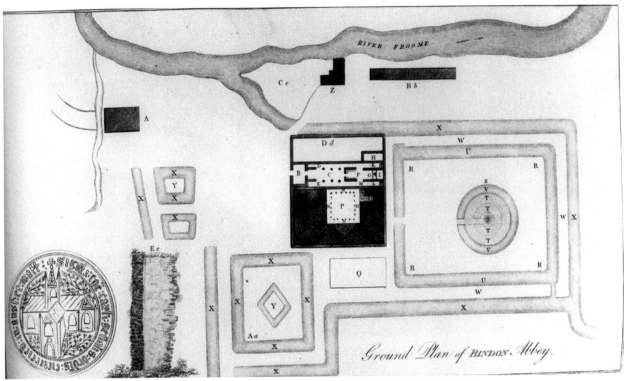

Figure 6:4. The water gardens at Bindon Abbey (after Hutchins 1861, facing 353).

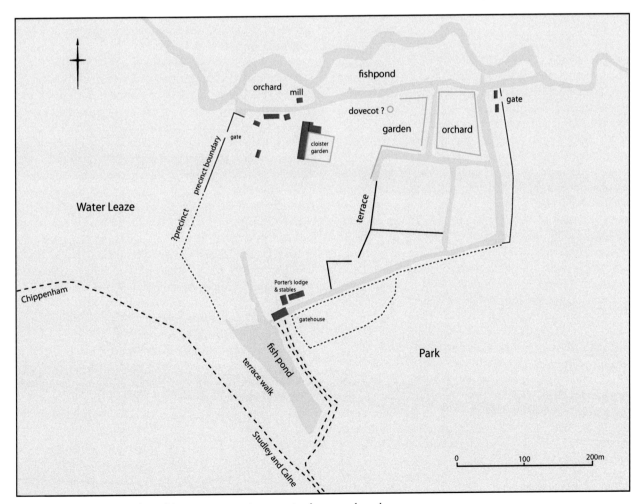

Figure 6:5. Interpretaive plan of the post-suppression mansion house and gardens

or conegre, in the 'greate ortchyearde' [great orchard]; the orchard was enclosed on the east and south sides by a stone wall and on the north side by the river (WSA: 473/258. 26). This orchard may have been the one to the east of the cloister garden (Fig 6:3f).

Water was a common theme in many sixteenth and seventeenth gardens as it was in medieval landscapes. These 'water gardens' were used for recreation and places where fish were bred. A plan of Welbeck Abbey (Notts) of 1629 shows well the form and intricacy of these gardens. Water flowed through the gardens to the south and east of the house along a series of canals and ponds and what has been described as a 'curious arrangement of a row of small rectangular pools linked by a central channel' (Whittle and Taylor 1994, 57. Another example, albeit later, is at Bindon Abbey (Dorset); here the garden is derived from the medieval ponds and moats in much the same way as at Stanley (Fig 6:4). The gardens probably date to 1600-1611 and comprise two main components. To the east of the house was the largest garden; it was rectangular in form and double moated with a circular mount in the centre. The second component lay to the south-west of the house where there was another moated garden with a diamond-shape moat around. Detached from these two gardens are further moated areas, which may be medieval (*ibid.*, 56; Hutchins 1861).

The Park

Although there is no specific documentary evidence for a wilderness garden at Stanley, small parks juxtapose the more formal gardens may reflect the notion of a wilderness. Such parks were a feature in the Tudor landscape and were seen as a contrast to the more formal gardens beside the house; they were not the hunting parks of the medieval period, but can be seen as places of natural beauty and statements of exclusion and exclusivity, a physical and metaphorical buffer between the agrarian landscape and the 'gentrified' landscape. At Stanley, a park lay on the eastern side of the precinct and was known as Stanley Park in 1567 (Fig 6:5; WSA: 1213/20). It probably included small clumps of trees and ponds and, given the topography and earthworks, there would also have been riverside walks and water meadows, all elements that provide a contrast to the formal gardens and add to a feeling of tranquillity and recreation.

Parkland names on a nineteenth century map confirm the location of the park and that it was about fifty-five acres (22ha) at this time. In 1607 there was a dwelling in Studley named 'Lodge'; this building was possibly associated with the park (WSA 473/258.38). Within the former precinct further field names, Home Park and Horse Croft, suggest they also formed part of the park, or were perhaps a wilderness garden. A similar small park existed at Hailes (Glos) in 1587 while at Croxden (Staffs) there was a small, detached park and rabbit warren in the eighteenth century (TNA: PRO, MF1/59; Brown 2009).

The approach to the Abbot's lodging from the south is very elaborate and manipulated and appears to be integrated with the 'canals'. The entrance was along the causeway (as it was in the medieval period) and through the gatehouse, which appears to have survived until at least 1617 since a lease of this date stipulates that a cottage was 'lying and being at the abbey gate in Stanley' (WSA: 473/258.46). A large lake, probably a medieval fishpond, defines the western side of the causeway, and beyond this, the flat ground would have been an ideal terrace walk. From the gatehouse the ground is rising, but the upper storey of the mansion house would have been visible and would have been approached from its western side.

Religious Symbolism in Stanley's Gardens

Religion was part of everyday life in medieval and post-medieval society. This symbolism can best be seen in their literature and art that illustrate their perceptions of the garden. The descriptions of the medieval enclosed garden, for example, are epitomized by the Marian *hortus conclusus*, the enclosed pleasure garden, that typically has a well or fountain at its centre symbolising the 'fountain of life' and Mary's role in bringing life to the infant Jesus; it is a metaphorical image of the garden as paradise or as the aristocratic garden of courtly love (Henderson 2005, 73). Many paintings of the Blessed Virgin Mary show her and the infant Jesus in an enclosed environment, which is meant to emphasize her purity and the miracle of the virgin birth.

The symbolism of the gardens at Stanley in a post-medieval context can be recognized from the documents and archaeology. It stems from the fact that the family, and the region as a whole, was staunchly Puritan and their ethos of work and pleasure has been demonstrated in the water gardens and fishing gardens of the period. The first point is that four specific elements to their garden were deliberately constructed and can be recognized from the earthwork plan: the enclosed garden; the water garden; orchard and warren, and the park. Their attitude to the garden is not only reflected physically but also in what they wrote, albeit scant. In 1555, in a lease of a fulling mill on the River Marden, Andrew Bayntun and Edward Bayntun reserved the right for 'fishing by draught net and casting net' (WSA: 473/258). Fishing was an important pastime for gentry families and it could be interpreted as being symbolic as a 'quietist fishing garden' (Everson 2007, 113-28). Later, in 1584, when part of the abbey was leased, it was agreed that Edward Bayntun and his wife would not forbid or deny William Anstie, his wife or friends 'to repose themselves in walking into the said orchard for their pleasure and recreation at all convenient times' (WSA: 473/258.26).

The Abbey Environs – its land and buildings

The manor of Stanley that the Bayntons acquired comprised tenements and land in Stanley, Nethermore, Loxwell, Studley, Chippenham, and a single tenement at Thickwood in Colerne. There were forty-nine copyholders

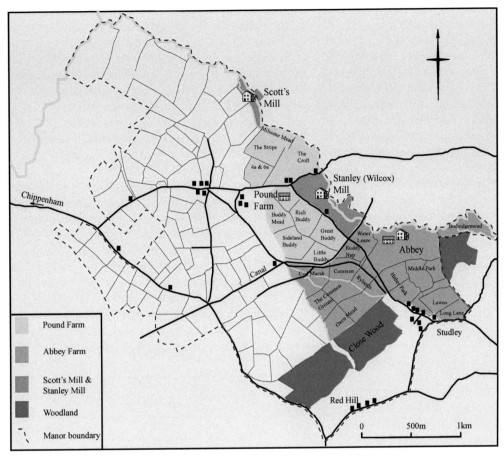

Figure 6:6. The extent of demesne at Stanley in 1536 represented by the shaded area of Abbey Farm and Pound Farm. Field boundaries are from the OS 1st edition map and field names from Stanley estate map dating to 1863 (Bowood estate maps).

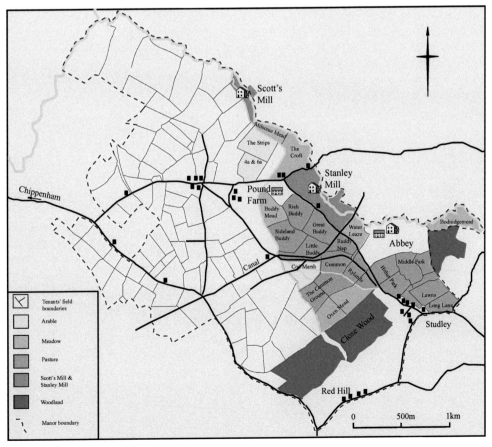

Figure 6:7. Land-use within the demesne at Stanley.

and thirty-five leaseholders in 1612 (WSA: 122/1). The manorial survey of this date, which is the earliest survey following the Suppression, is particularly useful since it lists the tenants with, in many cases, details of the property and land they held as well as the rents they paid. For every building the number of bays was noted and whether it was lofted (i.e. it had a first-floor). There were also details of any outbuildings. The survey also included Bayntun's other manors at Bremhill and Bromham although these are not analysed here (*ibid.*). Although the survey was undertaken in the early seventeenth century, many of the leases and copyholds date to the later sixteenth century and some from before the Suppression, and therefore reflect the later medieval landscape. Probate inventories and a hearth tax return, as well as a manorial account for 1539, supplement the survey and provide additional information for the buildings and the economy of Stanley.

The Demesne

The Augmentation Office survey of lands at Stanley Abbey in 1536 included rents from free and customary tenants that amounted to £39 15s 8d. The demesne was valued at £30 9s and was therefore about three-quarters the value of the tenants' land. The demesne covered an area of 425a (172ha) with 34a (8%) arable, 286a (67.3%) pasture, and 105a (24.7%) meadow; there was also an unspecified amount of woodland that was probably confined to Close Wood, and common of pasture in Pewsham Forest. Arable, therefore, accounted for only a small proportion of the land-use and when compared to the area under cultivation in 1415 when there was 149½ acres, it shows a dramatic decrease and conversion to pasture (Hare 2011, 61, quoting PRO: SC8/1054/9). The abbot's corn mill within the precinct was still held directly by the abbey and was worth 40s annually. There was also demesne at Chippenham and Nethermore valued at £4 2s 10d and £4 2s 4d respectively. (TNA PRO: E315/398).

The demesne at Stanley formed a consolidated block of land extending in an arc to the north, west and south of the abbey and probably included the nineteenth century farms of Abbey Farm (214a) and Pound Farm (210a) – a total 424 acres and within an acre of the 1536 amount (Bowood Estate map -Stanley; Christ College Mss. Estates 93/128; Fig 6:6). Field names from the schedules of these two farms, and the remains of ridge-and-furrow give an indication of the land-use at the time of the Suppression (Fig 6:7).

The majority of the enclosed fields have ditched boundaries and the arable lay in three closes, two to the north of what later became Pound Farm, with the other at Codmarsh. Evidence of ridge-and-furrow in the Buddy fields indicates the enclosing of the fields and change to pasture. The Buddy fields were ideally suited to cultivation since they are on higher ground and therefore better drained. In contrast, those closes to the south and bordering Close Wood are much lower and prone to waterlogging and therefore more suited to meadow or pasture.

Meadow was mainly concentrated along the riverbanks, although there were parcels at Buddy Mead and Oxen Mead. At Bodnidgemead, to the east of the abbey, there are the earthworks of a floated water meadow. It is unclear when the meadow was 'floated' but it was probably sometime in the early seventeenth century since a floated meadow on another of Baynton's estate, at neighbouring Bremhill, was the subject of complaint at the manorial court in 1630-1 (Bettey 2005, quoting WSA: 122/1). However, there is also a strong possibility that it overlies a much earlier system .

In 1539, just three years after the abbey's suppression, the only surviving sixteenth century manorial account roll provides evidence for the break-up of the demesne when part of it was leased to Robert Browne (alias Weare) of Marlborough. This land was described as pasture and included Great Buddy, Little Buddy, and Hode Close – land that later became part of Pound Farm. Two other closes had also been leased at this time to other individuals (WSA: 473/40.99). Eleven years later Browne increased his holding by leasing two further closes and the sheep house, presumably the former monastic sheep-house (WSA: 473/258.5).

Location	Rent
Chippenham	£3 - 4d
Stanley - Tenants	£29 15s 8d
Stanley - demesne	£23
Loxwell Grange	£9
Nethermore	£4 2s 4d
Studley	£5
Total	£73 18s 4d

Table 6:1. Rents received from the demesne and tenants' land in the Stanley region in 1539. The rents account for 70 per cent of the total income of the former abbey lands (WSA: 473/40.99).

The account shows that the total amount received per annum by Bayntun from the lands of Stanley Abbey and its territories elsewhere in 1539 was £115 12s 1d. Breaking this down we see that the demesne at Stanley was rented and in common with the 1536 valuation, this was less than the tenants' land, nevertheless it was still nearly a quarter of the total from all of Bayntun's former Stanley holdings, and when combined with the tenants' land it accounted for over 70 per cent of his income from the whole estate (WSA: 473/40.99; Table 6:1).

The Tenants' Land

Tenants in the manor of Stanley were either copyholders or leaseholders; there appears to be no freeholders. The leaseholders presumably held former monastic demesne.

Assuming the proportions of the tenants' land was similar to that of the demesne in 1536, i.e. 8 per cent arable, 67.3 per cent pasture, and 24.7 per cent meadow, the 1612 survey shows that, although cultivation fell from the medieval peak, there was virtually no change in the seventy-three years from 1536 (Table 6:2). The only major difference was between the pasture and meadow figures where the two terms may in fact be interchangeable. The size of the closes varied enormously in 1612 with many less than ten acres, while the largest was one of seventy-six acres. Enclosure was largely complete by the end of the sixteenth century at Stanley although there was still the occasional parcel of land being enclosed into the seventeenth century; for example, one such close was described as being 'lately enclosed' in 1613 (WSA: 473/258.42). The lord of the manor, Sir Henry Baynton, was an 'improving' landlord who facilitated enclosure. On his manors in 1619-1620 it was agreed that the tenants should have their lands:

'laid together in equall proportion by the generall consent and agreement of all parties aforesaid, to the intent as well as the said Lord as every of the said Tennants may enjoy from henceforth the plots of grounde allotted unto him in severaltye according to their former estates formerly granted to them' (Bettey 2005, xxix, quoting WSA: D1/39/2/8; 122/1 25 Sep 16Jas I).

	Pasture	Arable	Meadow	Total
Copyholders	209a	8.5a	25a	242.5a
Leaseholders	490.5a	107.5a	505a	1103a
Total	699.5a	116a	530a	1345.5a
Percentage	52%	8.6%	39.4%	100%
1536 demesne	67.3%	8%	24.7%	

Table 6:2. Tenants' agricultural land in the manor of Stanley in 1612 (data from WSA: 122/1). The demesne figures for 1536 are also shown.

The copyholders held less than a quarter of the tenants' land, and most of this was pasture. Of the forty-five copyholders, nineteen had rights of common, some without stint while in other cases the number of sheep, horses or cattle was specified. Thus Mathew Fowler, who had a two-bay lofted messuage, had common without stint, but no land; while Joanne Berryman who had a four-bay tiled and lofted messuage, a barn and stable of three bays and a two-bay ox-house, had common for 100 sheep and two horses. She also had twenty-eight acres of pasture. John Godwin had a five-bay messuage and ox-house, but his land amounted to forty-four acres of pasture and common for forty sheep and two horses. These latter two examples were, however, unusually large stints and presumably belonged to the wealthier yeomen. Other stints were generally much smaller, for six or twelve sheep with perhaps a horse or, in some cases, a cow.

As for the leaseholders, they held five times more land than the copyholders, but only two had common rights for their livestock. The amount of land they leased var-

ied a great deal with some having a mixed farming regime while others would not have been able to subsist from their land alone. William Rushwood, for example, had a two-bay messuage that was partly tiled called the Lodge, but only three acres of land, which was termed his garden. By contrast, Thomas Webb had a three-bay messuage with another dwelling of one-bay, which was lofted. His outbuildings included two cutts (a lean-to or penthouse), a two-bay barn and a lean-to workshop. There were two gardens, an orchard, and six acres of meadow, six acres pasture and 17.5 acres of arable land.

Some individuals held more than one lease and, although the majority are presumably for land in Stanley, at least one was for land in Thickwood in the parish of Colerne where the monks had formerly held land. Thus, although Bayntun had already disposed of most of his distant holdings, there were still small parcels in his hands.

The Tenants' Buildings

The period 1560-1640 was one of a transformation in vernacular architecture in what Hoskins described as 'the rebuilding of rural England' (Hoskins 1953, 44-59). More recent work, including regional studies and dendrochronology, would suggest a more varied and longer time-span (Johnson 2010, 88; Howard 2007, 2). The catalyst for this building transformation was not the Suppression, but the amount of building material that would be available would surely have provided an opportunity and impetus for change. As Howard says 'there were new houses built from scratch. But, far more importantly there was a lot of making new from old materials ...', he goes on to cite changes such as the flooring of open halls, insertion of fireplaces, glazing of windows, all 'customised old structures into modern dwellings'; but another, which he does not mention, would be the re-use of monastic material (Howard 2007, 2). At Stanley, this transformation is evident in a lease and from the 1612 survey where there are clearly open hall dwellings as well as those with one or even two floors. There is also evidence for the transformation of the some outbuildings, which did not form part of Hoskins's analysis. A lease of 1557 shows that John Wilcox, who leased Stanley Mill, 'lately erected and builded at the cost of the said John' a tenement (WSA 473/ 258.7). This was presumably at Stanley Mill since the lease included pasture that had been recently enclosed that adjoined the tenement and extended to a pond (the millpond?).

First, the manor houses on Bayntun's estates, as one would expect they were considerably larger than the tenants' dwellings; at Stanley, as we have seen, the manor house was ten bays long (*p. 105*). This was considerably smaller than the one at Bremhill, which was twenty-seven bays and presumably Malmesbury Abbey's former grange.

The tenants' dwellings varied in size between one to eight bays long and were referred to as either cottages or messuages (Table 6:3). The largest number were the two-bay

Bay	1		2		3		4		5	6	7	8	Totals
	Open	Lofted	Open	Lofted	Open	Lofted	Open	Lofted					
Copyholds	9	2	17	5	2	6	-	1	2	-	-	1	45
Leaseholds	1	2	4	6	3	7	1	-	1	1	-	-	26
Total	14		32		18		2		3	1	-	1	71
Percentage	19.7%		45.1%		25.4%		2.8%		4.2%	1.4%	-	1.4%	100%

Table 6:3. Number of bays in the dwellings in the manor of Stanley in 1612 (WSRO:122/1).

dwellings where there were 45.1 per cent, but the vast majority were one-three bays with seventy-nine per cent of the one-bay dwellings and 69 per cent of the two-bays held by copyholders. All the one-bay dwellings were referred to as cottages apart from a messuage in Chippenham that measured only 11ft, which seems remarkably small. Some of the lofted dwellings were part-lofted suggesting the retention of an open hall while others, particularly the mills, were double lofted, presumably with an attic over the first floor. The eight-bay house was in Chippenham and had four bays that were lofted; it was a barn conversion and it may have been converted soon after the Suppression when it was no longer needed as a barn. A probate inventory shows that it had a hall, a parlour, two butteries, two chambers at first-floor level and a kitchen (WSA: 122/1). Another property, Pound Farm, which was in the tenure of John Godwin was described as being a house and ox-house of five bays, four of them lofted, with a barn and wain-house of five bays, and a bake-house and stable of two bays. The phrase 'house and ox-house' perhaps suggests that this building may have been a longhouse (Harvey 1992, 32); alternatively the two buildings may have been in line and joined in some way.

It is noteworthy that, in addition to the manor house, there were thirteen other buildings that had tiled roofs in Stanley manor. This accounts for eighty-one per cent of the total number of tiled buildings on Bayntun's estates and in an area where the main roofing material at this time was thatch it would suggest that the tiles were taken from the disused monastic buildings (Harvey 1992, 32). It is also probable that tiles for some of the buildings at Bremhill also came from the abbey since the acquisition, or pilfering, of materials from the abbey was not necessarily confined to those who lived in the immediate environs of the abbey. At Hailes, for example, the commission of enquiry into the spoliation of the abbey found that some of the perpetrators came from a much wider area than Hailes itself (Shagan 2003, 162-96).

The hearth tax return in 1662 for Wiltshire is fragmentary but it shows that there were thirty-one dwellings with at least one hearth at Stanley, although by this time most dwellings probably had a smoke hood or some other means of providing a chimney (Table 6:4). There were also eight dwellings in Nethermore with hearths but there is no data for Loxwell (TNA: PRO E 179/259/29 part 2). Unfortunately it is impossible to demonstrate the progress of the abandonment of the open hall from the hearth tax since not all buildings are listed, and the detail for Chippenham does not specify those that were in the manor of Stanley.

Turning to the outbuildings. It is noticeable that none of the copyholders' one-bay dwellings had an outbuilding, nor did sixty-eight per cent of two-bay houses; this seems surprisingly large in a rural landscape with a dispersed settlement pattern where one would have expected at least one outbuilding. It may be that some of these dwellings were in Chippenham, although this seems unlikely since the survey specifically mentions when a property was there. The remaining two-bay houses had a barn measuring between one and five bays. Of the leaseholders, there is more evidence of a larger farming unit since only three had no outbuildings while the remainder had at least one; six of the seven three-bay houses had barns measuring between two and five bays. There were also two post-houses; it is unclear what these buildings were but one possibility is that they were open cart-sheds with a loft over the shed. There was also a bark-house 'standing on posts', suggesting tanning was undertaken – this building was presumably a survival of a monastic tannery. Other outbuildings of note include eight shops, and while it is possible that they were indeed shops, particularly if they were in Chippenham, another interpretation is that they were workshops such as for weaving.

The largest properties, apart from the mansion house, were those of the yeomen and yeoman/clothiers; people like the Wilcocke (or Wilcox) and Scott families, who held Stanley Mill and Scott Mill respectively for much of the sixteenth and seventeenth centuries. Although weaving was a cot-

Hearths	1	2	3	4	5	6	7	Total
Stanley	15	6	4	3	2	1	-	31
Nethermore	2	2	1	2	-	-	1	8
Total	17	8	5	5	2	1	1	39
Percentage	43.06%	20.5%	12.8%	12.8%	5.1%	2.6%	2.6%	100%

Table 6:4. Number of dwellings with hearths in Stanley and Nethermore in 1662 (TNA: PRO E 179/259/29 part 2).

tage industry, clearly it was undertaken at the mills as well. The probate inventories and leases are particularly informative as regards their holdings; that for Andrew Wilcocke shows that he had two looms and various grades of wool including coarse, fine, coloured and three broad cloths; he also had livestock, two pigs, six cows, two bullocks and a horse (WSA: 122/1). The fulling mill, which in 1612 was tenanted by Andrew Wilcocke, comprised a four-bay messuage with two pairs of stocks; it was tiled and double lofted. There was a two-bay barn that was also tiled. His land adjoining the mill included a backside (yard), garden and orchard and four acres of meadow, 15½ acres of pasture and fifteen acres of arable. In 1662 there were six hearths here, the largest number for any building in Stanley, even larger than the mansion house, which presumably had five hearths (TNA: PRO E 179/259/29 part 2)

Secularisation is, therefore, evident in the agrarian landscape and buildings at Stanley. The demesne, amounting to 425 acres, remained a consolidated block of land as well for the first few years following the Suppression but it was soon divided into two farms, Abbey Farm and Pound Farm. As for the tenants' land, leaseholders were by far the most numerous holding five times more land than the copyholders and evidence from elsewhere would suggest that many of these leases may have been taken out during the monastic period. Perhaps one of the main effects of the Suppression was that it provided a ready source of building material at a time of improvement of buildings in the country in general.

The Settlement Pattern

Evidence from late seventeenth and eighteenth century maps would suggest a largely dispersed settlement pattern at Stanley with a small hamlet at Studley. There was also a cluster of 'green-side' farmsteads at Huttes, and elsewhere dwellings were along roadsides, presumably close to their lands. The documentary evidence also points to buildings within or beside the precinct. There were about thirty-five dwellings by the later eighteenth century and it is probably an accurate picture of the mid sixteenth century landscape as well. The thirty-five dwellings is half the number in 1612; however, the survey included dwellings at Chippenham, Loxwell, Nethermore and Thickwood, which may account for much, but not all, of the discrepancy. The remainder may be made up from depopulation, which there undoubtedly was, not only of the abbot and monks, but perhaps also the eight corrodians whose fate is unknown. They may have continued to live within the precinct but whether the new lord was prepared to sanction this is a mute point. It is also probable that some of the smaller one-bay dwellings were abandoned during this period of 're-building'.

STANLEY'S GRANGES AND TERRITORIES

The granges and manors that the Bayntun's and Seymour's acquired following the Suppression continued to be leased and there was probably little change in the way the land was farmed. They were acquired as complete blocks of land, either as manors or granges.

Lord Seymour, who did particularly well out of the Suppression, acquired Richardson, Berwick Bassett, Broad Hinton, Midgehall, and Studley Grange from Stanley. His 'powerbase' in Wiltshire, however, was on the Marlborough Downs, the Pewsey Vale and along the Avon valley.

As for Sir Edward Bayntun, who acquired the remaining estates including the site of the abbey, he soon disposed of the more distant holdings leaving a core in the Chippenham Forest region. Speculators seem to be the principal recipients; Merecumbe Grange, for example, had three owners within twelve years of the Suppression and it appears to have been sold for quick profit. The grange, or tenement as it was then known, was initially leased in 1535 for sixty-four years at an annual rent of 26s 8d, but eleven years later Bayntun sold it to Nicholas Snell of Kington St Michael for £40, who sold it on in 1552 for £55 - a 37.5 per cent profit in just three years (*Cal. Anc Deeds vol 6*, C7260, C7261, C7618). Nicholas Snell also leased land from Bayntun at Stanley on favourable terms. He was clearly a wealthy individual who profited from the Dissolution. He also depopulated and emparked land at Kington St Michael, which lay to the north of Chippenham (Kerridge 1959, 48-9).

Estate Groups

Many former monastic farms throughout the country can be understood by studying their accounts and farm books, but another way that has been overlooked is an understanding of them in landscape terms - what we can see from the maps and on the ground - as well as the documents. It is clear that over time the fortunes of these former monastic farms varied and appear to be largely dictated by their size and relative value at the Suppression. Although all initially remained tenanted, the holdings fall into three main categories.

The first category was the small land-holdings. Many were less than sixty acres, such as Clopcote, Yatton Keynell, Easton and Costowe; all had low valuations in 1291 and 1535. Essentially these were family farms; three were in the 'Cheese' district of Wiltshire where the land was generally farmed from small, enclosed fields. The exception was Yatton Keynell, which was on the Cotswolds where the land was more suited to sheep grazing. These holdings appear to be unaffected by the Suppression.

The second group were those that continued to be farmed by the more prosperous yeoman farmers and minor county gentry, some of whom may well have been the monastery's bailiffs before the suppression. Their relative wealth is reflected in the two monastic taxations in 1291 and 1535 but can also be seen in the size of the land-holdings and residences; the house, for example, was noticeably more substantial and may have included an extensive garden layout such as at Berwick Bassett, Wapley, Midgehall, and Richardson.

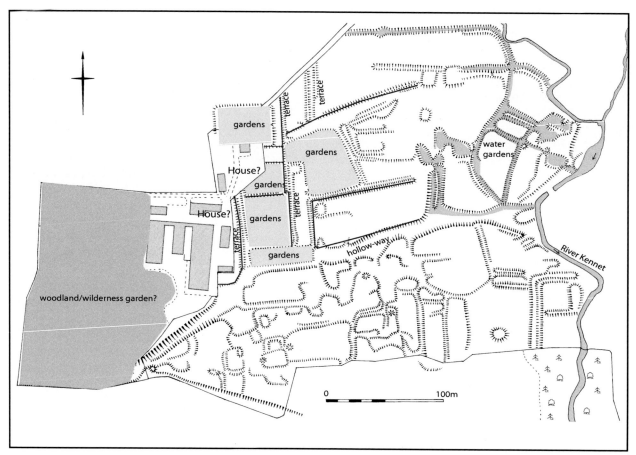

Figure 6:8. Interpretative plan of the possible layout of the gardens at Richardson (earthwork survey re-drawn from NMR: SU 07 SE 23. Crown Copyright Ordnance Survey. All rights reserved).

Midgehall had been leased to the Pleydell family in 1534 where the house stood on a moated site. Although there is no archaeological evidence of the layout of the buildings during the sixteenth and seventeenth centuries, a survey of 1607 describes it as comprising five acres with: 'a mansion house, barns, stables ox-houses, gardens, hop-yards, yards, and two rabbit warrens, one known as 'old cunnygar'. The farm, or perhaps more correctly, the manor, covered a little over 934 acres (378ha), with tenants' land of 193 acres (78ha) (WSA: 192/51).

Little survives from the medieval and post-medieval landscape at Richardson; however, as we have seen in chapter four the extensive earthworks show a complex development that are of at least two periods. To the south of a deep hollow-way there are the characteristic earthworks of building platforms, closes and a moated site dating to the medieval period and while it remains unclear when the medieval settlement was abandoned, it is likely to have been sometime in the sixteenth century when there were changes to the economy of the grange. However, it was never completely abandoned since in 1545, two individuals were taxed, the highest being Symond Baskerfeld who was termed 'gentleman' and presumably a yeoman; he paid 26s 8d, which was four times more than the other taxpayer (Ramsay 1954, 22). There is no mention of Richardson in the 1576 tax list but in Winterbourne Bassett, the parish in which Richardson lies, there was a William Baskerfeld who was assessed at £4, who may have resided at Richardson (*ibid.*, 103). Rather

than settlement desertion, there was settlement shift since to the north of the hollow-way some of the earthworks are more rectilinear and include terraces, enclosures and ponds, reflecting a garden layout of probable sixteenth or seventeenth century date going with a dwelling that was in the area of the modern cottages (Fig 6:8).

These gardens were probably established sometime during the later-sixteenth century or seventeenth century. By the mid eighteenth century they had been further adapted with an extensive orchard occupying much of the area, with small enclosed gardens near the house (BL: M.T.6.e.1.(1)).

Finally, the third group were those where the holdings remained intact after the Suppression, but the house may have been re-built or adapted at some stage into a more prestigious mansion house by a member of the local gentry, or farmer-landowners. Examples include Codrington Court and Heywood Grange.

Although nothing survives of the grand house, Heywood House or its early parkland that were built by the Earl of Marlborough in the first quarter of the seventeenth century, at Codrington there is evidence of the post-medieval landscape (Crittall 1965, 163). An indication of the former grange's layout is shown on an estate map that shows the house with its gardens set within a wider farming landscape (GRO: D1610/P43; Fig 6:9). The map dates to 1762; however, the layout of house and enclosed gardens is es-

Figure 6:9. Codrington Court, 1762 (GRO: D1610/P43).

sentially of the seventeenth century with none of the 'landscaping' which was so prevalent in the eighteenth century. The front of the house is on the north-eastern side. Extending from the front of the house is a formal avenue of trees, with another joining it at right angles and leading to the road. In front of the house is a small, enclosed garden with another, larger garden at the back - the 'private' side of the house. Extending from the rear garden are two 'walks', with an orchard in an attached rectangular enclosure. Even the name 'court' could be seen as having pretentions of grandeur, perhaps emulating the name of Henry VIII's Hampton Court. On the east side of the house was a rabbit warren defined by earthworks that were interpreted as possible pillow mounds (NMR: ST77NW11). A 'conygere' was associated with the manor house here in 1649 (BRO: DC/E/8/2 and DC/E/8/2/a).

In summary, therefore, although fragmentation of the former monastic estate occurred, it was initially of the more distant holdings, whereas the core estate in the environs of Chippenham remained largely intact. When property was disposed of it would appear that it was the whole of a holding. In the seventeenth century there was further fragmentation, and on some estates residences were improved or new houses built within a landscape of formal gardens and parkland. However, they were still primarily farm estates. Settlement shift is also apparent at Richardson and Langdon Wick, but this may have been the culmination a long process of population decline.

DISCUSSION

The sixteenth and seventeenth centuries saw dramatic changes in the landscape and society at Stanley, which can be seen as the 'secularisation of the landscape'. Some of these changes can be directly attributed to the Suppression while for others it was a contributory factor.

First, and most significant, the site of the abbey continued to be a place of lordship but on a much-reduced scale with only those buildings deemed necessary as a secular residence being retained. The new house was set within a landscape of gardens and parkland, and although it had all the hallmarks and pretensions of grandeur it was nevertheless still an active farming enterprise. The conversion to a Tudor house, however, only lasted until the mid seventeenth century when it was abandoned and replaced by a farmstead. Thus the house became a 'failed conversion'. Other monastic houses in Wiltshire also had mixed fortunes. Of the four Benedictine monasteries in the county only two were successful conversions, while of the five Augustinian houses Maiden Bradley was a 'failed conversion'. This was possibly because the Duke of Somerset had acquired it in 1537 and his principal residence was elsewhere.

Although it is not entirely clear why the site never succeeded as a mansion house, events in the wider region may point to the likely reasons. Perhaps the principal one was that it was always seen as a 'secondary' residence that was for the most part tenanted. Secondary residences were not uncommon; for example, Thomas Wriothesley bought Beaulieu Abbey in 1538, but he already had two other major houses one of which was Titchfield Abbey. Beaulieu was let in subsequent years although Wriothesley retained the rights to hunt and fish during his short visits (Howard 1987, 143). This also occurred at Stanley where Edward Bayntun retained the right to walk in the gardens beside the mansion house and fish in the river.

Another contributory factor concerning the status of the mansion house was the turmoil and declining fortunes experienced by the Bayntun family in the mid sixteenth century. Soon after his father's death, Andrew Bayntun (1515-1564), the new lord of the manor, was embroiled in financial difficulties from 1544-1563 and sold property in several of his manors including Stanley. The largest of these transactions was with Sir Thomas Seymour in 1545, which almost ruined him. When Seymour was executed in 1549, both men's property went to the Crown but during the reign of Queen Mary, Bayntun regained his former lands. He also had other troubles with debts to his father-in-law (Henning 1983, 409; Matthew and Harrison 2004a, 482-3).

Finally, Stanley was also quite removed from the main London to Bath road and in a damp, low-lying riverside location and not particularly picturesque. In contrast Bayntun's mansion at Bromham was close to the London road with extensive parkland reaching as far as the foothills of the Marlborough Downs, and at Spye Park the house was on high ground with commanding views over the surrounding countryside.

A second change that can be directly attributed to the Suppression was that of a 'dislocation' of settlement, of disruption and desertion. There was clearly some desertion, but equally there was some continuation of habitation. Within the precinct there would have been a wide range of individuals at the Suppression, not just the monastic community but others such as the seven corrodians, the schoolmaster, and servants, who were presumably accommodated somewhere within the precinct. Although we do not know where these individuals lived, the evidence from Cleeve Abbey may be an indicator. In 1536, of their five corrodians one was accommodated in the 'firmary chamber' another in the 'great chamber over the gate with other chambers adjacent', and another on the south side of the cloister (Williams 1991, 103-4). Clearly the monks at Stanley were evicted and moved to other monasteries – the major and high profile desertion - but where did the others go? Following the Suppression some of the buildings would have remained, but ultimately they would have been abandoned when there was no further use for them. Although there is little clear evidence, some buildings within the precinct at Stanley continued to be occupied even though the area had been 'gentrified'. In addition there were a couple of mills and some outbuildings that were staffed and presumably their dwellings were close-by. Laity who were resident in a monastery following the Suppression is illustrated well by the example of Tintern where some buildings were sublet by the new owner. In 1568, thirty-two years after its suppression, these included 'the laundry-house', a 'room above the gate of the abbey parlour', and several other buildings such as the gatehouse chapel, which had been converted into a dwelling (Williams 2001, 92). Clearly, the laity was quick to take advantage of the abandonment and it was probably a case of desertion coupled with limited settlement shift.

The tenants at Stanley were also affected by the Suppression, but whether as a direct consequence of the Suppression or factors that existed elsewhere in the county is unclear. As with the other county landed gentry such as the Herberts of Wilton and the Thynnes of Longleat, the 'newly rich', entry fines increased but rents were similar on all estates (Kerridge 1959, 61). The value of Stanley to the Bayntuns is reflected in the accounts of the 1560s. During this decade annual rents from Stanley manor and its dependencies amounted to about £730, while Bayntun's other manors at Bromham, Bremhill and Rodbourne added much more bringing the total to a little over £2,000; thus Stanley's contribution was thirty-six per cent of his revenue from his manors. There is also perhaps an indication of the influence Bayntun could expect to exert over the local population since a large number of the tenants are named in the lists (Matthew and Harrison 2004a, 484; Freeman 1988).

Tenancies at Stanley changed. This is most evident in the two surveys of 1612 and 1734 where the number of leases increased at the expense of copyholds; there was also an eight per cent decrease in numbers of tenants (Table 6:5). Copyholds decreased by twenty-one per cent, while leaseholds increased by the same amount; this allowed the lord of the manor to vary entry conditions and keep a greater control over his land.

Date/Tenure	Copyholds		Leaseholds		Total
	Total	%	Total	%	
1612	45	63%	26	37%	71
1734	27	42%	38	58%	65

Table 6:5. Number of tenancies at Stanley in 1612 and 1734. (WSRO: 122.1; 473/59

Clearly it cannot be demonstrated that this would not have occurred had the monastery remained, but using examples of Crown and ecclesiastical estates that were in existence from before the Dissolution there may be some hint of what might have occurred. Most significantly, it would appear that while rents on Herbert's and Seymour's estates rose sevenfold and ninefold respectively between 1510-1519 and 1600-1609, the rents from Crown land only rose threefold (Kerridge 1959, 62). As for ecclesiastical estates, analysis of the estates of the Vicars Choral of Wells Cathedral shows that they had a 'hands off' approach to management and that they were reluctant to make changes to their medieval style of leaseholds or improve their rent returns. A parliamentary survey in 1649 shows that rents had not changed since the fifteenth century. The most common form of tenure on their land in the post-medieval period was copyhold for three lives (Hill 1998, 1-25). This is in stark contrast to Stanley where there was a reduction of copyholds and increased entry fines.

Tenants, however, were able to take advantage of market conditions. Thus the leasing of the two mills was clearly an attractive and profitable proposition for the two clothiers since it enabled them to be more entrepreneurial and trade more widely, unencumbered by monastic administrators. John Wilcox, for example, not only sold his cloth locally, but also to the Blackwell Hall market in London where it was bought by German traders from Hamburg (Ramsay 1965, 26-7).

Finally, tenants were able to take advantage of a ready source of building material and other goods from the redundant monastic buildings and probably many new buildings and refurbished ones used material from the monastery. This was a bonus as far as those living in the vicinity of the monastery were concerned since the 'great re-building' would have occurred despite the Suppression.

In summary, therefore, the secularisation of the landscape at Stanley gathered momentum following the abbey's suppression, but it was also at a time of continuing and dramatic change throughout the country. These changes included the suppression of the 'old faith' that affected the fabric of churches and local communities alike. Rural housing was also undergoing improvement as people's expectations and notions of privacy changed. The agrarian landscape witnessed continuing innovation and improvement as more land was enclosed in the region and new crops and techniques introduced. The suppression of the monastery saw the eradication of a religious way of life that had existed for centuries, but in landscape terms it can be seen as an 'enabler' since it presented opportunities, particularly in the improvement of housing with superfluous monastic buildings being used as a source of building material. Secularisation is most apparent at the abbey and on the home grange demesne with the eviction of monks and monastic staff, the Abbot's lodging being converted into a mansion house with the attendant gardens and park, and the demesne being divided into two farms. The remaining land at Stanley, like most of its estates, was leased before the Suppression, and initially there was little effect on their tenures.

CHAPTER SEVEN

CONCLUSION

INTRODUCTION

The aim of this book has been to assess the impact of a Cistercian monastery on the landscape and how, in its turn, the landscape affected the monastery. Three key issues emerge from the study. First the methodology, which was a holistic landscape approach. Why was this approach taken and what were its advantages? The second issue concerns the traditional views of some previous researchers regarding the Cistercians and their attitudes to land acquisition and management. It questions whether the monks at Stanley conformed to the early ideals of the Order, or did they have to compromise? Finally, what effect did the suppression of the monastery have on the landscape?

METHODOLOGY

The methodology employed in this book is distinctive since no other study of a Cistercian monastery has employed the type of landscape approach to the depth that has been adopted here. As we have seen there has been a great deal of research into the standing fabric of monasteries and the excavation of the remains of their churches and conventual buildings, as well as charting the history of an abbey through the documents, but the area beyond the monastic complex, the precinct, has received scant attention, and far less research has been undertaken into the abbey's home grange or the territory that supported the monastery. Nor has there been any debate into the potential 'symbolism of place', which may shed new insights into the plantation of lordly residences such as abbeys, ecclesiastical palaces and castles.

Stanley Abbey is poorly documented and beyond a general history of the abbey little can be learnt and therefore our understanding of the impact of the Cistercian settlement on the region cannot be advanced using just the available documents. However, by linking the documentary evidence to the landscape evidence a more complete picture can be gained. The methodology recognises that the geomorphology of an area, and previous land-use, have a bearing on later land-use and may provide insights into why certain places were selected for settlement and others avoided, and how the land was exploited. As well as the pre-monastic landscape, the study of the post-monastic landscape enables an assessment of the relative 'control' the monks had on the environment in the final decades of the abbey's existence and the value of the land.

The excavation revealed the outline of the abbey; however, the earthwork evidence has been emphatic and crucial in our understanding of the abbey by revealing its extent and features within the precinct, which were hitherto unknown. It also shows how the abbey was transformed into a gen-

try residence with its attendant gardens and parkland. The map evidence, linked to the documents and place-names, was the basis for understanding the post-suppression environment at Stanley. The earthworks of granges has been equally rewarding in showing their extent and morphology. At Richardson the settlement was clearly confined to one side of a trackway, while extensive gardens associated with a later house occupied the other side. The earthworks also resemble a non-monastic settlement, and in the absence of supporting documentary evidence, the moated site could be interpreted as a secular manorial *curia*. Aerial photographs have also been invaluable in showing, for example, that many of the bland statements about how the Cistercians cleared and colonised land is far more complex, and while in some cases this was true, in other areas there is evidence that they incorporated former features such as 'Celtic' fields into their fields and that some land was more heavily exploited than others.

CISTERCIAN IDEALS AND THE REALITY

The second issue assesses to what extent Stanley conformed to the early ideals of the Order and questions whether they were distinctive from other Orders as well as exploring in what way they changed the landscape.

The monks who left Molesme and established a 'new monastery' (later known as Cîteaux) near Dijon were determined to adhere more strictly to the precepts of the Rule of St Benedict. In order to achieve this it entailed an entirely different socio-economic system whereby they were to be self-sufficient and not reliant on the rents or labours of others. To assist them in their endeavours, lay brothers were recruited to run the abbey's demesne farms, the granges. It has often been said that one of the most distinctive features of the Cistercians was the way they managed their territory, not from manors (these were initially prohibited) but from this network of granges. In their fully developed form the traditional view is that these were consolidated blocks of land separated from secular society. However, as this book has shown, while some granges were on the boundary of a parish and at some distance from habitation, others were within a village setting. In addition, as has been seen at Cistercian monasteries elsewhere, the monks soon acquired manors and Stanley was no exception, but the research at Stanley shows that on some of their manors they also had a grange either within the manor or beside it. The majority of Stanley's granges were consolidated blocks of land and separate from secular fields; thus they were able to exploit the land as they chose, but they also had the best of both worlds with their 'manor/granges' including demesne and tenants owing dues to the abbot, and an independent grange.

It is notable that there is no evidence that Stanley depopulated a settlement in order to establish a grange, which would suggest a degree of compliance and welcome by the inhabitants. This is in stark contrast to areas such as in the north of England where there was some depopulation (e.g. Beresford 1983, 152; Platt 1969, 93; Donkin 1978, 37-51).

In establishing their monastery the Cistercians sought 'desert' or 'wilderness' places far from habitation. Stanley's territory was spread widely over different topographies with varying resources. However, in an already exploited landscape in the south of England the monks had to compromise their ideals and while there is evidence of assarting, clearance and land drainage, some of the land they acquired was already under cultivation, and the monks may therefore not be as 'pioneering' as some would suggest. This combination of acquisition of already cultivated land and assarting is evident at other Cistercian monasteries, including those on the Continent. In a study of forty-three Cistercian monasteries in the south of France, for example, it was found that the properties they acquired were located 'almost entirely in already settled, cleared, and cultivated areas, not in wilderness' (Berman 1986, 11). Similarly at Plasy Abbey in western Bohemia, between 1150-1250 the monks acquired mainly cultivated land as well as woodland that had been assarted; also, of their eleven granges all but one occupied previously cleared land and at most the establishment of the grange entailed depopulation (Charvátová 1993, 134). In contrast to these two examples, in the newly colonised land to the east of the River Elbe in Germany the Cistercians were particularly active as 'truly pioneers in the eastward expansion of the German nation [...] into the newly conquered and sparsely peopled lands beyond the Elbe [where] they cleared the forests, they reclaimed the swamps, they drained the marshes, they built levees and dikes to confine the streams, and they made roads and bridges' (Thompson 1920, 77).

The distinctiveness of the Cistercians at Stanley, therefore, was in their grange economy and the establishment of their manor/granges. Land clearance, apart from within Chippenham Forest, appears to have been on a small scale, but the gradual accumulation of land into consolidated blocks and in a variety of landscapes ensured a successful agrarian economic base.

Revenues from churches were also amongst the early prohibitions of the Order. However, in the case of Stanley they held the advowson of two churches soon after its foundation. These may have formed the basis for expansion in the area since the abbey also held granges within the parishes. This link between church and grange can also be seen in the case of the Gilbertines. Golding, in his study of the Order, highlights the fact that they were influenced by the Cistercians in their Rule and many of their attitudes towards estate management; he also suggests that the interest in a church by the Order was an early stage of the establishment of a grange (Golding 1995, 394).

While Stanley held two churches from an early date, three others were appropriated in the fourteenth century specifically to relieve their financial problems, and it is perhaps significant that they did not hold granges within any of these parishes. They were, in effect, a means of quick, ready cash. In addition, the early statutes of the Order also prevented the monks from ministering at churches since this was also a source of income, but by the fourteenth century this was clearly not the case since, as far as Stanley was concerned, the pope sanctioned the appointment of monks as priests when he stated that 'upon the resignation or death of the incumbent, the Abbot could appoint his own monks to serve as vicars or appoint another secular priest who could be appointed and removed by the Abbot at his pleasure' (*Cal. Papal Registers Vol. 4*, 192).

The departures from the ideals of the Order occurred in the mid twelfth century, at much the same time as the death of St Bernard of Clairvaux and the founding of Stanley, and over the next century the monks effectively became feudal lords, but also retaining granges until they were leased from the early fourteenth century. These differences between the ideals and reality has been recognised by others and appears to have occurred at a time of rapid expansion and benefaction to the Order (e.g. Alphonso 1991, 3-30; Roehl 1972, 83-113).

EFFECT OF THE SUPPRESSION ON THE LANDSCAPE

The suppression of the monasteries was the largest transfer of land-ownership since the Norman Conquest, but what was the effect on the landscape? It would appear that in Stanley's case there was little effect since much of the land was already leased out and the changes that are evident at this time; enclosure of the common fields, changing farming practices, and improving building techniques, are mirrored on monastic and secular estates alike.

Although there were tenants on the abbey's home grange the demesne became the core of a new secular farming enterprise, but even this was separated into two farms, Abbey Farm and Pound Farm. As for the outlying territory, only the Marlborough Downs estates were still held by the abbey, but following the suppression they continued to be farmed in much the same way. It was only later, probably in the early seventeenth century that changes occurred when the grange buildings at Richardson were abandoned and a new residence was built a little distance from the grange. A similar situation can be seen at Langdon Wick (although the date of abandonment is unknown), when a new farmstead was built on the perimeter of the grange's outer court. These chalkland estates in many ways mirrored the secular estates on the chalk where manorial control was stronger than on the 'cheese' region of Wiltshire and where enclosure of the fields and wholesale conversion from pasture to arable did not occur until the eighteenth and nineteenth centuries.

The greatest effect of the Suppression was clearly on the abbey and the precinct when the buildings were largely destroyed and in their place a new secular mansion house was fashioned out of the west range. The process of change was protracted, with some monastic buildings surviving into the early seventeenth century. However, the notion of separation continued, although the precinct was abandoned, parkland formed a buffer between the mansion house complex and cultivated zone.

In summary, therefore, this book illustrates the potential of adopting a landscape approach to the study of a monastery, which could be replicated on other landscapes. By using such an approach a fuller understanding of the abbey and its territory has been gained - this would have been impossible if only documentary sources had been used. The survey and analysis of the earthworks within the precinct and on the granges have been a crucial part of this study since they reveal evidence of man's impact on the landscape, not only in the monastic period but also the post-dissolution period. The transcription and analysis of aerial photographs have also been an important element since they have revealed evidence of settlement, the extent of cultivation, and presence of water meadows in the region. These two strands of evidence, coupled with the documentary and map evidence, are all intrinsic elements in this landscape approach. The words of St Bernard of Clairvaux are most apt in this context when he said: 'Believe me who have experience, you will find much more labouring amongst the woods than you ever will amongst books. Woods and stones will teach you what you can never hear from any masters' (James 1953, 156).

BIBLIOGRAPHY

PRIMARY SOURCES

Bodleian Library (Bodl.)

Digby mss. 11

Bowood Estate

Estate maps of Stanley

British Library (BL)

Harl. ms. 6716
M.T.6.e.1.(1.) - A survey of Winterbourne, Rapson, Richardson, Upper Richardson alias Whyr, Summers's Hand alias Trotman's Farms [1760]

Bristol Record Office (BRO)

31965/STG/10 – Map of Manor of Stanley in parish of Bremhill (1862)
DC/E/3/2 – Manor of Codrington alias Codrington and Wapley
DC/E/3/2a - Manor of Codrington alias Codrington and Wapley

Chippenham College

Unpublished Field-walking notes

Devizes Museum (DM)

16.79 – Newspaper cutting from 'Daily News' about the discovery of the skeletons.
Register 1982

Institute for Historical Research, London

Seymour Papers – Microfilm vol. 12

The National Archive: Public Record Office (TNA:PRO)

E32/199 – Plea roll of Wiltshire forest eyre, 1263
E179/259/29 - Hearth tax returns for Stanley and Nethermore
E315/398 – Composite volume of particulars, valors etc. of monastic houses, 1536
E32/199/3 – Plea roll of Wiltshire Forest Eyre, 1263
MF1/59 – Map of Hailes 1587
SC2/209/56 - Halmote Sheldon and Louden 15, 16 Ed IV [1475-1476]

SC6/Hen VIII/3958 – Account of Nicholas Aleyn receiver general of the abbot, Christmas-Christmas 19-90 Henry VIII [1527-8]
SC6/1054/18 – Special Collections: Ministers' and Receivers' Accounts Langeden 20 to 21 Ed 1 [1292]
SC8/251/12533 – Petition relating to leasing of Cudrington, 1455
SC12/33/37 – Commissioners' Report on Stanley Abbey, 1536

National Monument Record Centre (NMR)

AF1071473 – RCHME: Fyfield and Overton Downs Mapping Project
AF1116517 – RCHME: The Avebury World Heritage Site Project, SU 17 SW
DoE Register 1979
LB UID 316191 – Listed Building unique identification number

Gloucestershire Record Office (GRO)

D 1610/P43 – A Survey and Map of the Manor of Wapley and Codrington and of Certain Parcels of Land lying in Dodington in the County of Gloucester belonging to Sir Richard Warwick Bampfylde Bart (1762)
D2311/T2 – Manor and Monastery of Hailes, 1624-1651

Somerset Archive and Record Office (SARO)

D\P\blag/20/1/1 - Blagdon Enclosure award and plan, 1787

Surrey History Centre (SHC)

G 97/4/9 – Pyford Manor Customal and rental 1330-1

Wiltshire and Swindon Archives (WSA)

106/1   - Sale Particulars of Meux Estates 1906
122/1 - Survey of the manors of Bromham, Bremhill and Stanley, 1612. Court book of manors of Bromham, Bremhill, Stanley, and Chittoe 1615-1638
192/51 - Survey of various places including Midgehall (1587-1607)
415/2 – Stone extraction Loxwell Quarry 1868
415/4 – Stone extraction Ash Hill Quarry 1895
415/8   - Valuation of Property in Chippenham and tithings of Allington, Tytherton, Stanley and Nethermore, c1822
415/272 - Schedule of deeds to documents relating to the estates of Joseph Neeld esq.

473 - Goldney Archive
740/2/1 - The Manor of Sheldon belonging to Wm Norris Esq [early eighteenth century]
873/350H - Map of the tithings of Stanley and Nethermore in the parish of Chippenham (1851)
873/351 - Exchange: Tithings of Stanley and Nethermore in the parish of Chippenham
1213/1 - Grant of meadow in Forest of Chippenham, 1151
1213/2 – Grant of land in Mercumbe, Blagdon 1151-1156
1213/3 – Gift of burgage in Chippenham, early thirteenth century
1213/7 – Gift of free alms, c1280
1213/20 - Bargain and sale by James Pagett, esq to Queen Elizabeth of the site of the late monastery of Stanley 28th April 1567
1259/22 – Three deeds of the fulling mill at Stanley (1554, 1623, 1649)
1780/4 - Survey and plans of the estates of Charles Wm Wyndham being part of the joint estates belonging to the Marquis of Granby, the Countess of Aylesbury and the said Charles Wm Wyndham [1779]
2454/7 - Plan of Loxwell and Ash Hill Farms and Loxwell Heath with the New Divisions situate in the Parish of Chippenham, 1824
2664 box 4 - Lacock Abbey archives
2664L - An exact plan of the Demean Lands and Manor of Lacock, with estates adjacent in the parish of Chippenham and the county of Wilts belonging to John Talbot esq, 1764
Tithe Award map and schedule - Preshute, 1843
Tithe Award map and schedule - Langley Burrell, 1840
Tithe Award map and schedule – Pewsham, 1840
Tithe Award map and schedule – Yatton Keynell, 1840

Wiltshire Buildings Record (WBR)

B6358 – Pound Farm, Stanley

Christ Church, Oxford

Ms Estates 93/128 – 20 May 1840. Chippenham, Schedule of tithe-free lands belonging to J. E. A. Starkey in the manors of Stanley and Loxwell

Oriel College, Oxford

Customs of the Manor of Wadley 1673-1773, Shennington 1693-1756
Plan of the Manor and Lordship of Wadley, Littleworth and Thrupp in the parish of Faringdon belonging to Oriel College. Copied from the Tithe Apportionment map 1852
Shadwell 678 – Wadley Manor, Faringdon

PRINTED PRIMARY SOURCES

Andrews' and Dury's Map of Wiltshire, 1773. facsimile edition. Devizes: Wiltshire Record Society 8
Astle T. Ayscough S. and Caley J. 1802. *Taxatio Ecclesiastica Angliae et Walliae, Auctorite Pope Nicholas IV, circa AD1291.* London: George Eyre and Andrew Strahan
Brewer J. S. 1879. *Registrum Malmuburiense. The Register of Malmesbury Abbey.* vol. 1
Brewer J. S. 1880. *Registrum Malmuburiense. The Register of Malmesbury Abbey.* vol. 2
Calendar of Ancient Deeds vol. 1
Calendar of Ancient Deeds vol. 3
Calendar of Ancient Deeds vol. 4
Calendar of Ancient Deeds vol. 5
Calendar of Ancient Deeds vol. 6
Calendar of Charter Rolls, Henry III, vol. 1, 1226-1257
Calendar of Close Rolls, Henry III, vol.1, 1227-1231
Calendar of Close Rolls, Edward I, vol. 4, 1296-1302
Calendar of Close Rolls, Henry III, vol. 2, 1231-1234
Calendar of Librate Rolls, Henry III, vol. 1, 1226-1240
Calendar of Librate Rolls, Henry III, vol. 2, 1240-1245
Calendar of Librate Rolls, Henry III, vol. 3, 1245-1251
Calendar of Librate Rolls, Henry III, vol. 4, 1251-1260
Calendar of Librate Rolls, Henry III, vol. 5, 1260-1267
Calendar of Librate Rolls, Henry III, vol. 6, 1267-1272
Calendar of Patent Rolls, Henry III, vol. 4, 1247-1256
Calendar of Patent Rolls, Edward I, vol. 4, 1301-1307
Calendar of Patent Rolls, Edward II, vol. 2, 1313-1317
Calendar of Patent Rolls Edward II, vol. 3, 1317-1321
Calendar of Patent Rolls Edward II, vol. 4, 1321-1324
Calendar of Patent Rolls Edward III, vol. 1, 1327-1330
Calendar of Patent Rolls, Edward III, vol. 2, 1330-1334
Calendar of Patent Rolls, Edward III, vol. 3, 1334-1338
Calendar of Patent Rolls, Edward III, vol. 5, 1340-1343
Calendar of Patent Rolls, Edward III, vol. 8, 1348-1350
Calendar of Patent Rolls, Edward III, vol. 10, 1354-58
Calendar of Patent Rolls Edward III, vol. 12, 1361-1364
Calendar of Patent Rolls, Richard II, vol. 1, 1377-1381
Calendar of Patent Rolls, Richard II, vol. 5, 1391-1396
Calendar of Patent Rolls, Richard II, vol. 6, 1396-1399
Calendar of Patent Rolls, Henry VI, vol. 4, 1441-1446
Calendar of Patent Rolls, Henry VI, vol. 6, 1452-1461
Calendar of Patent Rolls Elizabeth I, vol. 1, 1558-1560
Calendar of Entries in the Papal Registers Relating to Great Britain and Ireland: Papal Letters. vol. 1 A.D. 1198-1304
Calendar of Entries in the Papal Registers Relating to Great Britain and Ireland: Papal Letters. vol. 4 A.D. 1396-1404
Caley J. and Hunter J. (eds.) 1814. *Valor Ecclesiasticus temp. Henr. VIII auctoritate regia institutus.* vol. 2 London: Record Commission
Chibnall M. (ed.). 1973. *The Ecclesiastical History of Orderic Vitalis.* vol. 4:Books VII and VIII. Oxford: Clarendon Press
Clanchy M. T. (ed.). 1973. *The Roll and Writ File of the Berkshire Eyre of 1248.* Selden Society vol. 90 London: Selden Society
Cronne H. A. and Davis R. H. C. 1968. *Regesta Regum Anglo-Normannorum 1066-1154* vol. 3
Crowley D. A. 1989. *The Wiltshire Tax List of 1332.* Trowbridge: Wiltshire Record Society vol. 45 Trowbridge: Wiltshire Record Society
Dugdale W. 1825. *Monasticon Anglicanum.* vol. 5 Lon-

don: Longman.

Fenwick C. C. 2005. *The Poll Taxes of 1377, 1379 and 1381*, Part 3, Wiltshire – Yorkshire. Oxford: The British Academy

Fry E. A. (ed.). 1908. *Abstracts of Wiltshire Inquisitiones Post Mortem returned into the Court of Chancery in the reigns of Henry 111, Edward 1 and Edward 11*. London: British Record Society

Fry G. S. and Fry E. A. (eds.). 1901. *Abstracts of Wiltshire Inquisitiones Post Mortem: Charles 1*. Hertford: British Record Society for Wiltshire Archaeological and Natural History Society Record Society

Green E. (ed.). 1892. *Pedes Finium, commonly called Feet of Fines, for the County of Somerset, Richard 1to Edward 1*. Somerset Record Society vol. 6 London: Somerset Record Society

Henning B. A. (ed.). 1983. *The History of Parliament, The House of Commons1660-1690*. London : Secker & Warburg for the History of Parliament Trust

Hobbs S. 1998. (ed.). *The Cartulary of Ford Abbey*. Somerset Record Society vol. 85 Taunton: Somerset Record Society

Hobbs S. (ed.). 2003. *Wiltshire Glebe Terriers 1588 – 1827*. Wiltshire Record Society vol. 56 Trowbridge: Wiltshire Record Society

Hockey S. F. (ed.). 1974. *The Beaulieu Cartulary*. Southampton Records Series. vol. 17 Southampton: University Press.

Hockey S. F. (ed.). 1975. *The Account-Book of Beaulieu Abbey*. Camden Society 4th Series vol. 16 London: Royal Historical Society.

Hockey S. F. (ed.). 1991. *The Charters of Quarr Abbey*. Isle of Wight Records Series vol. 3 Newport: Isle of Wight Record Office

Kemp B. R. 1999. *English Episcopal Acta 18: Salisbury 1078-1217*. Oxford: Oxford University Press

Kirby J. L. (ed.). 1994. *The Hungerford Cartulary*. Wiltshire Record Series vol. 64 Trowbridge: Wiltshire Record Society

Kirby J. L. (ed.). 2007. *The Hungerford Cartulary. A Calendar of the Hobhouse Cartulary of the Hungerford Family*. Wiltshire Record Society vol. 60 Chippenham: Wiltshire Record Society

Latham R. E. and Meekings C. A. F. (eds.). 1956. 'The Veredictum of Chippenham Hundred, 1281' in N. J. Williams (ed.). *Collectanea*. Wiltshire Archaeological and Natural History Society Records Branch. vol. 12: 50-128 Devizes: Wiltshire Archaeological and Natural History Society

Letters and Papers Foreign and Domestic Henry VIII vol. 10

Letters and Papers Foreign and Domestic Henry VIII vol. 12, part 1 and 2

London V. C. M. (ed.). 1979. *The Cartulary of Bradenstoke Priory*. Wiltshire Record Society. vol. 35 Devizes: Wiltshire Record Society

Nichols J. 1841. *The Unton Inventories relating to Wadley and Faringdon Co. Berks in the Years 1596 and 1620*. London: Printed for the Berkshire Ashmolean Society by J.B. Nichols and Son

Ogilby J. 1971. *Ogilby's Road Maps of England and Wales: from Ogilby's Britannia (1675)*. Reading: Osprey

Ramsay G. D. (ed.). 1954. *Two Sixteenth Century Taxation Lists, 1545 and 1576*. Wiltshire Archaeological and Natural History Society Records Branch. vol. 10 Devizes: Wiltshire Archaeological and Natural History Society

Rich Jones W. H. (ed.). 1883. *The Register of St Osmund*. vol. 2 London: Longman

Sherbrook M. 1959. 'The Fall of Religious Houses'. in A. G. Dickens (ed.). *Tudor Treatises*. Yorkshire Archaeological Society Record Series vol. 125: 89-142 Wakefield: Yorkshire Archaeological Society Record

Waddell C. (ed.). 2002. *Twelfth-Century Statutes from the Cistercian General Chapter*. Cîteaux: Commentarii Cistercienses

Weaver F. W. 1889. *Somerset Incumbents*. Bristol: Jefferies and Sons

UNPUBLISHED SOURCES

Anon 1979. *List of Buildings of Special Architectural or Historic Interest*. North Avon District

Anon 1984. *List of Buildings of Special Architectural or Historic Interest*. North Avon District

Brown G. 1996. *Earthwork Survey of Stanley Abbey*. Swindon: English Heritage

Brown G. 2001b. *Chippenham Hundred: Settlement and land-use from the Sixth to the Sixteenth Century*. MA dissertation: University of Southampton

Brown G. 2002. *Earthworks at Buildwas Abbey, Shropshire*. Swindon: English Heritage Archaeological Investigation Report series AI/9/2002

Brown G. 2006. *Hailes Abbey and its Environs*. Swindon: English Heritage Research Department Report Series 29/2006

Brown G. 2008. *Dispersed Settlements on the Southern Mendip Escarpment: the Earthwork Evidence*. Swindon: English Heritage Research Department Report Series 72/2008

Brown G. 2009. *Croxden Abbey and its Environ*. Swindon: English Heritage Research Department Report Series 94/2009

Cattell J. 1996. *Studley House Farm, Studley, Calne Without, Wiltshire*. RCHME Historic Building Report. Report held at NMRC, Swindon

Hare J. N. 1975. *Lords and Tenants in Wiltshire, c1380-c1520, with Special Reference to Regional and Seigneurial Variations*. PhD thesis: University of London

Hill R. G. 1998. *The Estates of the Vicars Choral of Wells Cathedral (1591-1866)*. MA thesis: University of Bristol

Hunt A. and Stone J. 2003. *Griff, North Yorkshire, A Grange of Rievaulx Abbey*. Swindon: English Heritage Archaeological Report Series AI/14/2003

Jecock M. Burn A. Brown G. and Oswald A. 2011. *Byland Abbey, Rydale, North Yorkshire: Archaeological Survey and Investigation of Part of the Precinct and Extra-Mural Area*. Portsmouth: English Heritage Research Department Report Series 4/2011

Keil I. 1964. *The Estates of Glastonbury Abbey in the Lat-*

er Middle Ages*. PhD thesis: University of Bristol

Payne R. C. 1939. *Agrarian Conditions on the Wiltshire Estates of the Duchy of Lancaster, The Lords Hungerford and the Bishopric of Winchester in the 13th, 14th and 15th Centuries*. PhD thesis: University of London

Price S. J. 1971. *The Early History of Bordesley Abbey*. MA dissertation: University of Birmingham

Pearson T. Ainsworth S. and Brown G. 2003. *Haughmond Abbey, Shropshire*. York: English Heritage Archaeological Investigation Report Series AI/10/2003

Ramy R. L. 1996. *Abbot's Lodgings of the Cistercian Order in the Late Fifteenth and Early Sixteenth Centuries*. MA thesis: University of York

Register of Parks and Gardens of Special Historical Interest in England: Wiltshire. (revised version 2004)

White J. W. n.d. *Notes on Louth*. Louth Public Library

Wilcox R. 1987. *A Sampling Excavation at Manor Farm, Allington, Nr Chippenham, Wilts*. Chippenham College

PUBLISHED SOURCES

Akerman J. Y. 1857. 'Some account of the possessions of the Abbey of Malmesbury, in north Wiltshire, in the days of the Anglo-Saxon kings; with remarks on the ancient limits of the Forest of Braydon'. *Archaeologia* **37**.1: 304-15

Alphonso I. 1991. 'Cistercians and feudalism'. *Past and Present* **133**: 3-30

Anon 1902. 'Deed Relating to the Manor of Bromham, AD 1535-1579'. *Wiltshire Notes and Queries*. **3**:129-37

Anon 1987. 'Wiltshire Archaeological Registers for 1985'. *Wiltshire Archaeol Nat Hist Mag* **81**: 140-43

Anon 1988. 'Wiltshire Archaeological Registers for 1986'. *Wiltshire Archaeol Nat Hist Mag* **82**: 183-86

Anon 1990. 'Wiltshire Archaeological Registers for 1987 and 1988'. *Wiltshire Archaeol Nat Hist Mag* **83**: 224-35

Anon 1991. 'Excavation and Fieldwork in Wiltshire 1989'. *Wiltshire Archaeol Nat Hist Mag* **84**: 141-45

Anon 1993. 'Excavations and Fieldwork in Wiltshire 1991'. *Wiltshire Archaeol Nat Hist Mag* **86**: 158-64

Arneborg J. 2005. 'Greenland Irrigation Systems on a West Nordic Background'. *Ruralia. 5. Water Management in Medieval Rural Economy*. Prague: Institute of Archaeology, Academy of Sciences of the Czech Republic. 137-45

Arnold-Foster F. E. 1899. *Studies in Church dedications, or, England's Patron Saints*. **1** London: Skeffington and Son

Astill G. G. and Wright S. M. 1993. 'Perceiving patronage in the archaeological record: Bordesley Abbey' in M. Carver (ed.). *In Search of Cult: Archaeological investigations in honour of Philip Rahtz*. Woodbridge: Boydell Press. 125-37

Astill G. Hirst S. and Wright S. 2004. 'The Bordesley Abbey Project reviewed'. *Archaeol J* **161**: 106-58

Aston M. 1972. 'The Earthworks of Bordesley Abbey, Redditch, Worcestershire' *Med Arch* **16**: 133-36

Aston M. 1993. *Know the Landscape: Monasteries*. London: Batsford

Aston M. 1994. 'Medieval Settlement Studies in Somer-

set' in M. Aston and C. Lewis (eds.). *The Medieval Landscape of Wessex*. Oxford: Oxbow Books. 219-37

Aston M. A. and Munton A. P. 1976. 'A Survey of Bordesley Abbey and its Water System' in P. Rahtz and S. Hurst (eds.). *Bordesley Abbey, Redditch, Hereford-Worcestershire: First Report on Excavations 1969-1973*. British Archaeol Rep **23**: 24-37

Atthill R. 1971. (ed.). *Old Mendip*. Newton Abbott: David and Charles

Atthill R. 1976. (ed.). *Mendip: A New Study*. Newton Abbot: David and Charles

Attwater D. 1965. *The Penguin Dictionary of Saints*. Harmondsworth: Penguin Books

Austin D. 2004. 'Strata Florida and its landscape'. *Archaeol Cambrensis* **153**: 192-201

Baddeley W. St. Clair. 1908. *A Cotteswold Shrine: Being a Contribution to the History of Hayles, County Gloucester*. Gloucester: John Bellows

Barnwell P. S. Dunn C. Goodall I. and Pearson T. 2005. *Rievaulx: The Story of a Valley*, English Heritage fold-out

Barron R. S. 1977. *The Geology of Wiltshire: a field guide*. Bradford-on-Avon: Moonraker Press

Baskerville G. 1937. *English Monks and the Suppression of the Monasteries*. London: Jonathan Cape

Bateman C. 2000. 'Excavations along the Littleton Drew to Chippenham Gas Pipeline'. *Wilts Archaoel Nat Hist Mag* **93**: 90-104

Baulch C. 2005. 'Time for God – The Angelus' *Catholic Life: The Magazine of Catholic History and Culture*. Feb 2005: 8-9

Bayntun-Coward H. 1977. *Notes on the Bayntun Family*. Bath: George Bayntun

Bazeley W. 1899. 'The Abbey of St. Mary, Hayles'. *Trans Bristol and Gloucestershire Archaeol Soc* **22**: 12-285

Beresford M. W. 1959. 'Poll-Tax Payers of 1377' in E. Crittall, (ed.). *A History of Wiltshire*. **4**: 304-13. London: Institute of Historical Research

Beresford M. 1983. *The Lost Villages of England*. Gloucester: Sutton

Beresford M. and Finberg H. P. R. 1973. *English Medieval Boroughs: A Handlist*. Newton Abbot: David & Charles

Berman C. H. 1986. 'Medieval Agriculture, the Southern French Countryside, and the Early Cistercians' *Trans American Philosophical Society* **76** part 5. 1-179

Bettey J. H. 1989. *The Suppression of the Monasteries in the West Country*. Gloucester: Alan Sutton

Bettey J. 2000. 'Downlands' in J. Thirsk (ed.). *The English Rural Landscape*. Oxford: Oxford University Press. 27-49

Bettey J. 2007. 'The Floated Water Meadows of Wessex: A Triumph of English Agriculture'. in H. Cook and T. Williamson (eds.). *Water Meadows: History, Ecology and Conservation*. Macclesfield: Windgather Press. 8-21

Birch W. de G. 1875. 'Collections towards the History of the Cistercian Abbey of Stanley, in Wiltshire' *Wilts Archaeol and Nat Hist Mag* **15**: 239-307

Bishop T. A. M. 1936. 'Monastic Granges in Yorkshire' *English Historical Review*. **51**: 193-214

Blair J. 1988 (ed.). *Minsters and Parish Churches: the local church in transition, 950-1200*. Oxford: Oxford University Press

Blair J. 1991. *Early Medieval Surrey: Landholding, Church and Settlement before 1300*. Stroud: Alan Sutton

Blair J. 1992. 'Anglo-Saxon minsters: a topographical review' in J. Blair and R. Sharpe. (eds.). *Pastoral Care Before the Parish*. Leicester: Leicester University Press. 226-66

Blair J. 2001-2. 'Wells: Roman mausoleum, or just Anglo-Saxon Minster?' *Church Archaeology* **5 & 6**:134-7

Blair J. 2005. *The Church in Anglo-Saxon Society*. Oxford: Oxford University Press

Blair J. 2007. 'Transport and Canal-Building on the Upper Thames, 1000-1300'. in J. Blair (ed.). *Waterways and Canal-Building in Medieval England*. Oxford: Oxford University Press. 254-94

Blair J. and Sharpe, R., 1992, 'Introduction' in J. Blair and R. Sharpe (eds.). *Pastoral Care Before the Parish*. Leicester: Leicester University Press. 1-10

Bond C. J. 1973. 'The Estates of Evesham Abbey: a Preliminary Survey of their Medieval Topography'. *Vale of Evesham Historical Society Research Papers* **4**: 1-61

Bond C. J. 1979 'The Reconstruction of the Medieval Landscape: The Estates of Abingdon Abbey'. *Landscape History*. **1**: 59-75

Bond C. J. 2004. *Monastic Landscapes*. Stroud: Tempus

Bond C. J. 2005. 'The Location and Siting of Cistercian houses in Wales and the West' *Archaol Cambrensis* **154**: 51-79

Bond F. 1905. *Gothic Architecture in England: An Analysis of the Origins and Development of English Church Architecture from the Norman Conquest to the Dissolution of the Monasteries*. London: Batsford

Bonney D. J. 1980. 'Damage by Medieval and Later Cultivation in Wessex' in J. Hinchliffe and R. T. Schadla-Hall (eds.). *The Past Under The Plough*. London: Department of the Environment occasional papers **3**: 41-48

Bowden M. (ed.). 2000. *Furness Iron*. Swindon: English Heritage

Bowden M. 2001. 'Mapping the Past: O. G. S. Crawford and the Development of Landscape Studies' *Landscapes* **2,2**: 29-45

Bowles Rev. W. L. 1828. *The Parochial History of Bremhill in the County of Wilts*. London: John Murray

Bradley R. 2000. *An Archaeology of Natural Places*. London and New York: Routledge

Brakspear H. 1907. 'The Cistercian abbey of Stanley, Wiltshire'. *Archaeologia* **60**: 493-516

Brakspear H. 1908. 'Stanley Abbey'. *Wiltshire Archaeol Nat Hist Mag* **35**: 541-81

Branigan K. 1977. *The Roman Villa in South-West England*. Bradford-on-Avon: Moonraker Press

Braudel F. 1992. *The Mediterranean World in the Age of Philip II*. Harper-Collins: London

Brentnall H. C. 1923. 'Barton Farm in the Thirteenth Century'. *Report of the Marlborough College Natural History Society* **72**: 69-82

Britton J. 1814. *The Beauties of England and Wales*. **15**. London: Longman

Britton J. (ed.). 1847, *The Natural History of Wiltshire by John Aubrey (written between 1656 and 1691)*. 1969 edition, Newton Abbot: David and Charles.

Brown F. and Howard-Davis C. 2008. *Norton Priory: Monastery to Museum, Excavations 1970-87*. Lancaster: Oxford Archaeology North

Brown G. 2001a. 'Sheldon Manor: medieval settlement and land-use in the clayland region of north-west Wiltshire'. *Wiltshire Archaeol Nat Hist Mag* **94**: 209-17

Brown G. 2005a. 'Monastic Settlement and Land-use of the Marlborough Downs' in G. Brown D. Field and D. McOmish (eds.). *The Avebury Landscape: aspects of the field archaeology of the Marlborough Downs*. Oxford: Oxbow Books. 181-90

Brown G. 2005b. 'Langdon Wick: a grange estate of Stanley Abbey'. *Wiltshire Archaeol Nat Hist Mag* **98**: 35-48

Brown G. 2005c. 'Irrigation of water meadows in England' *Ruralia: Water Management in Medieval Rural Economy* **5**. Prague: Institute of Archaeology, Academy of Sciences of the Czech Republic. 84-92

Brown G. in prep. 'An eighteenth-century garden at Studley Farm, Calne'

Burton J. 1994. *Monastic and Religious Orders in Britain, 1000-1300*. Cambridge: Cambridge University Press

Burton J. 1998a 'The Estates and Economy of Rievaulx Abbey in Yorkshire'. *Citeaux Commentarii*. **49**: 29-93

Burton J. 1998b. 'The Cistercian Adventure' in D. Robinson (ed.). *The Cistercian Abbeys of Britain: Far from the Concourse of Men*. London: Batsford. 7-33

Burton J. E. 1999. *The Monastic Order in Yorkshire 1069-1215*. Cambridge: Cambridge University Press

Burton J. 2006. The Foundation History of the Abbeys of Byland and Jervaulx. York: Borthwick Texts and Studies 35

Burton J and Kerr J. 2011. *The Cistercians in the Middle Ages*. Woodbridge: Boydell Press

Canham R. 1982. 'Aerial Photography in Wiltshire 1975-81' *Wiltshire Archaeol Nat Hist Mag* **76**: 3-19

Carville G. 1982. *The Occupation of Celtic Sites in Ireland by the Canons Regular of St Augustine and the Cistercians*. Kalamazoo: Cistercian Publications

Carus-Wilson E. M. 1959. 'The Woollen Industry before 1550' in E. Crittall (ed.). *A History of Wiltshire*. London: Oxford University Press **4**: 115-47

Cassidy-Welch M. 2001. *Monastic Spaces and their Meanings: Thirteenth Century English Cistercian Monasteries*. Turnhout: Brepols

Chandler J. 1993. *John Leland's Itinerary. Travels through Tudor England*. Stroud: Sutton

Chandler J. 1996. 'Reviews'. *Wiltshire Archaeol & Nat Hist Mag* **89**: 154-60

Charvátová K. 1993. 'Settlement Patterns within the Domain of Plasy Abbey, Bohemia'. *Pamatky Archeologicke* **84**: 120-47

Chettle H. F. and Kirby J. L. 1956. 'Abbey of Stanley' in R. B. Pugh and E. Crittall (eds.). *The Victoria History of the County of Wiltshire*. London: Oxford University Press **3**: 269-275

Chew H. M. 1956. 'Abbey of Lacock' in R. B. Pugh and E. Crittall, (eds.). *The Victoria History of the County of*

Wiltshire. London: Oxford University Press **3**: 303-16

Clarke C. A. M. 2006. *Literary Landscapes and the Idea of England, 700-1400*. Cambridge: Brewer

Cleere H. and Crossley D. 1995. *The Iron Industry of the Weald*. Cardiff: Merton Priory Press

Codrington R. H. 1898. 'Memoir of the Family of Codrington of Codrington, Didmarton. Frampton-on-Severn, and Dodington'. *Trans Bristol Gloucestershire Archaeol Soc* **21**: 301-45

Constable G. 1964. *Monastic Tithes from their Origins to the Twelfth Century*. Cambridge: Cambridge University Press

Coope R. 1986. 'The 'Long Gallery': Its origins, development use and decoration'. *Architect Hist* **29**: 43-72

Coppack G. 1990. *Abbeys and Priories*. London: Batsford and English Heritage

Coppack G. 1993. *English Heritage Book of Fountains Abbey*. London: Batsford

Coppack G. 1998 *The White Monks: The Cistercians in Britain 1128-1540*. Stroud: Tempus

Coppack G. 2004. 'According to the Form of the Order: the Earliest Cistercian Buildings in England and their Context'. in T. N. Kinder (ed.). *Perspectives for an Architecture of Solitude: Essays on Cistercians, Art and Architecture in Honour of Peter Fergusson*. Tournhout: Brepols. 35-45

Coppack G. and Gilyard-Beer R. 1993. *Fountains Abbey*. London: English Heritage

Corney M. 2001. 'The Romano-British nucleated settlements of Wiltshire'. in P. Ellis (ed.). *Roman Wiltshire and After: Papers in Honour of Ken Annable*. Devizes: Wiltshire Archaeological and Natural History Society 5-38

Cossons A. 1959. 'Roads' in R. B. Pugh and E. Crittall (eds.). *A History of Wiltshire*. London: Institute of Historical Research **4**: 254-71

Courtney P. and Gray M. 1991. 'Tintern Abbey after the Dissolution' in E. Evans J. B. Smith and R. G. Livens. (eds.). *The Bulletin of the Board of Celtic Studies* **38**: 145-58

Crawley-Boevey A. W. 1887. *The Cartulary and historical notes of the Cistercian Abbey of Flaxley, otherwise called Dene Abbey, in the County of Gloucester*. Exeter: privately printed

Creighton O. 2009. *Designs upon the land: Elite Landscapes of the Middle Ages*. Woodbridge: The Boydell Press

Creighton O. and Liddiard R. 2008. 'Fighting Yesterday's Battle: Beyond War or Status in Castle Studies' *Med Arch* **52**: 161-69

Crittall E. 1965. 'Westbury' in E. Crittall (ed.). *The Victoria History of the County of Wiltshire*. London: Oxford University Press **8**:139-92

Crittall E. 1980. 'Wroughton' in D. A. Crowley (ed.) *The Victoria History of the County of Wiltshire*. Oxford: Oxford University Press **11**: 235-52

Cross C. and Barnwell P. S. 2005. 'The Mass in its Urban Setting' in P. S. Barnwell C. Cross, and A. Rycroft (eds.). *Mass and Parish in late Medieval England. The Use of York*. Reading: Spire Books 13-26

Crowley D. A. and Freeman J. 2002a 'Calne' in D. Crow-

ley (ed.). *The Victoria History of the County of Wiltshire*. Woodbridge: Boydell and Brewer **17**: 27-116

Crowley D. A. and Freeman J. 2002b 'Bowood', in D. A. Crowley (ed.). *The Victoria History of the County of Wiltshire*. Woodbridge: Boydell and Brewer **17**: 116-23

Cunningham W. 1922. *The Growth of English Industry and Commerce*. Cambridge: Cambridge University Press

Daniell J. J. 1894. *The History of Chippenham*. London: Houlton and Sons

Darby H. C. 1967. 'Wiltshire' in H. C. Darby and R. Welldon (eds.). *The Domesday Geography of South-west England*. Cambridge: Cambridge University Press 67-131

Dark P. 1999 'Pollen Evidence for the Environment of Roman Britain'. *Britannia* **30**: 247-72

Dark K. and Dark P. 1997. *The Landscape of Roman Britain*. Frome: Sutton

Darlington R. R. 1955. 'Translation of the Text of the Wiltshire Domesday'. in R. B. Pugh and E. Crittall (eds.). *The Victoria History of the County of Wiltshire*. Oxford: Oxford University Press **2**: 113-68

Desmond L. A. 1976. 'The Appropriation of Churches by the Cistercians in England to 1400'. *Analecta Cisterciensia* **31**: 246-66

Dimier M. A. 1982. 'Infirmeries cisterciennes'. in B. Chauvin (ed.). *Mélanges à la mémoire du Père Ansele Dimier*. Pupillin Arbois **2**: 804-25

Doggett N. 2001. 'The Demolition and Conversion of Former Monastic Buildings in Post-Medieval Hertfordshire'. in G. Keevill M. Aston and T. Hall (eds.). *Monastic Archaeology: Papers on the Study of Medieval Monasteries*. Oxford: Oxbow Books. 165-74

Doggett N. 2002. *Patterns of Re-use: The transformation of former monastic buildings in post-Dissolution Hertfordshire, 1540-1600*. Brit Archaeol Rep 331

Donkin R. A. 1958. 'Cistercian Sheep-Farming and Wool Sales in the Thirteenth Century'. *Ag Hist Rev* **6**, pt.1: 2-8

Donkin R. A. 1960. 'The Cistercian settlement and the English royal forests'. *Citeaux Commentarii Cistercienses* **11**: 39-45, 117-32

Donkin R. A. 1964. 'The English Cistercians and assarting c1128-1350'. *Analecta Sacri Ordinis Cisterciensis* **20**: 49-75

Donkin R. A. 1978. *The Cistercians: Studies in the Geography of Medieval England and Wales*. Toronto: Pontifical Institute of Medieval Studies

Donnelly J. S. 1954. 'Changes in the Grange Economy of English and Welsh Cistercian Abbeys, 1300-1540'. *Traditio* **10**: 399-458

Duffy E. 1992. *The Stripping of the Altars: Traditional Religion in England 1400-1580*. New Haven and London: Yale University Press

Duffy E. 2011. *Ten Popes who Shook the World*. New Haven and London: Yale University Press

Duggan A. P. and Greenslade M. W. 1974. 'The Abbey of Croxden' in M. W. Greenslade (ed). *The Victoria History of the County of Stafford*. London: Institute of Historical Research **3**: 226-30

Dunning R. W. 1985a. 'Old Cleeve' in R. W. Dunning (ed.). *The Victoria History of the County of Somerset*. Oxford: Oxford University Press. **5**: 39-54

Dunning R. W. 1985b. 'The Last Days of Cleeve Abbey' in C. M. Barron and C. Harper-Bill (eds.). *The Church in Pre-Reformation Society.* Woodbridge: Boydell Press. 58-94

Dyer C. 1994. *Everyday Life in Medieval England.* London: Hambledon Press

Dyer C. 1995. 'Sheepcotes: Evidence for Medieval Sheep Farming'. *Med Arch* **39**: 136-64

Dyer C. 1996. 'Seasonal Settlement in Medieval Gloucestershire'. in H. Fox (ed.). *Seasonal Settlement. Vaughan Papers.* Leicester: Leicester University Press **39**: 25-33

Dyer C. 2000. 'Woodlands and Wood Pasture in Western England'. in J. Thirsk (ed.). *The English Rural Landscape.* Oxford: Oxford University Press.97-121

Dyer C. 2002. 'Villages and Non-Villages in the Medieval Cotswolds'. *Trans Bristol Gloucestershire Archaeol Soc* **120**: 11-35

Eagles B. 1998. 'A Note on the Significance of Distribution of the Celtic Mounts' *Wiltshire Archaeol Nat Hist Mag* **91**: 40

Eagles B. 2001. 'Anglo-Saxon presence and culture in Wiltshire' in P. Ellis (ed.). *Roman Wiltshire and After: Papers in Honour of Ken Annable.* Devizes: Wiltshire Archaeological and Natural History Society 199-233

Ekwall E. 1968. *English River Names.* Oxford: Clarendon Press

Everson P. 1995 'The After-life of Monastic Houses: the earthwork evidence'. in C. Sturman (ed.) *Lincolnshire People and Places: essays in memory of Terence R. Leach, 1937-1994.* Lincoln: Society for Lincolnshire History and Archaeology 13-17

Everson P. 1998. '"Delightfully Surrounded with Woods and Ponds": field evidence for medieval gardens in England' in P. Pattison (ed.). *There by Design.* Swindon: RCHME 32-38

Everson P. 2001. 'Peasants, Peers and Graziers: The Landscape of Quarrendon, Buckinghamshire, Interpreted'. *Records of Buckinghamshire.* **41**: 1-45

Everson P. 2003. 'Medieval Gardens and Designed Landscapes' in R. Wilson-North (ed.). *The Lie of the Land.* Exeter: The Mint Press 24-33

Everson P. 2007. 'Reflecting a Stance: Establishing a Position; Moving Beyond Description and Function in Designed Estate Landscape?' in J. Finch and K. Giles (eds.). *Estate Landscapes: Design, Improvement and Power in the Post-Medieval Landscape.* Society for Post-Medieval Archaeology **4**: 113-28

Everson P. and Stocker D. 2003. 'The Archaeology of Vice-Regality: Charles Brandon's Brief Rule in Lincolnshire'. in D. Gaimster and R. Gilchrist (eds.). *The Archaeology of Reformation 1480-1580.* Leeds: Maney 145-58

Everson P. and Stocker D. 2007. 'St Leonard's at Kirkstead, and the Landscape of the Cistercian Monastic Precinct'. in M. Gardener and S. Rippon (eds.). *Medieval Landscapes. Landscape History after Hoskins* **2**: 215-30

Everson P. and Stocker D. 2008. 'Masters of Kirkstead: Hunting for Salvation' in J. McNeill (ed.). *King's Lynn and the Fens.* The British Archaeological Association Conference Transactions **31**: 83-111

Everson P and Stocker D 2011. *Custodians of Continuity? The Premonstratension Abbey at Barlings and the Landscape of Ritual.* Lincolnshire Archaeology and Heritage Reports Series No 11

Everson P.L. Taylor C. C. and Dunn C. J. 1991. *Change and Continuity. Rural Settlement in North-West Lincolnshire.* London: HMSO

Everson P. and Williamson T. 1998. 'Gardens and designed landscapes'. in P. Everson and T. Williamson (eds.). *The Archaeology of landscape. Studies presented to Christopher Taylor.* Manchester: Manchester University Press 139-65

Everitt A. 1986. *Continuity and Colonisation: the evolution of Kentish Settlement.* Leicester: Leicester University Press

Farmer D. 1978. *Oxford Dictionary of Saints.* Oxford: Oxford University Press, fourth edition

Fawcett R. and Oram R. 2004. *Melrose Abbey.* Stroud: Tempus

Ferguson P. 1983. 'The First Architecture of the Cistercians in England and the Work of Abbot Adam of Meaux'. *JBAA* **136**: 74-86

Fergusson P. 1990a. '"Porta Patens Esto': Notes on Early Cistercian Gatehouses in the North of England'. in E Fernie and P Crossley (eds.). *Medieval Architecture and its Intellectual Context: Studies in Honour of Peter Kidson.* London: Hambledon Press 47-59

Fergusson P. 1990b. *Roche Abbey.* London: English Heritage

Fergusson P. and Harrison S. 1999. *Rievaulx Abbey: Community, Architecture, Memory.* New Haven and London: Yale University Press

Findlay D.C. Colborne G. J. N. Cope D. W. Harrod T. R. and Staines S. J. 1984. *Soils and their use in south-west England.* Whitstable: Harpenden

Fleming A. 1998. *Swaledale: Valley of the Wild River.* Edinburgh: Edinburgh University Press

Fleming A. and Barker L. 2008. 'Monks and Local Communities: The Late-medieval Landscape of Troed y Rhiw, Caron Uwch Clawdd Ceredigion'. *Med Arch* **52**: 261-90

Foard G. 2001. 'Medieval Woodland, Agriculture and Industry in Rockingham Forest, Northamptonshire'. *Med Arch* **45**: 41-95

Fowler P. 2000. *Landscape Plotted and Pieced.* London: Society of Antiquaries

Fox H. 2012. *Dartmoor's Alluring Uplands: Transhumance and Pastoral Management in the Middle Ages.* Exeter: Exeter University Press

Fradley M. 2009. 'The Field Archaeology of the Romano-British Settlement at Charterhouse-On-Mendip'. *Britannia* **40**: 99-122

Freeman J. 1983a 'Ogbourne St Andrew' in D. A. Crowley (ed.). *The Victoria History of the County of Wiltshire.* Oxford: Oxford University Press. **12**: 138-51

Freeman J. 1983b. 'Winterbourne Bassett' in D. A. Crowley (ed.). *The Victoria History of the County of Wiltshire.* Oxford: Oxford University Press **12**: 184-92

Freeman J. (ed.). 1988. *The Commonplace Book of Sir*

Edward Bayntun of Bromham. Devizes: Wiltshire Record Society **43**

Freeman J. 2002. 'Berwick Bassett'. in D. A. Crowley (ed.). *The Victoria History of the County of Wiltshire*. Woodbridge: The Boydell Press **17**: 9-17

Fry A. H. 1940. *The Land of Britain: The report of the Land Utilisation Survey of Britain: Part 87, Wiltshire*. London: Geographical Publications

Gaimster D. and Gilchrist R. (eds.). 2003. *The Archaeology of Reformation 1480-1580*. Leeds: Maney

Garbett H. L. E. and Clapham A. W. 1924. 'Hundred of Faringdon'. in W. Page and P. H. Ditchfield (eds.). *The Victoria History of the County of Berkshire*. London: St. Catherine Press **4**: 486-97

Gelling M. 1978. *Signposts to the Past*. London: Book Club Associates

Gelling M. 1984. *Place-Names in the Landscape*. 1993 edition. London: Dent

Gerrard C. 2003. *Medieval Archaeology: Understanding Traditions and Contemporary Approaches*. London: Routledge

Gerrard C. and Aston M. 2007. *The Shapwick Project, Somerset: A Rural Landscape Explored*. Leeds: Maney. Society for Medieval Archaeology Monograph **25**

Gilchrist Clark W. 1894. 'The fall of the Wiltshire monasteries'. *Wiltshire Archaeol Nat Hist Mag* **28**: 289-315

Gilchrist R. 1994. *Gender and Material Culture: the Archaeology of Religious Women*. Routledge: London. 1997 edition

Gilchrist R. 1999. *Gender and Archaeology: Contesting the Past*. London: Routledge

Girouard M. 1976. *Life in the English Country House: A Social and Architectural History*. New Haven and London: Yale University Press

Goddard E. H. 1913. 'A List of Prehistoric, Roman, and Pagan Saxon Antiquities in the County of Wilts. Arranged under Parishes'. *Wiltshire Archaeol Nat Hist Mag* **38**: 153-378

Golding B. 1995. *Gilbert of Sempringham and the Gilbertine Order, c.1130-c.1300*. Oxford: Clarendon Press

Gough J. W. 1928. 'The Witham Charterhouse on Mendip'. *Somerset Archaeol Nat Hist Soc* **74**: 87-101

Gover J. E. B. Mawer A. and Stenton F. M. 1939. *The Place-Names of Wiltshire*. London: Cambridge University Press

Graham R. 1907. 'The Abbey of Flaxley' in W. Page (ed.). *The Victoria History of the County of Gloucester*. London: Institute of Historical Research **2**: 93-96

Grant R. 1959. 'Forests' in E. Crittall (ed.). *The Victoria History of the County of Wiltshire*. London: Institute of Historical Research **4**: 391-460

Greene J. P. 1989. *Norton Priory: The Archaeology of a Medieval Religious House*. Cambridge: Cambridge University Press

Greene J. P. 1992. *Medieval Monasteries*. Leicester: Leicester University Press

Greene J. P. 2001. 'Strategies for Future Research and Site Investigation'. in G. Keevill, M. Aston and T. Hall (eds.). *Monastic Archaeology* Oxford: Oxbow Books 4-8

Griffiths N. 2001. 'The Roman Army in Wiltshire'. in P. Ellis (ed.). *Roman Wiltshire and After: Papers in Honour of Ken Annable*. Devizes: Wiltshire Archaeological and Natural History Society 39-72

Griffiths N. and Robinson P. 1991. 'A re-examination of the tile designs from the medieval kiln at Nash Hill, Lacock'. *Wiltshire Archaeol Nat Hist Mag* **84**: 61-70

Gurnham R. 2007. *A History of Louth*. Chichester: Phillimore

Hall J. 2004. 'East of the Cloister: Infirmaries, Abbots' Lodgings, and other Chambers' in T. N. Kinder (ed.). *Perspectives for an Architecture of Solitud: Essays on Cistercians, Art and Architecture in Honour of Peter Fergusson*. Tournhout: Brepols 199-211

Hall J. and Strachan D. 2001. 'The precinct and buildings of Tilty Abbey'. *Essex Archaeology and History* **32**:198-208

Hare J. N. 1985. 'The Monks as Landlords: The Leasing of Monastic Demesnes in Southern England'. in C. M. Barron and C. Harper-Bill (eds.). *The Church in Pre-Reformation Society*. Woodbridge: Boydell Press 82-94

Hare J. 1993. 'Netley Abbey: monastery, mansion and ruin'. *Proc. Hants. Field Club* **49**: 207-27

Hare J. 1994. 'Agriculture and Rural Settlement in the Chalklands of Wiltshire and Hampshire from c.1200 – c.1500'. in M. Aston and C. Lewis (eds.). *The Medieval Landscape of Wessex*. Oxford: Oxbow Books 159-69

Hare J. 1999. *The Dissolution of the Monasteries in Hampshire*. Hampshire Papers 16

Hare, J. 2011. *A Prospering Society: Wiltshire in the later Middle Ages*. Hatfield: University of Hertfordshire Press

Harrison B. 1995. 'Field Systems and Demesne Farming on the Wiltshire estates of Saint Swithun's Priory, Winchester, 1248-1340'. *Agric Hist Rev* **43**: 1-18

Harrison S. A. 1999. *Byland Abbey*. London: English Heritage

Harvey B. K. 1992. 'An Early Seventeenth-Century Survey of Four Wiltshire Manors'. *Vernacular Architecture* **23**: 30-33

Harvey J. 1981. *Medieval Gardens*. London: Batsford

Hase P. 1994. 'The Church in the Wessex Heartlands'. in M. Aston and C. Lewis (eds.). *The Medieval Landscape of Wessex*. 47-81

Haslam J. 1984. 'The Towns of Wiltshire'. in J. Haslam (ed.). *Anglo-Saxon Towns in Southern England*. Chichester: Phillimore 87-147

Haslam J. and Edwards A. 1976. *Wiltshire Town: The Archaeological Potential*. Devizes: Wiltshire Archaeological and Natural History Society

Haslam J. Biek L. and Tylecote R. F. 1980. 'A Middle Saxon Iron Smelting Site at Ramsbury, Wiltshire'. *Med Arch* **24**: 1-68

Henderson P. 2005. *The Tudor House and Garden*. New Haven and London: Yale University Press

Henig M. 1999. 'A Silver Ring-Bezel from Gastard, Corsham'. *Wiltshire Archaeol Nat Hist Mag* **92**: 125-26

Hill B. D. 1968. *English Cistercian Monasteries and their Patrons in the Twelfth Century*. Urbana, Chicago, London: University of Illinois

Hilton R. 1985. *Class Conflict and Feudalism: Essays in Medieval Social History.* London: Hambledon Press

Hinton D. A. 1990. *Archaeology, Economy and Society: England from the Fifth to the Fifteenth Century.* London: Routledge 1998 reprint

Hoare R. C. 1812. *The Ancient History of Wiltshire.* **2**, London

Hoare R. C. 1819. *The Ancient History of North Wiltshire,* London

Hockey S. F. 1970. *Quarr Abbey and its Lands 1132-1631.* Leicester: Leicester University Press

Hockey Dom F. 1976. *Beaulieu, King John's Abbey: A History of Beaulieu Abbey Hampshire 1204-1538.* Old Woking: Pioneer

Hodges, R. 1991. *Wall-to-Wall History: The Story of Roystone Grange.* London: Duckworth

Holdsworth C. 1994. 'The Early Writings of Bernard of Clairvaux' *Cîteaux Commentarii Cistercienses.* **45**: 21-61

Hooke D. 1989. 'Pre-Conquest Woodland: its Distribution and Usage'. *Agric Hist Rev* **37**: 113-29

Hooke D. 1994. 'The Framework of Early Medieval Wessex'. in M. Aston and C. Lewis (eds.). *The Medieval Landscape of Wessex Oxford*: Oxbow Books 83-95

Hooke D. 1997. 'Lamberde leie, dillameres dic: A lost or living landscape?' in K. Barker and T. Darvill (eds.). *Making English Landscapes: Changing Perspectives.* Oxford: Oxbow 26-45

Hooke D. 1998. *The Landscape of Anglo-Saxon England.* London: Leicester University Press

Hoskins W. G. 1953. 'The Rebuilding of Rural England, 1570-1640'. *Past and Present* **4**: 44-59

Hoskins W. G. 1955. *The Making of the English Landscape.* London: Hodder and Stoughton

Hoskins W. G. 1959. 'Economic History'. in E. Crittall (ed.). *The Victoria History of the County of Wiltshire.* London: Oxford University Press **4**: 1-6

Howard M. 1987. *The Early Tudor Country House: Architecture and Politics, 1490-1550.* London: George Philip

Howard M. 2003. 'Recycling the Monastic Fabric: Beyond the Act of Destruction'. in D. Gaimster and R. Gilchrist (eds.). *The Archaeology of Reformation 1480-150.* Leeds: Maney. 221-34

Howard M. 2007. *The Building of Elizabethan and Jacobean England.* New Haven and London: Yale University Press

Hoyle R. 1989. 'Monastic Leasing before the Dissolution: The Evidence of Bolton Priory and Fountains Abbey'. *Yorks Archaeol Soc* **61**: 111-37

Huggins P. J. 1972. 'Monastic Grange and Outer Close Excavations, Waltham Abbey, 1970-72'. *Trans Essex Archaeol Soc* **4**: 30-127

Hutchins J. 1861. *The History and Antiquities of the County of Dorset.* London: Bowyer and Nichols

Iles R. 1984. 'The Medieval Landscape of the Southern Cotswolds' *Bristol and Avon Archaeology.* **3**: 39-46

Jackson J. E. 1862. *Wiltshire: The Topographical Collections of John Aubrey, AD 1659-70.* Devizes: Wiltshire Archaeological Society

James B. S. 1953. *The Letters of St Bernard of Clairvaux.* Stroud: Sutton. 1998 edition

James M. R. (ed.). 1983. *Walter Map, De Nugis Curialium, Courtiers' Trifles.* Revised by C. N. L. Brooke and R. A. B. Mynors. Oxford: Clarendon Press

Jamroziak E. 2003. 'Rievaulx Abbey as a Wool Producer in the Late Thirteenth Century: Cistercians, Sheep, and Debts' *Northern History.* **40** pt2: 197-218

Jamroziak E. 2005. *Rievaulx Abbey and its Social Context, 1132-1300: Memory, Locality, and Networks.* Tournhout: Brepols

Jones P. 1971. 'Italy', in M. M. Postan (ed.). *The Cambridge Economic History of Europe: The Agrarian Life of the Middle Ages.* Cambridge: Cambridge University Press **1**: 340-431

Jones R. and Page M. 2006. *Medieval Villages in an English Landscape.* Macclesfield: Windgather Press

Johnson M. 2002. *Behind the Castle Gate.* London and New York: Routledge

Johnson M. 2007. *Ideas of Landscape.* Oxford: Blackwell

Johnson M. 2010. *English Houses 1300-1800: Vernacular Architecture, Social Life.* Harlow: Longman

Kain R. J. P. and Prince H. C., 1985. *The Tithe Surveys of England and Wales.* Cambridge: Cambridge University Press

Kerridge E. 1959 'Agriculture 1500-1792' in E. Crittall (ed.) *The Victoria History of the County of Wiltshire.* London: Oxford University Press **4**: 43-64

Kerridge E. 1958-59. 'The Revolts in Wiltshire Against Charles 1'. *Wiltshire Archaeol Nat Hist Mag* **57**: 64-75

Kershaw I. 1973. *Bolton Priory: the economy of a northern monastery, 1286-1325.* Oxford: Oxford University Press

Kinder T. N. 2001. 'Living in a Vale of Tears, Cistercians and site management in France: Pontigny and Fontfroide'. in G. Keevill, M. Aston and T. Hall, (eds.). *Monastic Archaeology. Papers on the Study of Medieval Monasteries.* Oxford: Oxbow Books 37-53

Kinder T. N. 2002. *Cistercian Europe: Architecture of Contemplation.* Cambridge: Eerdams

Kirby J. L. 1956. 'Priory of Kington St Michael'. in R. B. Bugh and E. Crittall (eds.). *The Victoria History of the County of Wiltshire.* London: Oxford University Press **3**: 259-61

Klemperer W. D. and Boothroyd N. 2004. *Excavations at Hulton Abbey, Staffordshire 1987-1994.* Society for Medieval Archaeology Monograph 21

Knight J. K. 1999. 'Tintern Abbey and the Romantic Movement' *Monmouthshire Antiquary* **15**: 56-60

Knowles D. 1950. *The Monastic Order in England.* Cambridge: Cambridge University Press

Knowles D. 1959. *The Religious Orders in England.* Cambridge: Cambridge University Press 3 1979 paperback version

Knowles D. 1976. *Bare Ruined Choirs: The Dissolution of the English Monasteries.* Cambridge: Cambridge University Press

Knowles D. and Hadcock R. N. 1971. *Medieval Religious Houses England and Wales.* London: Longmans

Landsdowne, The Marquis of, 1927. 'A Roman Villa at Nuthills, Near Bowood'. *Wiltshire Archaeol Nat Hist Mag*

44: 49-58

Lawrence C. H. 1984. *Medieval Monasticism*. Harlow: Pearson Education 3rd edition 2001

Leclercq J. 1961. *The Love of Learning and the Desire for God*. New York: Fordham University Press

Leclercq J. 1970. 'The Intentions of the Founders of the Cistercian Order'. in M. B. Pennington (ed.). *The Cistercian Spirit: A Symposium in memory of Thomas Merton*. Dublin: MacGlinchey. 88-133

Lekai L. J. 1977. *The Cistercians. Ideals and Reality*. Kent Ohio: Kent State University Press

Lewis C. 1994. 'Patterns and Processes in the Medieval Settlement of Wiltshire'. in M. Aston and C. Lewis (eds.). *The Medieval Landscape of Wessex*. Oxford: Oxbow Books 171-93

Lewis C. 1999. 'Braydon: a Study of Settlement in a Parish-Edge Forest'. in P. Pattison D. Field and S. Ainsworth (eds.). *Patterns of the Past: Essays in Landscape Archaeology for Christopher Taylor*. Oxford: Oxbow Books 85-96

Liddiard R. 2005. *Castles in Context: Power, Symbolism and Landscape, 1066 to 1500*. Macclesfield: Windgather Press

Liddiard R. and Williamson T. 2008. 'There by design? Some reflections on medieval elite landscapes' *Archaeol J.* **165**: 520-35

Ludlow N. 2005. 'Whitland Abbey, Carmarthenshire: a Cistercian site re-examined, 1994-99'. *Archaeol Cambrensis* **151** (2002): 41-108

Lynam C. 1911. *The Abbey of St. Mary, Croxden, Staffordshire*. London: Sprague & Co

Mann J. 1959. 'Textile Industry since 1550'. in E. Crittall (ed.). *The Victoria History of the County of Wiltshire*. London: Oxford University Press 4: 43-64

Marsh A. E. W. 1903. *A History of the Borough and Town of Calne*. London: Castle, Lamb and Storr

Matarasso P. 1993. *The Cistercian World: monastic writings of the twelfth century*. London: Penguin Books

Matthew H. C. C. and Harrison B. (eds.). 2004a. *Oxford Dictionary of National Biography* 4. Oxford: Oxford University Press

Matthew H. C. C. and Harrison B. (eds.). 2004b. *Oxford Dictionary of National Biography* 6. Oxford: Oxford University Press

Matthew H. C. C. and Harrison B. (eds.). 2004c. *Oxford Dictionary of National Biography* 33. Oxford: Oxford University Press

McCarthy M. R. 1976. 'The Medieval Kilns on Nash Hill, Lacock, Wiltshire,' *Wiltshire Archaeol Nat Hist Mag* 69: 97-160

McDonnell J. 1963. *A History of Helmsley Rievaulx and District*. York: Stonegate Press

McOmish D. Field D. and Brown G. 2002. *The Field Archaeology of the Salisbury Plain Training Area*. Swindon: English Heritage

Meredith J. 2006. *The Iron Industry of the Forest of Dean*. Stroud: Tempus

Moore D. 2005. 'Ruined abbeys in romantic landscapes'. *Archaeol Cambrensis* **154**: 179-213

Moore J. S. (ed.). 1982. *Domesday Book: Gloucestershire*. Chichester: Phillimore

Moore J. S. 1990. 'The Gloucestershire section of Domesday Book: geographical problems of the text, part 4' *Trans Bristol Gloucestershire Archaeol Soc* **108**: 105-30

Moorhouse S. 2003. 'The anatomy of the Yorkshire Dales: deciphering the medieval landscape' in T. G. Munby S. Moorhouse and P. Ottaway (eds.). *The Archaeology of Yorkshire: an assessment at the beginning of the 21st century*. Yorkshire Archaeological Society Occasional Paper 3: 293-362

Morant R. W. 1995. *The Monastic Gatehouse*. Lewes: The Book Guild

Morgan M. 1946. *The English Lands of the Abbey of Bec*. Oxford: Clarendon Press. 1968 edition

Morris C. 1947. *The Journeys of Celia Fiennes*. London: Cresset Press

Morris R. 1983. *The church in British archaeology*, CBA Res Rep **47**

Morris R. 1989. *Churches in the Landscape*. London: Dent

Mowl T. 2004. *Historic Gardens of Wiltshire*. Stroud: Tempus

Neale F. 1976. 'Saxon and Medieval Landscapes'. in R. Atthill (ed.). *Mendip: A New Study*. Newton Abbot: David & Charles 75-101

Newman P. 2011. *The Field Archaeology of Dartmoor*. Swindon: English Heritage

Oliver Rev. H. A. 1881. 'Some Account of the Remains of a Roman Villa in the Parish of Bromham'. *Wiltshire Archaeol Nat Hist Mag* **19**: 299-302

Palmer M. and Neaverson P. 2005. *The Textile Industry of South-West England: A Social Archaeology*. Stroud: Tempus

Parker R. Ives T. and Allan J. 2007. 'Excavation and building study at Cleeve Abbey, 1995-2003'. *Somerset Archaeol Nat Hist Soc* **150**: 73-167

Parsons D. 1991. 'Stone'. in J. Blair and N. Ramsay (eds.). *English Medieval Industries*. London: Hambledon Press 1-27

Pearson T., forthcoming. 'Analysis of the precinct at Rievaulx'. *Council for British Archaeology Newsletter*

Pevsner N. 1963. *The Buildings of England: Wiltshire*. London: Penguin Books 1975 2nd edition

Pierce. T. Jones, 'Strata Florida Abbey'. *Ceredigion* **1**, 18-33

Piggott C. M. 1942. 'Five Late Bronze Age Enclosures in North Wiltshire'. *Proc Prehist Soc* **8**: 48-61

Pitt J. 2003. 'Malmesbury Abbey and Late Saxon Parochial Development in Wiltshire'. *Wiltshire Archaeol Nat Hist Mag* **96**: 77-88

Platt C. 1969. *The Monastic Grange in Medieval* England. London: Macmillan

Platt C. 2007. 'Revisionism in Castle Studies: A Caution' *Med Arch* **51**: 83-102

Pollard J. and Reynolds A. 2002. *Avebury The biography of a landscape*. Stroud: Tempus

Powicke M. 1950. *The Life of Ailred of Rievaulx by Walter Daniel*. Oxford: Clarendon Press

Pugh R. B. 1953 'Bradford-on-Avon'. in R. B. Pugh and E.

Crittall (eds.). *The Victoria History of Wiltshire*. London: Oxford University Press 7: 5-51

Rackham O. 1976. *Trees and Woodland in the British Landscape*. London: Dent

Rackham O. 1980. *Ancient Woodland its history, vegetation and uses in England*. London: Edward Arnold

Rackham O. 1986. *The History of the Countryside*. London: Dent

Raban S. 1982. *Mortmain Legislation and the English Church 1279-1500*. Cambridge: Cambridge University Press

Ragg F. W. 1906. 'Translation of the Berkshire Domesday'. in P. H. Ditchfield and W. Page (eds.). *The Victoria History of the County of Berkshire*. London: St. Catherine Press 1: 324-69

Ramsay G. D. 1965. *The Wiltshire Woollen Industry in the Sixteenth and Seventeenth Centuries*. London: Oxford University Press

Ramy R. L. 2004. 'An Archaeology of Hospitality: the Stoneleigh Abbey Gatehouse'. in R. Bearman (ed.). *Stoneleigh Abbey: The Home, Its Owners, its Lands*. Hereford: Stoneleigh Abbey Ltd. 62-81

RCHMS 2008. *In the Shadow of Bennachie*. Edinburgh: RCHMS

RCHM(Wales) 1982. *An Inventory of the Ancient Monuments in Glamorgan: Medieval Secular Monuments. 3 part 2: Non-defensive*. Cardiff: HMSO

Reynolds A. 1999. *Later Anglo-Saxon England*. Stroud: Tempus

Riley H. 2006. *The Historic Landscape of the Quantock Hills*. Swindon: English Heritage

Riley H. and Wilson-North R. *The Field Archaeology of Exmoor*. Swindon: English Heritage

Rivet A. L. F. and Smith C. 1979. *The Place-Names of Roman Britain*. London: Batsford

Rippon S. 1994 'Medieval Wetland Reclamation in Somerset'. in M. Aston and C. Lewis (eds.). *The Medieval Landscape of Wessex*. Oxford: Oxbow 239-53

Rippon S. 2006. *Landscape, Community and Colonisation*. CBA Res Rep 152

Roberts B. and Wrathmell S. 2000. *An Atlas of Rural Settlement*. London: English Heritage

Robinson D. M. 1980. *The Geography of Augustinian Settlement in Medieval England and Wales*. Brit Archaeol Rep 80

Robinson D. (ed.). 1998. *The Cistercian Abbeys of Britain: Far from the Concourse of Men*. London: Batsford, 2002 edition

Robinson D. 2002. *Tintern Abbey*. Cardiff: CADW

Robinson D. M. 2006. *The Cistercians in Wales: Architecture and Archaeology 1130-1540*. London: The Society of Antiquaries of London

Robinson D and Harrison S. 2006. 'Cistercian Cloisters in England and Wales'. *JBAA* 159: 131-207

Robinson P. 1992. 'Some Late Saxon Mounts from Wiltshire'. *Wiltshire Archaeol Nat Hist Mag* 85: 63-9

Rodwell W. 2001. *The Archaeology of Wells Cathedral: Excavations and Structural Studies 1978-93*. London: English Heritage

Roehl R. 1972. 'Plan and Reality in a Medieval Economy: The Cistercians'. *Studies in Medieval and Renaissance History* 9: 83-113

Roux J. 2005. *The Cistercians*. Toulouse: Fournié

Rudder S. 1779. *A New History of Gloucestershire*. Dursley: Alan Sutton 1997 re-print

Saunders M. 1959. 'Stone Quarrying'. in E. Crittall (ed.). *The Victoria History of the County of Wiltshire*. London: Institute of Historical Research 4: 247-50

Sawyer P. H. 1968. *Anglo-Saxon Charters: An Annotated List and Bibliography*. London: Royal Historical Society

Scott R. 1959. 'Medieval Agriculture'. in E. Crittall (ed.). *The Victoria History of the County of Wiltshire*. London: Oxford University Press 4: 7-42

Scrope G. P. 1855. 'History of the Wiltshire Manors subordinate to the Baronry of Castle Combe'. *Wiltshire Archaeol Nat Hist Mag* 2: 261-89

Seaby W. A. and Woodfield P. 1980. 'Viking Stirrups from England and their Background'. *Med Arch* 24: 87-122

Service M. 2010. 'The Home Estate, Granges and smaller properties of Waverley Abbey' *Surrey Archaeol Collect* 95: 211-57

Shagan E. H. 2003. *Popular Politics and the English Reformation*. Cambridge: Cambridge University Press

Shadwell C. L. and Salter H. E. 1926. *Oriel College Records*. Oxford: Clarendon Press

Smith A. H. 1937. *The Place-Names of the East Riding of Yorkshire and York*. Cambridge: Cambridge University Press

Smith N. 2005. 'Medieval and Later Sheep Farming on the Marlborough Downs'. in G. Brown D. Field and D. McOmish (eds.). *An Avebury Landscape: The Field Archaeology of the Marlborough Downs*. Oxford: Oxbow Books 191-201

Stalley R. 1987. *The Cistercian Monasteries of Ireland: An Account of the History, Art and Architecture of the White monks in Ireland from 1142 to 1540*. London & New Haven: Yale University Press

Stevenson J. H. 1980. 'Enford'. in A. Crowley (ed.). *The Victoria History of the County of Wiltshire* .London: Institute of Historical Research 11: 115-34

Stocker D. and Stocker M. 1996. 'Sacred Profanity: the theology of rabbit breeding and the symbolic landscape of the warren'. *World Archaeology* 28: 265-72

Story Makelyne T. 1909. 'An Ancient Wiltshire Custom' *Wiltshire Notes and Queries*. Devizes: George Simpson. 6: 331-36

Styles D. 1956. 'Priory of Bradenstoke' in R. B. Pugh and E. Crittall (eds.). *The Victoria History of the County of Wiltshire*. Oxford: Oxford University Press 3: 275-88

Tatton-Brown T. 1994. 'The Medieval Fabric'. in M. Hobbs (ed.). *Chichester Cathedral*. Chichester: Phillimore 25-46

Taylor C. C. 1989. 'Somersham Palace, Cambridgeshire: A Medieval Landscape for Pleasure'. in M. Bowden D. Mackay and P. Topping (eds.). *From Cornwall to Caithness: Some Aspects of British Field Archaeology*. Brit Archaeol Rep 209: 211-24

Taylor C. 2000. 'Medieval Ornamental Landscapes'.

Landscapes 1: 38-55

Taylor C. Everson P. Wilson-North R. 1990. 'Bodium Castle, Sussex'. *Med Arch* 34: 155-7

Taylor H. M. and Taylor J. 1965. *Anglo-Saxon Architecture*. London: Cambridge University Press 1

Thirsk J. 1967. 'The Farming Regions of England'. in J. Thirsk (ed.). *Agrarian History of England and Wales, 1500-1640*. Cambridge: Cambridge University Press 4: 1-112

Thompson M. 2001. *Cloister Abbot and Precinct*. Stroud: Tempus. 2007 reprint

Thompson J. W. 1920. 'The Cistercian Order and Colonisation in Medieval Germany'. *The American Journal of Theology* 24 (1): 67-93

Thorpe L. 1978. *Gerald of Wales: the Journey Through Wales and the Description of Wales*. London: Penguin. 2004 edition

Tingle. M. 1991. *The Vale of the White Horse Survey*. Brit Archaeol Rep 218

Tonkin J. 1997. 'After the Dissolution'. in R. Shoesmith and R. Richardson (eds.). *A Definitive History of Dore Abbey*. Little Logaston: Logaston Press. 153-54

Tramontin Don Silvio. 2006. *The Life of St. Anthony of Padua and his Basilica*. Venezia: Storti Edizioni

Turner J. 1981. 'The vegetation'. in M. Jones and G. Dimbleby (eds.). *The Environment of Man: the Iron Age to the Anglo-Saxon Period*. Brit Archaeol Rep 87: 67-73

Turner S. 2006. *Making a Christian Landscape*. Exeter: Exeter University Press

Underdown. D. 1985. *Revel, Riot and Rebellion: popular politics and culture in England 1603-1660*. Oxford: Clarendon Press

Upham M. 2006. 'Brightley Abbey'. *Devonshire Association. Report and Transactions* 138: 151-64

Vellacott C. H. 1969. 'Lead Mining'. in W. Page (ed.). *The Victoria History of Somerset*. London: University of London 2: 362-79

Very D. and Brooks A. 2002 *The Buildings of England, Gloucestershire 2: the Forest of Dean*. Third edition, New Haven and London: Yale University Press

Waddell C. 1994. 'The Cistercian Institutions and their Early Evolution'. in L. Pressouyre (ed.). *L'espace cistercien*. Paris: Comité des travaux historiques et scientifiques 27-38

Waddell H. 1998. *The Desert Fathers*. New York: Vintage

Wager S. J. 1998. *Woods, Wolds and Groves. The woodland of medieval Warwickshire*. Brit Archaeol Rep 269

Waites B. 2007. *Monasteries and Landscape of the North York Moors and Wolds*. Stroud: Tempus

Walsham A 2012. *The Reformation of the Landscape: Religion, Identity, and Memory in Early Modern Britain and Ireland*. Oxford: Oxford University Press (2012 paperback edition)

Walton P. 1991. 'Textiles' in J. Blair and N. Ramsay (eds.). *English Medieval Industries*. London: Hambledon Press 319-54

Wardrop J. 1987. *Fountains Abbey and its Benefactors, 1132-1300*. Kalamazoo: Cistercian Publications 91

Watkin Dom A. 1956. 'Abbey of Malmesbury'. in R. B.

Pugh and E. Crittall (eds.). *The Victoria History of the County of Wiltshire*. London: Oxford University Press 3: 210-31

Watkins A. 1994. 'Merevale Abbey in the Late 1490s'. *Warwickshire History* 9 (no 3): 87-105

Whitelock D. 1961. *The Anglo-Saxon Chronicle*. London: Eyre and Spottiswoode

Whittle E. and Taylor C. 1994. 'The Early Seventeenth-Century Gardens of Tackley, Oxfordshire'. *Garden History* 22.1: 36-63

Williams D. H. 1984. *The Welsh Cistercians*. Tenby: Cyhoeddiadau Sistersiaidd

Williams D. H. 1990. *Atlas of Cistercian Lands in Wales*. Cardiff: University of Wales

Williams D. H. 1991. 'Layfolk within Cistercian Precincts'. in J. Loads (ed.). *Monastic Studies. The Continuity of Tradition*. Headstart History 87-117

Williams D. H. 1997. 'The Dissolution'. in R. Shoesmith and R. Richardson (eds.). *A Definitive History of Dore Abbey*. Little Logaston: Logaston Press 149-52

Williams D. H. 1998. *The Cistercians in the Early Middle Ages*. Leominster: Gracewing

Williams D. H. 2001. *The Welsh Cistercians*. Leominster: Gracewing

Williams D. H. 2004. 'Abergavenny Conference on the Cistercian Landscape'. *Archaeol Cambrensis* 150: 249-53

Williams D. H. 2004. 'Cistercian Grange Chapels'. in T. N. Kinder (ed.). *Perspectives for an Architecture of Solitude: Essays on Cistercians, Art and Architecture in Honour of Peter Fergusson*. Tournhout: Brepols. 213-21

Wilson D. H. 1991. 'Old gardens from the air'. in A. E. Brown, (ed.). *Garden Archaeology* CBA Res Rep 78: 20-35

Wilson-North R. and Porter S. 1997 'Witham, Somerset: from Carthusian monastery to country house to Gothic folly'. *Architect Hist* 40: 81-98

Wilson A. R. and Tucker J. H. 1983. 'The Langley Charter and its Boundaries'. *Wiltshire Archaeol Nat Hist Mag* 77: 67-70

Winkless D. 1990. *Hailes Abbey Gloucestershire*. Leckhampton: Thornhill Press

Woodward G. W. O. 1966. *The Dissolution of the Monasteries*. London: Blandford Press

Wright S. 1976. 'Historical Notes'. in P. Rahtz and S. Wright (eds.). *Bordesley Abbey, Redditch, Hereford-Worcester: First report on excavations 1969-1973*. Brit Archaeol Rep 23: 16-24

Yorke B. 1995. *Wessex in the Early Middle Ages*. London: Leicester University Press

Young C. R. 1979. *The Royal Forests of Medieval England*. Leicester: Leicester University Press

Youngs S. 1995. 'A Pennanular Brooch from near Calne, Wiltshire'. *Wiltshire Archaeol Nat Hist Mag* 88: 127-31

Youings J. 1971a 'The Church'. in J. Thirsk (ed.) *The Agrarian History of England and Wales, 1500-1640* 4: 306-56

Youings J. 1971b. *The Dissolution of the Monasteries*. London: George Allen and Unwin